RIDING OLD TRAILS

BY

JAMES CURTIS

© Copyright James Curtis, 1976

All rights reserved

Second Printing 1977

Revised Edition 1983

Publisher - ROCKY MOUNTAIN BOOKS
Box N, Windsor, CO 80550

CONTENTS

INTRODUCTION

CHAPTER ONE	-	TALL IN THE SADDLE	1
CHAPTER TWO	-	SADDLE UP	35
CHAPTER THREE	-	HOT IRON	63
CHAPTER FOUR	-	THE HOME PLACE	87
CHAPTER FIVE	-	THE LADY OF THE HOUSE	123
CHAPTER SIX	-	THE WOOLLY BOOGERS	163
CHAPTER SEVEN	-	CHUCKS ON	187
CHAPTER EIGHT	-	PROMENADE	209
CHAPTER NINE	-	A SIDE TRIP	223
CHAPTER TEN	-	THE WINDS OF CHANGE	239
CHAPTER ELEVEN	-	END OF AN ERA	269

EPILOG

The influence of individual character extends from generation to generation. — The world is molded by it.

—Macleod

DEDICATED
TO
JOHN WAYNE

Cattleman and Traditionalist

*

*In appreciation for his efforts
in keeping the spirit of the
Old West alive*

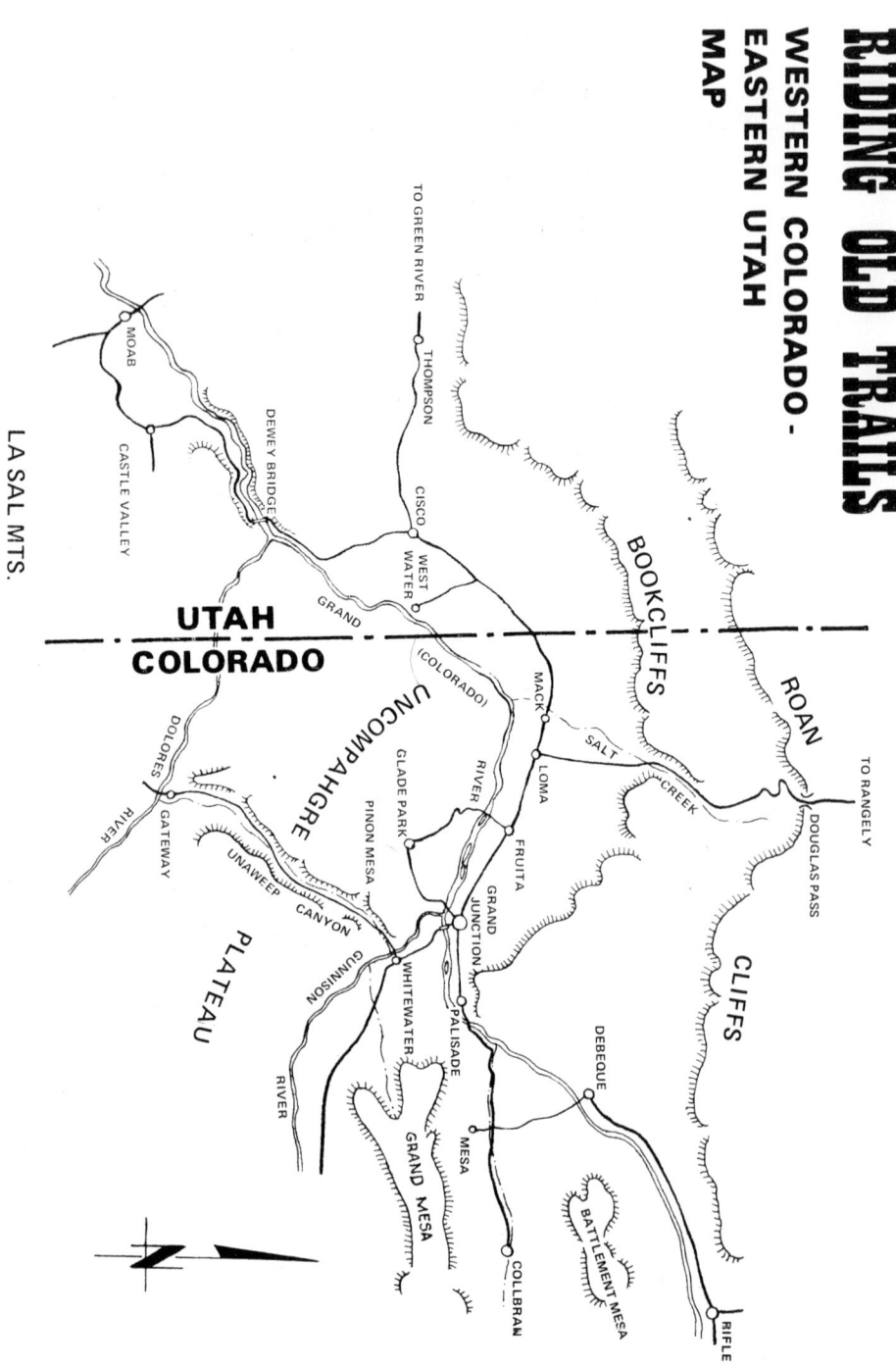

INTRODUCTION

The Old West passed by at a rapid pace, and few participants on the scene had the time to pause in the midst of building a life on the frontier in order to preserve records. Certainly, most of the early pioneers were fully immersed in each new day as it happened and generally unaware of their part in one of the most colorful and heroic sagas of man's movement across the face of the earth. Now, years later, there are increasing signs of concern. Don't let the facts get lost! Preserve the records! Capture the color! Set it all down on paper, before the cast is gone, and it is too late to document the story.

In order to do this properly, it is necessary to stress the importance of individual effort in the building of the West. For if one thing stands out in our national life, it is that the record of the great westward movement was one of sorties and retreats by determined individuals.

At the very beginning of that national life, nine out of ten Americans lived on farms where they grew barely enough to feed their own families. It was a time when farm work was done by the muscle and grunt method; hard work, large families and survival all went together — hand in hand. But however much they might preach the gospel of making it by the sweat of your brow, it has always been common knowledge that a great many early Americans were in constant communion with a grand purpose. They were looking for something more, something better.

Some, obviously, had a great desire, an all-consuming impulse, if you will, to become richer and stronger than anyone else. Others, just as obviously, simply wanted to do what they wanted, when they wanted, and to do it entirely on their own. The records show, however, that a majority dreamed purely of land — free land, good land, more land. So, with single-minded purpose, like a portly man much addicted to the pleasures of the table, each of the seekers pointed west. The frontier was somewhere just over the horizon, and they not only had dreams and ideas, but the gumption to act on them. The operative word was — hope.

It is abundantly clear that the "don't-give-up spirit," the "try-anything spirit" was a primary ingredient in this country's formative years. Nowhere was this more true than in the individual American's itch for land. It reached its peak with The Homestead Act of 1862. The primary purpose of The Homestead Act was to open the vacant lands of the vast American West to agricultural settlement. In order to qualify for a homestead, a person had to be a citizen of the United States, at least 21 years of age or the head of a household, and own less than 160 acres under cultivation. After living on the land for six months, it could be purchased for $1.25 per acre; or after five years of residence, a title could be acquired for a $15.00 filing fee. More than one-million families received a homestead title to over two-hundred forty-eight million acres of public land in this manner. The practice of homesteading on vacant land continued well into the mid-1900s; clearly and truly, for many Americans, the lure of land was like an unquenchable thirst. Not everyone who came west, however, was suited to the life of a sodbuster.

For many people the true symbol of the West is and has always been the old-time cowboy with his constant, almost arrogant rejection of the ways of the outside world. The frontier ranches, the wide open spaces, the unending struggle between man and nature bred a stubborn individualism which not only included an open admiration for personal skill and self-reliance, but stressed independence and unconventionality. The way men lived, the country itself, the method of earning a livelihood all contributed to this individualism. It was a big empty country, and cowboys liked it, or they would not have been there. On some ranges, it was considered a circumstance, if you met one person on a day's ride, and a happening, if you met two. It was no wonder that in this big empty land people put a premium on neighborliness in a way not always understood by outsiders.

These early-day Westerners had a complete life mode; they established their own rhythms; created their own styles; invented their own humor. Filled with a sense of purpose, they built and bred and fueled a unique lifestyle on a great sea of grass. Within that old frontier way of life, they enjoyed the luxury of being individuals. It was — when all is said and done — a good life in a very rough and difficult time.

This collection of stories tells of the old ways; of a life fast fading into memory and never to return. It is the history of a special people as they once lived in their isolation and self-sufficiency. History such as this survives only in the memories of people who lived it. It is the stuff of legends. We seek here to preserve those legends.

*   *   *

CHAPTER ONE

TALL IN THE SADDLE

*It almost seems as if they'd found
The chosen way, the favored ground.*

In the summer of 1950, the Colorado high country experienced an invasion which centered on the Molas Divide area near the old mining town of Silverton. Here, in the very heart of the southern Rockies where rough ridges and jagged peaks seem to claw at the sky, Hollywood location experts decided to film a story of early-day fur traders in Montana entitled, "Across The Wide Missouri." It was, of course, a logical site.

"Across The Wide Missouri" was a major motion picture effort produced by Robert Sisk for Metro-Goldwyn-Mayer and directed by a hard-nosed, outspoken man named, William Wellman. The cast was headed by Clark Gable, and included such well-known names as John Hodiak, Ricardo Montalban, Adolph Menjou, and old-time action star, Jack Holt.

The script of "Wide Missouri" cast the dynamic Gable as the

rugged leader of a band of wild mountain trappers who schemes to gain safe access to the wilderness by marrying an Indian princess. In a classic scene, Gable returns to the tepee of his bride after a long celebration with his men; he is unshaven, dirty and quite rank. The daughter of the chief refuses him entrance with an absolute flood of indignant gibberish. In obvious distress, Gable turns to Adolph Menjou, who plays the part of a French guide and interpreter.

"What'd she say?" asks the great lover in an injured tone.

"She say, you stink," replies the impeccable Menjou in his best French accent. "And, by gar, you do stink!"

Needless to say, in the very next scene Gable was bathing in a cold mountain stream and shaving his accumulated beard; and from here on in, it was no contest. No tepee flap in the history of the West could have remained closed to a clean-shaven, freshly bathed, buckskin-clad Clark Gable. He was larger than life, an embodiment of the Western myth and Yankee dynamism. It is a picture tied tightly to the end of the frontier old and the beginning of tradition.

The impact of this tradition on successive decades of American life and progress has amply proved the frontier's existence in the hearts and minds of Americans. In a classic sense, the frontier ethic has been the only mythological tissue available to this nation over the years. The man on horseback, the conquest of nature and the law of the gun have appealed from the first. The American legend evolved in stories of people caught up in the ordinary business of life. Very often they were told in terms of the individual, but in the end each story became an integral part of the whole.

Americans, and especially rural Americans, have always been storytellers. The stories covered a variety of subjects. Some were raunchy tales filled with mirth. Others were chronicles of action, danger, and frontier lore. Mostly, they were stories of everyday life -but often exaggerated and expanded through repeated telling. Not a few, in the early days of this nation, were outright fabrications told by some of the most magnificent liars ever to sit around a campfire. These tellers of tall tales were known as mountain men. They were trappers and fur traders for the most part, and they lived in a time when animal furs were the currency of the frontier. And when the American frontier reached the known limits at or near the Mississippi River, hesitation was slight. Almost to a man, this rugged group dropped off the edge and headed for the far mountains; to a place somewhere to the west where all trails came out of the fog. But this was a tough breed.

Soon stories came trickling back: stories of mountains five miles high, of contorted rock formations painted a dozen shades of crimson or vermillion, of a mountain range 180 miles long and 50 miles wide composed of solid rock salt and drained by a river which flowed salt water for 600 miles. Then from out of the mists came eerie, unreal tales of mysterious underground rumblings, bubbling mud pots and steaming holes that spouted hot water to the heavens even in mid-winter. To skeptics back in the "States," Colter's Hell* was on the rainbow edge of fantasy; it was all a bit much. But a little doubt has never been able to stop a trend with momentum, and the stories continued. If anything, the wilderness vocabulary became systematically more ambiguous.

Yellowstone Park

The tales grew taller. Men who were "half horse — half alligator" fought "injuns" and "grizzlys" with their bare hands and killed game at such distances that the meat invariably spoiled before they could reach it. The country they roamed was filled with phenomena, strange and unnatural. There were glass mountains that magnified distance like a telescope, and great stone forests where "putrified birds sat on putrified limbs and sang putrified songs." Make no mistake about it — the West of the mountain man was one helluva place. And aberrations and all, the stories of its wonders helped to open the floodgates of the deluge to come.

History records that the westward movement in the early days was due to a combination of forces and pressures supplemented by the actions of various individuals. Certainly the presence of Jefferson at the time of Lewis and Clark and the Louisiana Purchase must be taken into account. Still, it is abundantly clear that the progress of settlement which had been driving back the frontier ever since the revolution was the result of individual initiative. The frontier was a great leveler, and early Americans always placed a premium on ingenuity and physical prowess; talent had no use for class or caste, nor did it waste time on legalities. So while politicians probed the heights, and editors fought their wars of words, the history of this country was being decided by ordinary people, going west. In the process, they took American interests to the Pacific in force. It was not really all that simple, of course, but we shall leave the complexities to accredited historians; our purpose here is thematic. No matter how the continental westering is detailed, however, the fact remains that manifest destiny was constantly booted along the trail by massive doses of American individualism.

While it is undoubtedly true that most people see the past in terms of their own interests, it does seem equally clear that few, if any, have ever cut themselves off, as a gesture of disapproval, from their wealth and all the attendant impurities of the market-place. Embellishment is a part of human nature. But once the pale abstractions and half-baked philosophies have been shorn of their scholarly trimmings — it's back to the basics; back to where it must be acknowledged that the community of life exists in material things. This fact is true today. It was true in the time of the mountain men.

The American free-trapper galloped full-tilt out of the shadowy trails of legend into the annals of folklore. His was an elusive image conjured up by storytellers and embellished by time. Behind the mists, however, there is ample evidence to show that the legendary fur-trading mountain man was a ring-tailed free enterpriser of the first degree. His primary reason for invading the wilderness was economic. For by the standards of time, fur-taking was a lucrative occupation. To put this fact in proper perspective, it must be noted that Nineteenth Century America was not a place of overflowing abundance for all. Most families lived on farms and scratched a meager living from the soil. The best that could be said for the average man was that the future held promise, and the country was growing all the time. By 1890, the United States had 60 million people and led the world in practically all the necessities of life. And at that particular time in our national life, 11 of the 12 million families in this country lived on an average income of $380 a year. Prosperity is definitely a matter of perspective.

To the mountain man of the early West, prosperity meant beaver in plentiful supply. Beaver fur had a ready market of $3.00 a pound in the mountains, and a prime pelt often weighed 1½ pounds or more. Five dollars a skin at a time when $100 cash could keep a man for the better part of a year, was better than a license to steal. In rapid order, companies were formed, and men and supplies headed for the high country. And while it may have been high adventure for many, it was certainly not all fun and games.

The Rocky Mountain beaver is a fur-bearing mammal with a unique lifestyle and an appetite for the bark of the high country aspen tree. The beaver has always been a sociable cuss, and where the environment is favorable for growth, the number of families in an area is bound to increase. The limiting factors are food and seclusion. The Rocky Mountains of the early 1800s had a plentiful supply of both. The first trappers to reach a new and secluded area in those days often found entire colonies living in close harmony. Working together, the little animals had in some instances improved and extended their interwoven dams to the length of a modern football field. And when nearby food supplies were depleted, the entire colony would turn out to dig canals to a new grove of trees. Some of these canals might be up to three feet wide, hundreds of feet long, and deep enough to float pre-cut limbs and poles down to the central pond. It's hard to believe that such ingenious creatures could have a weak spot, but they do, and it has to do with physical attraction. For whatever else they might be, it is pure fact that beavers are extremely well versed in the arts of love — and sociability.

The average adult beaver is nearly two and one-half feet long, stands one foot in height, and weighs in at about forty pounds. The body is plump, the hind feet webbed, and the two front teeth on either jaw look like sharp enameled chisels. To top it off, each comes equipped with a broad, flat scaly tail about ten inches long. Obviously, the attraction is not on the surface. But under the skin of the lower belly, the beaver has a pair of rather special glands which secrete a musklike substance called, castoreum. It is the essence of love that finally does them in.

The mountain man of the Rocky Mountain fur-trading days was smarter than a beaver — usually. At any rate, any trapper worth his salt always carried among his "possibles" a substance made primarily from beaver castor glands which was known as "medicine." This substance was liberally sprinkled around each trap-set where its pungent odor not only killed the man scent, but caused naturally wary, super-smart creatures of the wild to throw caution to the winds. The ultimate sociability was at hand, and glassy-eyed lovers went to the target like a moth goes to a flame.

Beaver trapping by its very nature was an uncomfortable and physically exhausting business. Traps were set along animal runways and usually in the water in order to eliminate signs. They were anchored to a stout pole firmly set in mud bottoms, and when sprung, the animal would invariably drown while struggling to get free. Mountain men spent a great deal of their working life standing tail-deep in icy mountain streams, and most of them ended up with bent backs, stiff limbs and "rheumitiz" in every joint. The wilderness life imposed a maximum tax on strength and resourcefulness, but these were remarkable men, They had the capacity to enter an unknown wilderness, the willingness to dare, to make judgements, and take risks. Survival in strange country required a curious mixture of open-mindedness and skepticism, a capacity to adjust to unfamiliar conditions. It required, too, an analytical understanding of the lay of the land. For this was Indian country — the land of the Arapaho, Crow, Snake, Flathead, Nez Perce, Blackfoot and Sioux. In many cases, it was also territory claimed by the British in the north, and Mexico in the south and west. All of which slowed the adventurers from the "States" not one whit.

The Mountain man was able to survive, because he adapted. He possessed the free and undirected mind of the individual. He blended into the landscape, lived off the land, fought when necessary, and learned the secrets of the western wilderness. And then as the demand for furs increased and the number of trapping parties grew, he engaged in cutthroat competition for the remaining beaver streams in the far mountains. It was a competition which could involve trickery, theft, and outright physical combat. For this was indeed a tough breed.

No matter how rough the times or bitter the squabble, however, there always came a time of truce. Each summer during the "glory days" of the mountain man era, they all came together at rendezvous time. The old-time Rocky Mountain Rendezvous was an outdoor get-together held at some prearranged spot for the purpose of trading the year's fur catch for supplies and cash in form of credit recorded in company books at St. Louis. The trade goods came in on pack mules or horses and consisted of beads, blankets, calico cloth, rifles, knives, tobacco, powder-lead, traps and diluted alcohol which was sold as "sippin' whiskey', at $4.00 a pint. Everyone came, including the Indians. Rendezvous was a place where everyone met on common ground.

The first rendezvous was held in 1825 at Henry's Fork on the northern drainage of the High Uinta Mountains — now part of the Flaming Gorge Country in southern Wyoming. Here at a spot not far from where this picturesque stream empties into the Green River, the pattern for future trading sessions was set. It was all a bit like a country fair with booths set up displaying the trade goods for barter, but with the added attraction of whiskey kegs for openers. It was a time for letting off steam; a place where men with unweaned egos and a variety of appetites could find release in gambling, drinking, horse races, shooting at a mark, or competing for the favors of Indian women who invariably accompanied their men to the trading place. After two weeks of get-together, hell-raising, and trading the year's catch, a halt was called, and the various parties went their own way after setting a meeting place for the following year.

Records show that William Ashley returned to St. Louis with more than $50,000 worth of pelts obtained at that first get-together on Henry's Fork. While the second rendezvous was held in the Cache Valley of northern Utah, the most popular spot in subsequent years seemed to be in the upper valley of the Green River, at the foot of the Wind River Mountains. It is a matter of record that the time of the mountain man — the wild, fur-trading, free-roaming mountain man did not last for long. Beaver fur hats for men went out of style in the early 1830s when silk became the rage, and by the mid-thirties, the annual meetings at rendezvous were no more.

But while the Rocky Mountain Fur Company, the American Fur Company and others passed into oblivion, many of the men involved in those legendary times went on to greater fame in the years to come. For the tracks of the furtrader's pack horses now became the wagon trails of the pioneer emigrants. And now also the names of the mountain men who pointed the way truly became legend. There was Bill Williams — of whom it was said no one in his right mind would turn his back on in a tight fix. To old Bill — meat was meat. And Kit Carson, who led Fremont, the great pathfinder of the West, over trails the mountain men trod for years. And there was Jim Bridger (probably the greatest of them all) who built a fort on the Blacks Fork River in southern Wyoming which became a key stop on the overland route of the pioneers. Destiny — all of this? One cannot help but wonder. In any event, it was time for the "builders" of the West to take over; time for the wagons to roll.

The American trek west on the several overland trails was a time of excitement, discovery and revolutionary changes. With the quest for free land and the subsequent discovery of gold, everyday Americans became adventurers by right of movement and participation. In the end, the great overland push to the Pacific was the fundamental background for the rise of the cattle trade, and when the dust finally settled the era's symbol was the American cowboy. In the course of years the image of the lonely cowboy riding the wide prairie has become part of a modern mythology. Much of this myth was undoubtedly created through the magic of motion pictures. The evidence was clear from the beginning.

In 1903, Edwin S. Porter and the Edison Company produced a motion picture entitled, "The Great Train Robbery." It was a landmark film which introduced crime and action to moving pictures while telling a story. And although filmed entirely in New Jersey, this elemental story of robbery, killing and final shoot-out with the law was a "Western." An era was about to begin.

The time of the Western moved swiftly into place, and myth and legend moved just as fast. In no time at all the strong, silent Western hero of the screen emerged, and one of the first to hit it big with his name over the title was William S. Hart. Bill Hart was a veteran stage actor who took to Westerns in 1914 like a duck takes to water, and by 1916 had made the medium his own. In terms of the times, Hart's pictures were excellent. They had adult themes and strong story lines. Writers and critics loved (and still love) to cite the realism of Hart and his films. Ramshackle buildings, baggy britches and clouds of dust in background shots were considered by many to be proof of this authenticity. It was not necessarily so. For the West was not all stark and drab, nor was it peopled by hard-eyed avengers or unshaven rascals up to no good. Hart's realism was stereotyped and unchanging. Like most actors of his time, he emoted with his face; it was an expressive face — long, sad and mobile. And Lordy — how that man did suffer! Real cowboys were far more likely to tie one on and head for the nearest bawdy house. One might conclude from this that genuine cowboys were just plain hell-raisers. Such a generality would, however, be as misleading as an advertisement for a Mexican gold mine.

Cowboys on the whole were, in fact, as varied in character as the entire band of pioneers who made up the Old West. Some of them were brave, others were cowards; some were modest and quiet, others could on no account shut their mouths to stop the drip. In the final analysis, it does seem clear that each point of view must be understood in the context of its own time and direction. Certainly this is true in any real-life story of the West. With this thought in mind, let's return for a moment to 1903 and an incident related by old-time cowboy, Cecil Gross, of Cody, Wyoming:

"In 1903, Ed Walsh and I sold some wild horses we had caught and took the money we got from them and went to Ouray, Utah, and bought a bunch of Indian horses from the Utes. We were on the north side of Green River at Ouray. There was no bridge across Green River, and we had to cross them on a ferry boat. We took them to Rifle, Colorado, and shipped them to Hutchinson, Kansas. They were pretty wild. When we started, we had some Utes help us get them on the ferry and get them started. We held them in a corral that was on the south side of Green River and on the north side of White River. After we got started, we had them off of their range, and we made it to Rifle pretty good. We had three carloads. We shipped them to Hutchinson and sold them. We fed in Pueblo on the way to Hutchinson. We were gone a month. That was in July, 1903. I was sixteen years old."

It is easy to see that even in 1903 the point of view depended very much upon the angle of viewing. In old New Jersey, Americans were trying to catch and preserve the spirit of the Old West on film. At the same time this was happening, Americans in a still wild and remote part of the West were actually living the old ways. The high-powered experts, past and present, who persistently claim the Old West died in the 1880s could be talking through their hats. There are some who claim things were just getting started along about then. And there are some — by hell — who insist the old spirit has never died out. It is, of course, all a matter of perspective. At any rate, ol' Bill Hart continued to grind out "Westerns" in his own particular style, and his popularity increased with each new release. But times do change, and back in the wings a new-style whirlwind was about to take over. The new man had, in fact, been around for some time.

In 1911, a two-reel western movie was shot on location high in the Rocky Mountains of Southern Colorado. Featured was Tom Mix, a man destined to become a legend in the soon-to-boom make-believe world of Hollywood. Tom had gotten started in film-making when the Selig Company shot a documentary short on location in Oklahoma. The picture was entitled, " Ranch Life in the Great Southwest," and while Tom's part in its production is vague, there is no doubt that it started him out in the business of film-making. Between 1911 and 1917, he personally produced nearly one-hundred Western shorts for the Selig Company. In most of them, Mix himself was the star, author, and director. While the pictures produced were not especially memorable, they did give this high spirited cowboy an opportunity to demonstrate his expert horsemanship and daredevil action skills.

In 1917, William Fox offered him a contract, and Tom Mix took off like a shooting star. His pictures were slick and full of action. He rode a horse named, Tony, who was invariably smarter than the villain and to some of us far better looking than the heroine. Tony could climb stairs, untie knots, jump over cars, unlatch gates, and if need be, fight or outwit the bad guys. The combination of man and animal was showmanship at its best, and by 1920, the formula had proven its worth. Tom Mix and Tony became the most popular team in the movies.

The popularity of the Mix films lasted for the better part of a decade. They played in first-run theatres to packed houses all over the world. By the mid-twenties, Tom Mix was in the top-ten moneymakers along with Mary Pickford, Doug Fairbanks, and Charlie Chaplin. Certainly, one reason for the tremendous success of Tom Mix and Tony was the practice of shooting each film on location, far from the studios of Hollywood. The authentic backgrounds which seemed to deliberately exploit the rugged beauty of the West soon became a trademark of the Mix pictures. no baggy britches, ramshackle buildings or fake scenery in a studio back lot here. Tom obviously loved the West, and sheer photographic beauty was a planned part of the entertainment package. To zero in on some particular spot and weave that locale into the plot of the picture was an integral part of that plan. Did love of the land play a part in the success of this effervescent cowboy who, through deliberate action, brought the wonders of the West to millions? One might as well ask if scenic splendor contributed to the Western legend. Both questions are posed for assessment as we zero in on a particular spot in this story of people who settled a land.

The land consists of an area in the intermountain West commonly designated by natives as the Western Slope. In more specific terms, it covers a region of Colorado River drainage country along the border of western Colorado and into eastern Utah. These geographic facts are closely woven into the fabric of our story. For in the beginning, there were formidable obstacles to overcome, and the border country would settle hard.

There were some who claimed that Colorado was created by accident, since it had no natural boundaries and was assembled from portions of the four existing Territories of Kansas, Wyoming, Utah, and New Mexico. In any event, the central Rockies were a staggering barrier, and long after army expeditions and emigrant trains had established overland routes to the north, Colorado was still one of the wildest, most awe-inspiring and strikingly beautiful geographical areas on the face of the earth. Then, in 1859, 50,000 goldseekers moved into the "Pikes Peak" region. It had taken the discovery of gold to open the gates of the Colorado mountains. It took the Civil War to make Colorado a separate territory, however.

When news of the secession reached the Rocky Mountains, Colorado became a divided camp. On February 28, 1861, a war measure was hastily passed by the United States Congress to insure that Colorado remained safely in the Union. Shortly thereafter, President Lincoln appointed Colonel William Gilpin the first Governor of Colorado Territory.

In 1873, President Ulysses S. Grant made a good will tour which included a visit to the gold fields in the Rocky Mountains. Upon his return to Washington, he suggested to Congress that Colorado just might be ready for statehood. Grant's conclusion was based on some very solid evidence. The Colorado miners had prepared for his visit by covering the sidewalk to the Teller house in Central City with bars of pure silver. It was an act of pure genius. Said the President, "This Territory possesses all the elements of a prosperous state!"

Three years later, on August 1, 1876, Colorado became the 38th state to enter the Union. It had been eighteen years since the first goldseekers had come to the base of the mountains and settled on Cherry Creek. But although the gates had been breached, the inner areas remained wild and remote, and practical men were obliged to conform to the possible.

The 1870s saw several attempts to set up agricultural colonies. One of the first was a cooperative formed by a man named, Carl Wulsten. Wulsten moved 100 German families to an isolated valley in the Wet Mountains south of the present-day community of Canon City. The group included a doctor, a clergyman, and a schoolmaster. A special point had been made to exclude all lawyers, but there were "twenty fair-haired German girls, all young and good-looking." This uncommonly shrewd approach seems to have focused on the basics in all areas, save the weather.

The new colony had planted the fields and built cabins, but an early frost hit the 7500 foot upland valley, destroying both crops and the cooperative spirit. By the following spring, most of the members had moved to Denver, or the surrounding goldfields. They had learned the hard way that nature can be indifferent to time and man's fate.

A second colony was founded in the Cache LaPoudre Valley

north of Denver along the main route leading to Cheyenne and the Union Pacific RR. It was settled by a group of New Yorkers and in the beginning was called the Union Colony. Two of the original founders were Nathan Meeker and a man of letters, named Pabor.

The new colony at the foot of the Rockies was promoted by the New York Tribune, and its publisher, Horace Greeley, who encouraged cooperative settlement of the land and total abstinance from hard liquor. Memberships in the cooperative community were sold to "temperance men of good character" for a fee of $150. The first year for the new settlers was lean and hard going.

W. E. Pabor wrote of this difficult time:

> *"The chosen ground was unbroken for miles, the wind had blown off the light soil, leaving gravel. Fifty to a hundred persons arrived daily without enough blankets or provisions, and in the whole town, there was but one well. Some seemed to forget that it was the work of a colony needed to create a city; they expected to see one already built. They remained to curse only so long as the next train east delayed its going."*

Yet, in spite of hard beginnings, the community survived. By the second year, those who stuck it out were on their feet and looking optimistically to the future. Eventually, the colony ceased to be commonly owned, and its name was changed to, Greeley. The success of Greeley started a rush to build new cooperative towns at the eastern foot of the mountains. The future beckoned, and the country responded. "Go West, young man", became the national byword. It would still be several years, however, before Nathan Meeker and W. E. Pabor moved on to become involved in new settlements on the sunset side of the Rockies. There were two major obstacles to the western movement; one was the Ute Indians; the other a great natural barrier known as, The Continental Divide. But the frontier formula had by now created a keen sense of directional time.

In 1880, by a treaty with the government, the Ute Indians surrendered all claims to the lands now included in the Counties of Mesa, Delta, and Montrose. By midsummer of 1881, the Utes had been moved to a new reservation in Utah, and this area on the western slope of the central Rockies was finally opened to settlement. A group led by George A. Crawford, a former territorial governor of Kansas, promptly filed for a townsite on a point of land in the Grand Valley, near the junction of the Grand and Gunnison Rivers. The new town was officially incorporated and named, Grand Junction, on October 10, 1881. In spite of obstacles, the barriers were coming down. And all the while, the settlers — promoters and businessmen, sodbusters and cattlemen were coming over or around the big divide into the newly-opened country. They all came — the fiddle-footed and the restless — the land-grabbers who would settle in only long enough to prove title and sell out — and the solid, tough as rawhide cattlemen who would stand stubborn and stiff-necked through the hard years and stay to make homes for their women in this isolated land. They came, the land-hungry, from all points of the compass — from the east and the midwest, and as many more direct from the Old South. And most of them were as diverse in make-up and character as the land they came to claim.

There can be little doubt that diversity was a basic factor in the settlement of the West. This was the time of the doer — of the rugged individualist. In those early years, the realities of pioneer life demanded an intense practicality. The price of survival was ingenuity, and early-day settlers were usually willing to try anything. Confident and resourceful, they improvised to meet conditions, and then proceeded to Americanize the results with practical efficiency. And while concern for a neighbor was a definite part of the frontier way of life, most settlers shared the same aggressive desire to do what they wanted, when they wanted, and without interference from anyone. This diversity factor — the difference in attitude, outlook, and individual — is an integral part of our frontier heritage. Certainly, the Rocky Mountain country was settled by hard-nosed individualists possessing every degree of cussedness known to God or man. Rugged and direct, they lived in a time when the risks and dangers of daily life had to be met boldly. Those who made it became specialists in the art of survival. Then, slowly, out of the mists and shadows that gather over all persons and events with the passing of time, they also become part of an ever-growing legend.

For years, the symbol of the West has been the man on horseback. In the United States, the image of the lonely cowboy riding the wide prairie has become part of a modern mythology. Much of this myth was probably created through the magic of motion pictures. Certainly, it was helped along by an accumulation of exaggerated fiction written to attract attention, rather than telling the facts. Early writers of pulp fiction never failed to assure readers of the truth of their melodramatic extravaganzas. But overstatement created confusion, and eventually a new group of writers tried to discredit the aura of glamour surrounding the West. Their efforts were nothing more than exaggeration in reverse and simply added to the confusion. In any event, it now seems clear that somewhere along the line, tradition became thoroughly mixed with legend. The truth probably lies somewhere in between.

Legend has it that all cowboys on the frontier wore their guns low and were either paragons of virtue or rustlers. In the vernacular of the movies, they were either good guys or bad guys. But was it all that simple? Let's take a look.

Old-time rider, Mose Burkitt of Fruita, Colorado, relates the following incident which took place about 1910:

> "*We were on a summer ride in West Salt Creek — Bart Howell and Johnnie Miller were repping for the North Side; Bill Cobb, Sam Moore, and myself for East Salt Creek; Ed Gordon, Gibb Webb, and Bert Hubbard for West Salt Creek.*
>
> "*We had had a long hot ride on the desert; nothing to eat or drink since early morning and were coming back up the canyon in the evening and stopped at the water trough at Carbonera to get a drink and water our horses. About that time, the bell rang calling the Greek section hands on the Uintah Railroad to supper. We watched things for awhile, and one of the boys said, 'It's a damn shame when good hard-working Americans have to go hungry while they import Greeks* and feed them three squares a day.' Another said, 'That's right, and I think we ought*

* Anyone who spoke a foreign language — probably from — "It's Greek to me."

to see what we can do about it.'

The windows of the cook shack were all wide open, and when we went in, the Greeks were just setting down to supper. Sam Moore pulled his .45 and said, 'I'm going to shoot once through the ceiling; once through the floor, and the next time right down this row of seats,' demonstrating with his gun just in case any of them didn't understand English.

When Sam shot through the ceiling, the Greeks went out through the windows two at a time, and we sat down to eat. After we had all had a good meal, Bart Howell (sitting at the lower end of the table) wanted some coffee, and when he got up to get it, Bert Hubbard said, 'Bring me the spuds.' Bart had the spuds, but turned the bowl upside down over Bert's head, and said, 'Here's your spuds!' About the time Bert got the spuds out of his eyes, Ed Gordon, sitting next to Bert, turned the gravy bowl over his head and said, 'Have some gravy, Bert!' About that time, Bert became undone, and the ruckus started. Bill Cobb joined them, and the rest of us went the way of the Greeks and let the four have at it. By the time they had fed each other what was left of the pie, jelly, syrup, etc., they had lost most of their shirts, and the cook shack was slightly out of repair. As it was getting late, we didn't have time to leave things as we found them. It was an old-time custom of the cow country that if you ever ate at a neighbor camp and didn't wash the dishes, you better never go back.

P.S. I forgot to mention that the Greeks had some beer in the horse trough — the kind that makes a jack rabbit chase the bear."

The legend of the cowboy is filled with inconsistancies. Certainly an accurate account must include such high-spirited hijinks, but let's expand on that legend a bit more. Catherine Moore of Grand Junction, Colorado adds this account to the mosaic:

"In 1902, my grandfather, Charles Sieber, was shot from his horse and killed by one Joe Harris, over a dispute about a wrong-branded calf. Several years later, Harris was shot from his horse and killed by Joe Pace, one of grandfather Sieber's cowboys who had this remark after the killing, 'That's for Charlie Sieber.'

Joe Pace was a tough hombre from Texas. In those days, lots of outlaws came to this country to hide out, and Grandpa always hired them. Some stayed and helped settle this area and behaved like good citizens.

After grandpa was murdered in 1902, the Thatcher brothers took over the Sieber Cattle Co., and it became known as the T. Cattle Co., and was managed by F. D. Parks.

As long as grandfather Sieber was here, the sheep were kept out of this country. In 1908, they finally made it. A swinging bridge was built across the Colorado River two or three miles below the Rio Grande pump house, which was on the river five miles south of Cisco, Utah. Forty-thousand head of sheep, belonging to the Goslin Sheep Co. were pushed across this bridge onto the Sand Flats in one night. As time went on, some of the old cow men changed over to sheep, and now the sheep outnumber the cattle in this once, sheep-free country.

Bob Fuller died in about 1901. Joe Pace, who was Bob Fuller's cousin, bought in with Mrs. Fuller, and they ran cattle for many years in this area. Mrs. Fuller died in about 1930. Joe Pace sold the outfit to Jim Luster in the late 1930s.

As a child, I adored Joe Pace and spent a lot of happy days at their summer camp. Joe would go out and gather a half-dozen calves, put them in the corral for me to ride. If I stayed on one, he would cheer, but if I went off, which I usually did, he would laugh and tell me to try another one. This was the summer the first sheep were brought onto Pinon Mesa, and how we hated them. I was ten and Leola was 15. Every day, we got on our horses, took the dogs, and hunted up a sheep herd. Back and forth through the herd we ran our horses, hollering and sicking the dogs. We would scatter those ewes and lambs for a long ways, and never once did we see a herder. They were too scared of Joe Pace."

Mrs. Moore's graphic recollections of those early days point with unerring aim to another facet of the old legend. It had to do with land use. Rivalry for water and grass on the open range of the West led to many conflicts in which stockmen often took the law into their own hands. The sharpest and most lasting of such conflicts were between cattlemen and sheepmen. This clash of interests was in many sections the cause of bitter range wars. Such clashes can be understood only in the context of existing circumstance; they should be discussed, therefore, in terms of time and place and conditions. For in the beginning, as has been noted, the border country settled hard. There were some, however, who could see beyond the initial hardships. In 1886, for example, Charles W. Haskell, Editor of the Mesa County Democrat, wrote this eloquent description of the new land west of the Great Divide:

>"On the Western Slope of the Rocky Mountains, on the border line separating Colorado from Utah, lies the County of Mesa. So situated on the extreme western edge of the great range of the Continent, and joining the plains and extensive valleys of Utah, its physical features partake of the nature of both, and within its borders are mountain ranges, high plateaus, covered with luxuriant grasses and coniferous forests, immense rivers, with numerous tributaries, and valleys, fertile and extensive.
>
>As a result, Mesa County is adapted to mining, grazing and farming. Within its mountains and canyons are found extensive veins of coal, iron, copper and silver, but awaiting development from the miner. Its extensive plateaus and elevated parks and valleys covered with luxuriant grasses afford stock a range for summer and winter, not to be surpassed. While the lower, and more extensive valleys, with their fertile soil, abundance of water for irrigation, and mild, equitable climate, permit the farmer to devote his attention to the successful production of either grain, fruit, or vegetables.

Through the southern portion of the County passes the Uncompahgre Plateau; the Grand Mesa and Battlement Mountains extend along the northwest, while along the northern boundary line extend the Book Cliffs; all converging toward one great valley, the Grand Valley of Mesa County. These plateaus and mountains are spread out on their summits to extensive parks and large forests. For summer ranges for cattle, these parks cannot be surpassed; and the foothills and valleys, formed by the streams which drain them, afford ranges for winter equal to the former in the luxuriant growth of grasses, if not in extent of surface.

The Uncompahgre Plateau is drained on the south and west by the Dolores River, and from the north and east by the Grand and Gunnison Rivers. The Grand Mesa is drained by the Grand, the Gunnison, and Plateau Creek; Battlement Mountains and the Book Cliffs are drained directly by the Grand River.

This river is the largest in the state. It is not only the largest river, but contains a larger volume of water than all the other rivers combined. Competent observers estimate that the water supply of this large river is sufficient to irrigate 500,000 acres of land. Confluent with it at Grand Junction is the Gunnison River, a river only surpassed, within the state, by the former in volume of water; and in the south is the Dolores River, ranking only next to the Gunnison in the amount of water flowing between its banks.

These rivers possess numerous tributaries with fertile valleys which form the grazing and farming portion of the county.

These tributaries and valleys along the Grand are the Parachute and Roan Creeks on the west side, and the Cactus, Blue Stone and Plateau Creeks on the east side.

Along the Gunnison are the Kannah Creek and Whitewater Valleys, extending several miles along the creeks from which they are named. The largest valley, however, in the county and one of the largest in the state is, Grand Valley.

This valley contains an area of 150,000 acres of tillable lands with the most fertile of soils, and with a water supply far beyond what can ever be used for irrigation. Commencing at the mouth of Hog Back Canyon, about fifteen miles above the junction of the Grand and Gunnison Rivers, the Grand Valley extends along the former river for a distance of forty miles, with a width varying from five to fifteen miles."

It was a natural fact of life that such glowing reports would eventually reach to the far side of the mountains. As time passed, word continued to go out on the wonderful future of the Grand Valley. It told of two large irrigating canals and several thousand acres in fruit, hay and grain. It mentioned another — to be known as the Highline — which would irrigate many more thousands of acres. All one had to do was pre-empt 320 acres, and when the new canal was finished, the land would be worth several thousand dollars. It sounded too good to be true.

In the spring of 1891, a young man from the East named, Whiting, came over the mountains to see for himself. He stopped off in Fruita, a small town located twelve miles down valley from Grand Junction. In later years, he described the scene at the time of his first arrival:

> "Grand Valley was about seventy-five miles long and from fifteen to thirty miles wide, mostly flat, lying at an altitude of about five-thousand feet, and surrounded by high mountains. It was a desert, covered with low brush and grass, which made good cattle range. Several cattle men had their ranches and homes near Fruita. They had very little snow in the winters, the days were warm and pleasant, but the nights were very cold for about two months, the thermometer registering zero. To the south and west for forty or fifty miles was desert and mountains, inhabited by wild cattle, horses, and game. This was called, "The Range," where everybody pastured their stock they were not using, sometimes not seeing them for a year at a time, and then taking days or weeks to find them.
>
> There was nearly always plenty of excitement in that little village, Fruita, being the headquarters of the range. On holidays, Saturday nights and Sundays, there was always a bunch of cowboys celebrating, and although there were no saloons there, they always had plenty of whiskey. After having a few drinks, one, two or four men would ride their horses at a gallop right down the main street, yelling and shooting in the air just for fun. This might happen in the daytime, or any time between the dark and daylight. They also made a racetrack of the main street, betting either money, or one's horse against the other

> —*the loser handing the bridle of his horse over to the winner. Sometimes, they bet one or a dozen head of cattle, but with all this, during two years I was there, there was not one murder. There were, however, a few shooting matches out on the range, when they would get in a row over the pasture, in some certain part of the range, or one outfit stole the other's cattle or horses. It was an unwritten law among them that if one outfit (or brand) were using a certain part of the range, no other outfit could come in and use the same territory. If they did not heed the warning, either the cattle or cowboys were shot on sight, and they were shot dead, because 'dead men tell no tales,' and it was nearly always impossible to find out who did the shooting; consequently, they had a law all to themselves."*

Now, while young Whiting's estimates of size, distance and direction may have been off a bit, it must be admitted that his overall descriptive powers were excellent. And while his observations on shooting matches and range fights could very well have been exaggerated, the several statements do have a certain ring of authenticity. Consider this follow-up incident related by Mr. Whiting as an illustration of rough times on the open range:

> *"One day a message came from Cap Davis who was running cattle in a canyon thirty-five miles down the Grand River on the border of Utah to send him three cheap coffins, as it had become necessary to kill three men. It was commonly reported that Davis was a gunman and had already killed several men, but in*

such secrecy that it could not be proved that he did it. He would never stop at a hotel, and when going any place, he camped by his wagon, trusted no one, and always had his two 44s ready. For some time previous to the shootings mentioned, he had been suspected of stealing cattle and putting his brand on them, so these three fellows were watching him and caught him in the act. When they started to go away, he shot all three of them, then gave himself up to the authorities, and at the trial claimed they got in a row, said the three men drew their guns on him, and he shot them in self-defense. All three were dead and could not contradict it, so he could not be convicted."

No matter how you slice it, this is meaty material. Like an old-time distilled beverage aged in the barrel with two pounds of fine-cut tobacco to the gallon, it has the flavor of individuality. To this adventurer, the Old West was not only real, but near at hand. To him, the little village of Fruita, Colorado was at the center of that exciting world; it was the headquarters of the "Range." There can be little doubt that others saw the area in a different light, for it was about this same period that Editor Haskell, twelve long country-miles away in Grand Junction, wrote:

"On the border land of Mesa County and of the state, in the state, in the Grand Valley, lies Fruita, founded by W. E. Pabor and his associates, in the spring of 1884. The year previous, an attempt had been made to lay out a town on the same site, by Grand Junction parties, to be named, Fairview; but the organiza-

tion was not perfected, and the land where the town of Fruita now is, was pre-empted by four men named Steele, Ross, Sutton, and Downer.

When Mr. Pabor came into the valley as the agent of the Colorado Loan & Trust Company, his examination of the soil led him to believe that the land, lying from eight to fifteen miles west of Grand Junction, was eminently suited to fruit growing; and that the similarity of soil, climate and altitude to Utah Valleys, lying a hundred miles beyond, indicated that the peach, apricot and possibly foreign varieties of grapes could be successfully grown.

In the fall of 1884, Steele, Ross, Downer and Sutton, having proved up on their lands, were bought out by Mr. Pabor, in behalf of a Town Company; and Fruita was surveyed by A. J. McCune and patented. The town site proper, comprises eighty acres, in the center of which is a park named after the President of the Town Company. On the north and east are laid out five and ten-acre fruit tracts, which have been set out to a variety of standard and small fruits, while the residence blocks of the town site have been set round with Box Elder, Maple, and Cottonwood trees, planted 15 feet apart; these in a few years will make a beautiful village of Fruita."

W. E. Pabor was a pioneer editor, a builder of towns, and a poet. There were some who maintained he also had the gift of prophecy. Certainly, his view of the future was optimistic as he wrote of the Fruita area in his poem, **We Are All For Colorado:**

"Nowhere is there such a valley,
Nowhere is there such a town;
with such promise for the future
Crowned with riches and renown.
Happy homes and prosperous people
Growing richer year by year —
Come, oh come across the mountains,
Health and wealth await you here.

See the mighty river giving
Water to the thirsty land;
See the peach and apple orchards,
And the farms on every hand;
Blue the blossom of the alfalfa —
See the berries, blushing red;
Come, then, to the Sunset valley
Where the roan cliffs lift their head."

It is quite clear that Mr. Pabor did not visualize this bright new center of the world as the headquarters of the range. His interests were in other areas; he was obviously a dreamer. But visionaries were necessary to the opening of a new land. They were prime movers in a time when what happened to one group was of tremendous consequence to the others. For this was a period when the resources and events of any new region were closely bound together and each individual destiny was indelibly woven into the fabric of the whole. It is in such context that we continue with sketches and commentary in this story of old-time cattlemen who settled on the rugged mountain country west of the divide.

*   *   *

DISPATCH

Grand Junction, Colorado
November 22, 1882

An event of great interest occurred at this date. The arrival of the first locomotive, and completion of railway communications with the outside world. The sight of this, the first train in the valley, caused much rejoicing among the people. It was like the arrival of an army sent to relieve a beleagured city.

During the latter part of the month, a census of the city was taken, showing a population of 524.

CHAPTER TWO

SADDLE UP

Now, all you young maidens, where'er you reside,
Beware of the cowboy who swings the rawhide,
He'll court you and pet you and leave you and go
Up the trail, in the spring, on his wild bronco.

The American cowboy emerged from the Old West as a distinct, larger than life character. As the legend formed, he not only became an integral part of our national heritage, but in the minds of many, the sum total of what a genuine man should be. How did such a thing come about? Why such universal appeal?

No matter how you approach it, the cow business was a tough old game, and hardship, isolation and danger were the substance of a cowboy's everyday life. The average puncher spent most of his time in the open. His job was working cattle, and the hours were long and the wages low. It is hard to find glamour in sleeping on the ground and rising at dawn, or in sweating through burning summer days or freezing in winter blizzards. But let a man once get the range in his blood — the silent dawns and the fiery sunsets, the howl of a coyote and the whisper of the wind on a starlit night — let a cowboy get it all in his system, and he was likely to stay with it until the end.

Old-time punchers have long been pictured as being strong, silent, clannish and reserved with strangers. This may have been true as a surface point, but as is usual with men of the outdoors, there was another side to the coin. For on their home ground, no more fun-loving, hard-cussing group ever existed. Perhaps it was because of the way they lived that most of them saw the humorous side of life. At any rate, cowboy humor was a fact of life, and it expressed itself in extravagant, picturesque speech, practical jokes, and in tall tales that invariably grew with the telling.

One custom common to the entire western range country was the use of nicknames. No matter what a man's given name might be, sooner or later, he would be tagged with some descriptive label such as, Tex, Speck, Rusty or Slim. Once branded with such a "handle", the victim was usually marked for life.

Another outstanding characteristic of the cowboy was the standard reaction when a friend or bunkmate took a tumble or got caught in a tight fix. Any unfortunate or awkward situation, be it moral or physical and short of death was invariably greeted with a bellylaugh. It was a reaction grounded in the basic range country attitude that any man had a right to strut his stuff the best he could, but he ought not get caught with a wet finger in the sugar sack. Such an attitude reflected the life that cowboys lived, and the lusty he-man quality of it all can probably be best summed up in an old cowboy jingle:

> *Last week when Slim got throwed*
> *I thought the boys would bust;*
> *We liked to died a-laffin'*
> *To see him chewin' dust.*

Now the scene is set. And we had better let some of those old hellraisers tell it in their own words.

Mose Burkitt:

I was raised on a hay, grain, and fruit ranch, but that looked too much like work for me, and I had got a taste of riding from helping with a bunch of range horses my father had acquired from C. C. "Windy" Johnson. They told me all a cowpuncher had to do was "eat, sleep, and ride a pony." Sounded good to me, until I found out by experience that it was mostly – ride a pony, postpone a good many of your meals, and meet yourself getting up in the morning when you went to bed at night.

In the spring of 1902, I was thinning beets alone one day when I heard horse bells and saw a bunch of horses coming down the road. It was Burns Fisher headed for the spring ride. He said, "Come on and go on to the round-up, Mose."

I crawled over the fence and said, "Catch that bed horse." (He was fooling, but I wasn't). I rode the bed horse down to Jim Turner's house in Cleveland where they all met. Jim staked me to a saddle, and Burns gave me a horse, and we went to Mack where we spent the first night. The next morning, Al Sayles and Doc Gavin each gave me a horse, so I was pretty well mounted. We rode what they called a "greasy sack" outfit, packed tents, bedding, Dutch Ovens, everything

on a string of pack horses. We started on West Salt Creek, covered the East Salt Creek country and over into the Big Salt Wash where Charley Ray had a camp which was later bought by Tom Cuddy and Matt Lane. Among those previously mentioned on the ride that I remember were Tom Cuddy, Lee Ashley, Bert Mahanny, and Doc Kirk.

I didn't draw any pay, but I sure earned my bacon and beans washing dishes, peeling spuds, dragging wood and chopping it, day herding and jingling horses. Seems like I was on a horse jingle about every morning. The ride lasted about a week or ten days, and when I got home, the beet field was just like I left it.

Ute Osborn: On the range near Hunter Mine.

We used the rims and desert for horses and calves while the snow was on the ground. Ollie Pysert worked for us. He and I were camped in our winter cabin near the Hunter Mine. One day, we were riding on the desert and got to the cabin for dinner. Ollie went to the horse pasture in the rims to get us a fresh horse while I got dinner. Soon, I heard Ollie screaming for help; he had killed a rattle snake, put his foot on it and started cutting the rattles off; the snake turned his head up over Ollie's finger. He grabbed his finger and ran down the trail; I met him almost to the cabin. I took a spool of heavy batchler's thread, wrapped the finger above the knuckle-pulling and wrapping until I had pulled the flesh and skin to the bone.

While I was getting a horse, he started to town on mine. He met Bose Hartman and fainted and fell off; Bose revived him, put him back on his horse, and started him on his way. I soon caught up with him, and he started to faint. With my quirt, I pursuaded him to hang on. We got to our winter quarters – a house near the Starr Schoolhouse; there, I gave him a bottle (about a quarter-full) of whiskey. We made it on to Roan where Mr. Roan ran a store, gave him a quarter half-pint more of whiskey and went on to Grand Junction on dirt roads. It rained hard all the way. We stopped in front of the Orson Adams bank, went upstairs to Dr. Bull's office where with a knife, Bull slit his finger from the thread to the end. When the green and red blood quit running, Doc had Ollie suck his finger until it was white as cotton. Bull then doctored it and sewed it back together. Doc said no one could have done better and thought no poison had got past the thread. He got well with no ill effects.

Lester Starr – Fruita, Colorado:

I always wanted to be a cowboy, so I hired out to Bart Owens in the spring of 1916. He had just shipped in a thousand-head of Old Mexico steers. We started from Fruita to Douglas Creek Pass. It took about two days to get to the foot of the Douglas Creek Pass. That was my first experience night-herding. Just below the R. O. Brown place, they put I and another boy on at 3:00 AM. John Hudson was the foreman. His instructions were whatever you do, hold them, and he rode off to the wagons. Well, I and this other boy got by pretty good, until about daylight, and then we couldn't do a thing. They started drifting up the canyon. Well, I wanted to be a cowboy, and I knew I'd get canned, if we wasted them, but they got away from us. When John Hudson caught up with us, I was in the lead on top of Douglas. The steers scattered all over that cone. I was blue, tired, and hungry walking beside a blowed-up horse. I knew I would probably get canned that day. John rode by and said, "You're a hell of a cowboy. I told you to hold them." The last night, everything was lovely.

I stayed on the job for a couple of months, and then they wanted me to work on the ranch, but I could do that in Grand Valley. I came back to Fruita. The next spring, I went to work for Tom Cuddy and worked for four or five years and had a few head of my own. I finally quit up there and went to farming in Grand Valley.

Frank Moore — Glade Park:

We came here in 1903, and my dad was a horse trader. If he didn't trade every day, he thought it was lost. Until I graduated in 1912, I spent the summers out riding for some outfit. I spent two years with Lee Ashley, one year with Burns Fisher, two years with Louis Goucher up on Lanes Range, a year with Charles Turner on Willow Creek, and here with Austin Boy on Meadow Creek. In the spring of 1912, I took the first steady job of cowboying with Ed and Lew Young. I have got them to thank, because they worked me 18 hours a day; we ate when we had a chance. I thought there must be an easier way of making a living, so I quit and went to irrigating orchards.

In the spring of 1913, I started to work for the government and put in thirty years surveying. When I was working on the survey, we were chaining down through the pinons and cedars one day and heard the brush cracking and looked around, and there was a pretty good-looking girl running down there. I got a pretty good description of her and hunted her up. We went together off and on for three or four years and finally married. But the first pair of shoes she had, we always had to put sand in them, so as to get her to wear them. She had gone barefooted for so long, I just couldn't keep those shoes on her.

After leaving government work in 1945, I decided to make an honest living, so we went out to Nevada and worked for five years for the people that bought out the old UC Land & Cattle Co. All this time, Katherine and I were accumulating a little land up on Pinon Mesa as we could get a few dollars together. We came back to Colorado in 1950, and have been living here ever since.

Jake Goss — Fruita, Colorado:

The Goss family came here to Mesa County in 1887. We came in a couple of wagons, along with the Turners, Oscar and Charlie, a boy and three or four girls and the old lady. We located in Fruita. Everybody then run the range cattle in town, and we had another town adjoining it called, Cleveland. They would steal the post office from Fruita and take it to Cleveland. Then, they would steal it from Cleveland and take it back to Fruita. Fruita finally won out. They were closer to the depot. Cleveland had a hotel, blacksmith shop, big store, a shoeing outfit, and a church or two. Finally, Fruita got all of it. The cattle came right into town in the wintertime. My brother-in-law caught a cow in town that was on the fight and threw her and broke her neck. He got off and got her head out from under her and was standing there holding on to her tail and had it fastened under her hind leg. There was a fellow named Murphy, who was not too bright, and my brother-in-law got him to come and hold her so he could get back to his horse. Then, he got on his horse and rode off, leaving

Murphy to hold the cow down. Murphy looked around every place and finally let go and run as fast as he could. There was a lot of people watching him, but the cow was already dead. I took Murphy to the Flying W. I worked him on the ranch, and the boys took him snipe hunting, and he got so scared of the old cow hide he was dragging that he hid under a foot bridge and stayed there for about two hours before I could find him. A couple of days later, the boss Hank Carr, tried to get him to feed the hogs some hay, but Murphy said, "I might be crazy, but I sure won't feed good hay to the hogs."

Looking back in hindsite, it is quite clear that Mose Burkitt was following a trend of the times when he jumped the fence to go cowboying. This last great frontier issued a special call to the young and the adventurous. But while there was a common bond between all who answered the call, cowboys differed as much as other humans in their various capacities. There were, for example, certain men in every cow camp who excelled at telling droll stories which helped pass time away in a pleasant manner. Storytelling was part of their birthright, and some of them practiced the gift with considerable artistry. Humor was basic to most rangeland stories, but the specialist always gave them certain individual touches, because of the way he handled the material. The natural storyteller could make the wildest exaggerations with a perfectly sober face, and cowboys loved it. Most favorite tales were told over and over, such as the classic story about a puncher who made a trip to Kansas City as the representative of a western Colorado cattleman. Upon his return, he made much of the hospitality he had received. The mayor, he bragged, had met him at the station with a brass band, and a special committee rode him in style to the best hotel where they gave him "a genuine Missouri breakfast" which consisted of a big ring of baloney, a bottle of rye whiskey and an ol' houn' dog.

"And what," he was always asked, "was the ol' houn' dog for?"

"Why to eat that God damn baloney — of course!" came the sober-faced reply.

Cowboys never grew tired of the punch line, and it, too, became part of the legend.

Legend in the Colorado-Utah border country would not be complete without the story of Charlie Glass. Charlie was a black cowpuncher who gained notoriety when he killed a Basque sheepherder in a gunfight during the range disputes of the early 1920's. A trial was held in Moab, Utah, and Charlie pleaded self-defense. Although he was acquitted by a jury of twelve, the true story of Charlie Glass remains controversial. He is truly a legend of the West. Our story of Charlie is related by one who knew him — Mrs. Enola Mock:

> Let us meet Charlie at home on the range. As he stands at the edge of a circle of cowboys around the campfire, we see that he is taller than most of the boys, and that he is well built with strong shoulders. He is genial and friendly, but never forward.
>
> He is dressed in sober and sensible clothes with no show of flashing color or fancy rodeo designs on his boots or chaps. His full-flowered stamped saddle bears evidence that he chooses for quality and use — so do his spurs that are not fashioned and decorated just to clank down Main Street for show.
>
> He rides a good string from the company-owned horses, for his

boss knows that he has the ability and knowledge to handle and take care of a horse. He eases up onto his saddle with the grace and agility of a good rider, and as he reins his horse away from the corral at a walk, we know that he is a real cowhand and not one of the modern screen version who spur away at a full gallop.

His bed roll is as good as the rest, and he spreads it down in the bunk house or on the tent floor alongside of those of the rest of the boys. When the company manager comes from town, Charlie waits to eat, until the boss has left the table. Otherwise, he sits down with the boys, sharing in their conversation and jokes of the day as they enjoy the meal.

He willingly helps with the camp work and chores as he tells you, "When I quit ridin', I'm gonna buy a silver-mounted Ford and a red plow."

And so it was here on the range where I met Charlie at a spring roundup in May, 1909. The *S + and other cattlemen were holding a roundup bunch on a point across the river just south of Fruita that day. Knowing that there would be a lot of cowboys over there to work the cattle, and that they would cook a good dinner on a campfire in dutch ovens, several of us girls decided, without invitation, to join them for the day. Those of us who had no horses of our own rented horses from Bagshaw's livery stable.

We were introduced to Charlie, one of the cowboys of the old West that gave it its color and atmosphere, a character respected by all his associates. He came to this country during the early 1900's. He was a native of Oklahoma with Cherokee blood in his veins. During his early life, he rode in Oklahoma and other parts of the Southwest,

---

* Called locally the S Cross

but it was in New Mexico near Roswell where Frank Parks became acquainted with him and persuaded him to come to Colorado to work for the S+ Company on Pinon Mesa where he rode for a number of years.

Cattlemen, former employers, acquaintances and friends all agree that fiction could produce no more colorful or picturesque a character than Charlie Glass. As a cowpuncher, those who worked with him declare he was expert as anyone in the game, a good rider, and a topnotch man with a lariat. The fact that he was one of the very few negro cowboys in the West, and the only one here, added to his notoriety. He was a familiar figure at Western Colorado rodeos where he took an active part in the events.

The dominant features of his character were his loyalty to his friends and employers, his courtesy, unselfishness and dependability. These traits of character were so marked that he was a welcome visitor in every camp, and his associates recognized his true worth. He never failed their trust or failed them in their need. When others hesitated to go, it was Charlie who stood with his hat in his hand all the time, winter or summer, when he talked with me on the streets in Grand Junction or elsewhere when we stopped to visit. It was Charlie who would not permit a cowboy to eat until my plate was filled and brought to me when I sat in the round up circle. And it was Charlie who made the coffee at the Summer Camp dances on Pinon Mesa, but who never came in where we were dancing, either to dance or as a spectator. And it was Charlie whose face spread with shocked surprise when he saw me standing in the door of his cabin on Westwater as he rode up in the late afternoon.

I've often wondered what thoughts went through his mind.

It was he who got mad and really mad when a careless packer failed to pack his sour dough jug right, and it tipped over, spilling its contents into the panyard. He was not so much disgusted about the mess, as he was about the loss of his sour dough which he needed to make biscuits for the boys on the ride. It was Charlie who was a gentleman when he came to our ranch and sat at our table well-mannered and quiet as he ate with us as our friend.

After leaving the S+, Charlie worked for Oscar Turner as his foreman for sixteen years. He worked also for Wallace Cunningham and H. S. Tracy in eastern Utah. While in Colorado, he worked also for Frank Parks and others spending a short time up around Axial Basin.

"Wherever Charlie Glass rode and worked, there is sorrow at his passing," so says his obituary, "and friends feel that a comrade has ridden on ahead to greet them when they come."

Among us, his friends, we often spoke of him as, Nigger Charlie, not in any disrespect at all, but rather we used this name with an intimate, friendly tone to distinguish him from the other Charlies. He had his faults, yes, so we all have, but they were not malicious as were those of some sheepherders who poisoned the quarter of beef he had at his camp while he was gone on a ride on the desert not far from Cisco. There had been disputes with the sheepherders who had encroached on the cattle range where Charlie was running cattle for his employer, and so they sought to get rid of him. But, this night, he cut a piece of beef from the quarter and fed his hungry dog. Before he cooked some for his own supper, the dog promptly died.

Later in the range trouble, or range wars they were sometimes called, Charlie killed, persumably, one of those same sheepherders. At a long and spectacular trial at Moab, Utah, he was acquitted when it was proven he had acted in self-defense. He met his tragic death at Cisco, Utah where he spent most of his time in his later years, although he kept an apartment room in Grand Junction where he stored his few belongings. And this is how it happened.

The men involved succeeded in persuading Charlie to go with them, against the advice of a friend. They got him drunk, and then took him for a ride in a light pick-up truck which was overturned, presumably, in an accident a short distance from Cisco. Charlie was the only one killed, supposedly with a broken neck. However, at the mortuary, there was found another wound just above the ear across the head horizontally that had fractured his skull causing a brain hemmorhage. A rod or bar had caused this injury. He was about 65 when he passed away on February 22, 1937. He was not married and had no immediate survivors who could be located, though at one time, his mother lived at Roswell, New Mexico.

His funeral was held at Fruita at the Starks Funeral Home which was filled to capacity with his friends. There were no negroes there, nor was there a section reserved for the family, for we, his friends, were his family. There were many floral tributes with red roses placed on his casket. Reverend Methvin paid a touching tribute to his memory, closing with that beautiful poem, "I Know Not What His Creed May Be." There was a tear in every eye as the Misses Barbara and Joan Taylor sang, Rock of Ages, Down De Road, and Old Faithful. The pallbearers were old-time friends: Ute (M. U.) Osborn, Claude Taylor, Don Weimer, A. B. (Bert) Mahanny, Lew Young, and Leslie Tomlinson. He is buried in Elmwood Cemetery in Fruita where a small monument marks his grave. When you go there on Decoration Day, you will find flowers left by friends who haven't forgotten him.

Here are some stories:

At a cowpunchers' reunion and rodeo, Charlie had a red, white and blue shirt for the occasion. Some of the kids made fun of him, so he said, "See here, kids, no white peoples got a shirt like this and darned few colored peoples."

When he was track walking for the Rio Grande RR through Ruby Canyon west of Mack, Colorado, some one asked him how it went. He answered, "Alright, only it was darned monopolis!"

When he got the news that Oscar Turner was dead, he just sat down on the curb of the street by the Grand Valley Bank at Grand Junction and cried, regardless of passersby. This was Charlie.

Harry Brown — Vernal, Utah

I used to live in Fruita, Colorado and graduated from high school here in 1912. Right after that, I went out into Utah and started to work for Charles, Oscar and Albert Turner. At that time in that country, there weren't many roads. Every place we went, we had to pack our bed and camp on a pack horse. In the spring of 1913, there was five or six of us going down to the low countries to drift cattle up. We had these pack horses. Sy Nearing was working there, too, and we got about where we were going to camp. Of course, we all got our ropes down to catch a pack horse, and Sy was riding a big blue horse that would buck him off about every time he rode him. He took his rope down, and this old horse bucked him off, and Sy got up. He was *pretty mad. He said he would ride that horse, if it took him all night. He got back on the old horse, and the horse bucked him off again. He got up and got on him again.*

There was a fellow there by the name of Vint Dennis. He was quite a tease, and he rode up to the side of Sy, and Sy was kind of holding the horse up, and he said, "Well hang them in him, Sy," and so Sy drove them (spurs) right in him, and the old horse bucked him off again. He was still pretty mad. He caught the horse and got on again, and Vint rode up beside him again and said, "Hang them in again Sy."

Sy said, "Oh, let the old sonuvagun go to the devil!"

I guess in those days there was hardly a wagon road over that mountain. All the fellows there would have to trail their cattle to Mack to ship them. Then, in later years, they trailed them to Grand Junction to the sugar factory. It used to take us all the way from 6 to 8 days that we would be on the trail with a beef herd. It would be about 90 miles to Grand Junction. Now, we have roads, and the fellows can load up the cattle and have them on the scales in four or five hours here in Grand Junction. The ranchers over in that country had to go over the mountains and across the desert up to Fruita or Grand Junction to get supplies. They would come in about twice a year, fall and spring. When you went back over in the fall, you were done. You couldn't get out except on horseback. You couldn't get the wagons over the mountain.

Shorty Gross — Fruita, Colorado

My folks came to Fruita in 1885, and I landed in 1896. In 1904, *my older brother and I run a town herd out of this town. We would pick up those milk cows every morning and take them out along the lanes and on the hills to graze. Got them back to their owners in time to milk every night. We were paid $1.50 per month for each cow. At the peak, we had 58 cows in the herd. That was good money in those days. I lost my father in the fall of 1900, so I grew up more or less on my own. I run around with the Fisher kids and Raymond Skelly – they had the old Straddle X Camp in Hay Canyon. Old Cheesey Fisher and I decided, if we were going to be decent hands, we had to have a little practice riding broncs. We used to go out on the desert and corral them ponies, ride the little ones without a saddle and saddle the bigger ones. So, we broke a horse of Mose Burkitt's our way. He was broke to catch him and saddle up. Then, when you crawled aboard, you wanted to set pretty tight in the saddle. They were gentle, until we made them wild. I worked around on various ranches – wherever I could get a job that would buy a pair of britches and a few groceries.*

In 1917, I went over on White River, and built me up a ranch over there. Sold out in 1948, and moved back over here. I spent a lot of time with the Fishers and Fisher kids. Franz Muhr was in on some of that horse taming, whether he will admit it or not. Don Weimer was another. The late Walter O'Connor was a pretty good rider. Then Mose can tell you about his sharp little bay horse that was so gentle to catch and saddle up. The first rodeo was right out in the flats up here around 1914 or 1915. The round-ups were just plain old hard, rough-and-tumble work and lots of dirt and dust. Old Al Sales done the cooking most of the time. But when Jay Nearing was the cook, you had something to eat. My God, he cooked the best bread and meat that you ever tasted and the best bread pudding. Sy Nearing did a little cooking also, but he couldn't even wash dishes for his dad.

Franz Muhr — Fruita, Colorado:

I am not old enough to know any history very far back. I couldn't tell it to you anyway, unless I was leaning on a corral fence or something. I worked here and there for cattlemen, including Mose Burkitt and R. O. Brown. Finally, I bought Mose Burkitt out. I don't remember what year that was, but about 1919. I run it then until about 1926, and then Mr. Mogensen and I went into a partnership, and we continued that for ten to twelve years. I still have a few cattle, but I farm mostly.

It is perfectly obvious at this point that cowboys were indeed as varied in outlook and general character as they were in physical make-up. Even personal skills varied to a degree, although all were expected to be proficient in the regular duties incident to the raising of cattle. A good cowhand was often required to be a veterinarian, a blacksmith, a fire fighter, a nursemaid, or a midwife. But above all, he was a horseman. He might be on duty as a line rider, bog rider, fence rider or bronc buster, but first and foremost — he was a rider.

Cattleman were great sign-watchers. On the range, outriders rode anywhere and everywhere. They checked on the condition of water and grass, and kept a wary eye on the general condition of the cattle. Always they watched for tracks of livestock, predators or strange riders. The wrong kind of hoofprint in the wrong place might send a cowman traveling out of his way for half a day, just to see what a strange rider might be up to. To a good tracker, each sign told a story as plainly as if it had been drawn in a picture book. The trail might lead to a wolf den, a bog hole, or into the next county, but it was usually noted and checked. For on the range, the preservation of property and one's own good health just might depend upon noticing signs and figuring out what they meant. There were many phases in the craft of cowboying, and as in all crafts, some men were more proficient in one area and some in another. While many were all-around hands, most cowboys knew their own limitations.

John Dowling of Grand Junction sums it up in a brief statement:

> *I started by running horses on Pinon Mesa in 1903 with the S Cross outfit. We started out in April and would ride from Yellowcat to the Mountains. I always considered myself to be a bronc rider and rode in a great many tournaments. Never could rope much. The last cow work I done, I helped Lew Young trail cattle from here to the east end of Pinon Mesa down between the rivers. Then, I went railroading over on the narrow gauge out of Cimmaron. Retired off the Western Pacific in 1957. I guess I've always been a cowboy at heart.*

Harry Knight of Grand Junction rode for the Tom Currier outfit of Collbran and Grand Junction for many years. A cowboy for most of his life, Harry's best remembered incident has to do with his part in helping a government trapper named, Roberts, run down the great killer-wolf known as Bigfoot. It was a tracking job which required skill, perserverance, and a knowledge of the country. Harry Knight had received early training for the job.

The Knight family had come to Mesa County in 1901 in a one-wheeled cart pulled by a team of mules. Once settled into the area, they had made a business of hunting wild horses in the Bookcliff Mountains. On one hunt, Dave and Charlie Knight caught 72 head. They all became expert at tracking; and they knew the country.

In 1924, Harry married Nettie Stolze who during their courtship was housekeeper for the George Currier family. After they were married, they lived in a log cabin which Tom Currier had bought for $800. It was located high above the Dry-fork area of the Bookcliff Mountains and had no modern conveniences. It was from here that Harry helped trapper Roberts track and run Bigfoot and his mate to their final rendezvous. The hunt did not end with the death of the pair, however.

Says Harry Knight:

The only way to get rid of wolf trouble is to get 'em all. An' that means the pups. We knew the female had a litter hid out up in the rims, an' we had to find 'em. Well, we backtracked an' finally found a den, an' I went in after them pups. That den was in solid rock, an' it narrowed down in the back, so I couldn't reach the little devils. I had to get a stick with a crook on the end of it, and then I reached in and twisted, until I caught one and dragged him out. It took quite awhile, but I finally got them all, and that was the end of the wolf trouble in this part of the "Books".

To the old-time cowboy, a good cow horse was the primary tool of his trade. On a working ranch, there were four main jobs for horses: roping, cutting, riding circle, and standing night guard. There were usually specialists in each cowboy's string, suited by nature and training for the different kinds of riding done in cow work. A horse well-trained for cutting a herd or standing night guard, might be of little value for roping. A horse used for riding circle needed a lot of bottom and endurance. A rider might be fifteen miles or more from the wagon when he started hazing cattle out of the brush and draws, and by the time he drove his gather back to the holding ground, he had covered a lot of country. It took a good strong horse for this kind of riding.

There were no branding chutes in the early days, and all cattle, big or little, were roped and stretched out either in corrals or on the open range. A good roping horse went into top speed from the first jump and stopped the minute the rider made a catch. The instant the roped animal fell, a top horse would pull against the rope and keep it taut. A tight rope prevented the cow from getting up, and even if the rider dismounted, a well-trained horse would maintain that pull on the rope. The best roper, no matter how expert he might be, owed much of his success to the training of the animal he rode.

It has been said that a top cutting horse was like having a second set of brains at the roundup. Once such a horse identified the animal to be removed, he could, quite literally, take that particular critter out of the herd by himself. Some horses became so proficient that they could actually cut without a bridle. In any event, most riders worked with a loose rein, since a well-trained horse anticipated every move and possessed the ability to spin and turn faster than the cow. A cutting horse did not get to be a special animal without a lot of training, and a top horse was a cowboy's pride.

Franz Muhr was one who broke and trained a good many horses over the years. One particular horse — a palomino out of Kentucky Gold Dust stock — was fast and unusually smart. Franz tells of being able to move a fair-sized herd by putting the palomino on drag while he, afoot, and the dog took the swing positions. The good word about this horse got around, and one day a representative of the world famous movie cowboy, Tom Mix, came out to take a look. The man from California evidently liked what he saw, for he offered $900. Says Franz:

> *"That was an awful lot of money in those days, but I sure as hell turned him down. That ol' horse just wasn't for sale."*

Mr. Muhr was, of course, leaning on a corral pole at the time.

The importance of the horse in the winning of the West cannot be overstated. The importance of horsemanship is not quite so obvious. For the fact remains that many riders, who might stick like glue in all kinds of terrain, were not necessarily horsemen in the full sense of the word. This point is brought out in sharp detail when one compares Western films of the Twenties, Thirties and Forties with a majority of "movies" — Western in theme — produced in the Fifties, Sixties and Seventies. And here, once again, the legendary Tom Mix can be used as a prime example.

Insofar as Westerns were concerned, Tom Mix dominated the Twenties in a thorough fashion. His influence was felt throughout the industry during his active period and would continue to be felt for twenty years to come. If ever anyone became a legend in his own time, it was this man. Yet, it's reasonable to suggest that a major reason for the tremendous success of the high-spirited Mix was his insistence upon sharing the spotlight with his equally high-spirited mount, Tony.

Throughout his peak years, and even into his sound pictures for Universal in the early Thirties, Tom made it a practice to alternate between plot Westerns, action or fun-Westerns and "Tony"-Westerns. Thus Zane Grey's, **The Lone Star Ranger** might be followed by a picture called, **Softboiled,** and **The Last of the Duanes,** (again a Zane Grey), by **Oh You Tony.** In the mid-twenties, at the absolute height of his career, Tom filmed **Riders Of The Purple Sage** on location under the very shadow of Mt. Whitney in the picturesque Owens Valley of California. In it, he played, Lassiter, the grim-faced gunman of Zane Grey's most famous story. Tony had little to do in this one, save run like the wind a time or two, but in the last reel just before he rolls the huge boulder which annihilates his pursuers and seals off the hidden valley forever, Lassiter removes the saddle and bridle and says goodbye to his mount. The scene was not in the original story, but in a touching, fleeting moment, it proved to be pure magic on film.

In the next year (1926), **The Great K & A Train Robbery** was shot on location in the Royal Gorge country near Canon City, Colorado. This time, Tony was up to his ears in the action. In one key scene Tom, playing a railroad detective, decides to look for clues in a large Spanish Castle-type home. He enters on foot, leaving his mount at the gate. In short order, Mix is cornered by several of the robber gang. Tony, meanwhile, has jumped the gate, crossed the courtyard, clattered up the marble stairs to the second floor and enters the upper foyer just in time to nudge one of the villains out an open window. The jump, fer Chrissake, is real. They land in the swimming pool, then out the far side, across the courtyard, over the gate — and fadeout.

In terms of fast-moving action and downright rousing fun, the aforementioned picture was among the best of the silent era. In terms of solid production values and sheer photographic beauty, however, **Riders Of Death Valley,** shot on location in California's famed desert valley in 1932 must top the list. "Riders" was second in a series of nine "talkies" Tom made for Universal Pictures in the early nineteen-thirties. Although both horse and cowboy were getting a bit "long in the tooth" by 1932, this was a Mix classic. The plot action builds dramatically as Tom probes the desert wasteland to find and rescue the heroine, played by the fair Lois Wilson. Trapped by the villains, Tom sends Tony for help. When the horse arrives back at the ranch, he is put in the stable while the cowhands speculate on Tom's whereabouts. Tony, wonder horse that he was, unlatches the box stall gate, hunts up each of the hands on the property, and by rearing, running and wheeling convinces them to follow him. The long sequence of riderless, unguided animal threading his way over hills and gulleys, along ridges and weaving a way through giant desert cactus at full gallup was sheer poetry in motion. One did not necessarily have to be a horse-lover or Western film devotee to thrill at the nick-of-time rescue. It was fun; good, lively entertainment, and it was done professionally. And therein lies the point in this entire matter of declining influence of the Western.

Tom Mix was a horseman, and in the entire context of the term this meant, trainer, as well. When he stepped to the saddle, his mount knew immediately what was expected. The command might be transmitted by voice, knee pressure, weight shift or by rein, but the response was quick and precise. When he did a jump or flying mount, the action was planned, rehearsed, almost choreographed like a Gene Kelly dance number. Tony was sharp, but he was sharp by command of his trainer. And everything was done in fast action, to please the eye and to give the illusion of spontaneity.

What a far cry from a vast majority of today's Western theme productions with their milling, undisciplined horseback scenes in which the horse may well decide the course of action. It's a clear echo of the prevalent current attitude that most of the heroes of historical tradition, and especially Western Tradition, were vastly overrated and need debunking. Something valuable has been lost in the process.

We do know that at the peak of its influence on American attitudes and values, the Western film was presented by people who knew which end of a horse got the oats. Most were men. Most were horsemen. Those who were not, fell by the wayside — or, if they survived, damn-well became horsemen in short order.

It may not be necessary to be a cowboy to portray a cowboy on film; but one ought to be a horsemen.

*   *   *

DISPATCH

1882 – Grand Junction, Colorado

During the spring of this year, the Grand Valley has been literally over-run with cattle thieves. 193 head of stolen stock were run into the country from Utah, and disposed of in various ways. Sixty head are said to have been sold to parties near this place, and about one-third recovered by the parties from whom they were stolen. The "gang" was composed in part of the following named persons: Doc Bangs, Geo. Howard, Tom Worthery, Buffalo Dan, John Mathews, Buckskin Jack and others. Geo. Howard, the leader, was killed at Whitewater by Sheriff Bowman and party, and this, was a vigorous pursuit of the outlaws, caused the breaking up of the worst band of cattle thieves that ever infested Western Colorado. Two of the band are now doing service for the Territory of Utah, in the penitentiary.

CHAPTER THREE

HOT IRON

A short-handled iron
Works like a charm;
And one more brand,
Won't do no harm.

In the beginning, land was free for the taking.

The pioneer cattleman usually established a ranch headquarters along some water course, and then simply took proprietary control over large areas of adjacent range. He assumed the right of prior use would protect his claim to the land. It was a right which had been established by possessing and putting to use an unclaimed wasteland. His stand was backed by frontier precident; the time-honored principle of "first in time — first in right" applied by tacit agreement. Viewed in context of time and circumstance, the concept was not only practical but necessary. For the cattle business in the early-day West was built on a foundation of cheap cattle, free grass, and low operating costs.

And open range was definitely the key to the entire operation.

Now at this particular time, it might be well to point out that an old-time range cow was a contrary critter and under certain conditions could be highly mobile. A rancher's claim to ownership of a particular animal was based almost entirely on the legibility of a brand burned on the hip or rib. Since cattle running at large on unfenced range were bound to mix, keeping an accurate tally was difficult to say the least. As cattle numbers increased, gathering strays and branding became ever more important; and this in essence was the basic function of the roundup.

To the old-time cowman, one of the most unforgettable sounds on the range was the resounding chorus made by a bawling herd that had been assembled for branding. Branding was hot, hard, and tedious work. To make a permanent mark in an animal's hide, the branding iron had to be heated white-hot. A brand had to be put on properly. If it were not burned deep enough, or if the iron was too cold, a brand could fade out or "hair over"; if the iron was held on too long, the brand could blotch. Any such imperfection might cause problems, since certain brands could look very much alike under adverse conditions. This was especially true at large roundups where branding irons were likely to be numerous.

It has been said that in the old days, many a herd was built up with no capital but hope, energy, and a steady hand. One old timer, who shall remain nameless, put it this way:

"The most valuable property in the range country, countin' totals, was cows. They walked around on four legs in out-of-the-way

places, and it was commonplace knowledge that many respected citizens considered it all right that they themselves had started with nothing but a running iron, a rope, and an easy conscience. But, of course," he added with a sly grin, *"they didn't approve of the same methods in others after they had made their own piles."*

On the face of it, one might conclude that some of those old boys did indeed have — many irons in the fire. But — of course — it's only hearsay.

West and south of Grand Junction lies a large mesa consisting of approximately 600,000 acres. It is known in general as, Glade Park. However, Glade Park proper is only a small portion of this country. Before the post office was established in 1910, the mesa was broken in sections and known to the old timers as, Big Park, Little Park, West End, Pinon Mesa, Little Dolores, Beezer Creek and Coats Creek. Catherine H. Moore tells of this area in the early days:

Until 1910, this was strictly cattle country. At one time, the Seiber Cattle Co. alone ran 30,000 head, and all the stock was wintered out. There were very few fences. Everyone's cattle went where they pleased — in the summer on Pinon Mesa — and all over the area known now as Glade Park. In the winter, they were pushed down on the benches toward the river. The Sand Flats and the Sinbad country in Utah also were used.

I have heard my father say when he came here in the 80's, that any place they rode through the high parks, grass dragged upon the stirrups. In the 90's, this country suffered a severe drought, and by that time, it was so heavily overstocked that most of the small outfits went out of business. The Sieber Cattle Co. took 400 head of cattle to White Canyon in Utah (now in the Canyon Lands Park). Emery Knowles was one of the men sent down there to look after the cattle. I have heard him tell with a chuckle about riding into Butch Cassidy's camp and being asked to get off and eat. He said that he knew he was eating S Cross beef, but he ate it and didn't complain.

One of the men who spent a considerable amount of time in this high park area was John C. Mock. Mr. Mock was a top rider in every sense of the word. He was born in 1884 on the Mock home ranch, located on the Arkansas River near Fowler (which was called Oxford in the early days of Colorado). John Mock started young, and by the time he was twenty-two had worked for cattle ranches on the eastern slope of the Rocky Mountains in Colorado, Montana and Canada. Mrs. Enola Mock tells of his coming to the western slope of Colorado:

In the fall of 1906, Johnie returned to Colorado to work for the Circle Diamond of the same Bloom Land and Cattle Company near Trinidad for about a year. It was here that Frank Parks watched Johnie breaking horses and said, "If you ever want a job, I have one for you at Grand Junction."

But Johnie returned to Canada in the spring of 1908 to work for Ogle, an Englishman and a squaw-man, who raised horses at Woody Mountain, Canada. Ogle offered Johnie an all-expense-paid trip to England, if he would stay with him, but the winters were too hard in Canada, he thought, and there were too many little half-

breeds; besides England was too far from home, so he turned down the trip and came to Grand Junction, August 8, going to work August 10, 1908 for Frank Parks, Manager of the S Cross outfit on Pinon Mesa. Thatcher Brothers of Pueblo owned the outfit then, though it was still sometimes called, The Sieber Cattle Company.

However, he took time off the winter of 1908 and 1909 and joined a wild west show called, The King Brothers. He was their trick rider and bronc rider. They travelled through the states of the deep south before returning in 1909.

It was while he was with the King Brothers Show that Buffalo Bill offered Johnie a chance to join his show that was leaving soon to tour Europe. Had he accepted Buffalo Bill's offer and gone to Europe, what might have been the future course of his life? This was just another opportunity he sacrificed when he didn't go, but came back to Pinon Mesa and was made range boss of the S Cross Co. which ran several thousand head of cattle. He stayed with this outfit, until they quit business the fall of 1910.

Now, Johnie's job as range manager, wagon boss, or range boss, as he was called here, was to run this particular outfit on the range. He hired and fired the men who worked under him; he had to know the range, its feed qualities and carrying capacity, its boundaries, and where and when to put the cattle thereon. He decided what to gather for beef and when to ship in the fall. He had to determine what cattle could winter out, and which ones had to be taken to the Company Ranch on Glade Park and fed. He organized the various round-ups and rides of the year, maintaining the wagons and keeping sufficient teams and cow horses for all the work. There were new horses to be broken and added to the cavvy, so "snapping broncs" was a part of a cowboy's job, if he could do it.

Johnie bought the grain for the horses, and the groceries for the cowboys, and maintained the summer camp on the mountain, and one place where they had a house and corrals. He had to keep a constant eye on the cattle rustlers, and try to find and reclaim the cattle, if they got off with them.

Now, let's take a look at the S Cross spring round-up of about 1909, before and after. Two big wagons; lumber wagons, they were called with usually about three side boards, added to make deeper loading capacity, were greased and made ready. The one which hauled the groceries, the pots, dutch ovens and tin dishes had a chuck-box built in the back end which was to cook's kitchen cabinet; the door which closed it tight when traveling let down to make a work table when needed. The cook had to know how to "skin" or drive two teams called a "four-up." Then the bed wagon likewise with two or three side boards was piled high with the cowboy's bedrolls and grain for the horses and was also pulled by two teams.

The S Cross with their wagons, cowboys and cavvy of possibly 80 horses more or less, started the spring round-up down near Thompson Springs, Utah to ride the desert (that part of the open range of Eastern Colorado and Eastern Utah lying between the Colorado River on the south and the Bookcliffs on the north). It extended well up the valley to several miles east from north of Fruita. Most of the cattlemen of the two states here, wintered their cattle on the desert, and the purpose of the round-up was to gather all the cattle, numbering in the thousands of head, so that they could be taken to their summer ranges. And so, as they worked up the desert eastward, the various cattlemen who had their headquarters in the north side or the south side joined the S Cross wagon and helped with the ride, cutting their cattle out as they reached their home rangelands.

Camp was moved each day and set up at a place designated by the range boss. Here they drove the day herd and held them, until the cattle from the day's ride joined them. All the outside men and the S Cross cowboys ate dinner at the S Cross wagon; then went out and worked the bunch, cutting out the cattle which were not to be driven on. The wrangler brought the horses, grazing them along. Each day's program was the same, until the S Cross crossed the river at Fruita with all the southside cattle.

There were rules of the range to be followed. There was a leader for each of the two groups who rode the circles. Johnie, as boss, was always one leader, while the second leader was chosen each day – by right of the number of cattle owned, or the man whose range bordered the territory to be ridden that day. Each leader scattered his men to ride where he directed them.

Another rule: when the cook was getting a meal, all men except his helpers, were supposed to stay out of his way. If they didn't, but got close enough to hinder him, Johnie told him to take the pot hook and clean them out.

Rule no. 3: Breakfast was ready at 4:00 AM, and a little earlier for the boys who went out on "Cocktail Guard" at four o'clock in the morning. This guard relieved those who had held the herd from 2:00 to 4:00 AM on the Graveyard Shift. Third guard was from Midnight to 2:00 AM. Second Guard from 10:00 PM to Midnight, and First

Guard from 8:00 PM to 10:00 PM. The cowboys who were to day herd the bunch were chosen by the range boss before the men on Cocktail left camp. A night horse, it is said, could tell time about as well as a clock, knowing when his guard was up, and he would be turned loose to the night hawk.

It was against the rules to bring horses into camp and tie them to the chuck wagon or leave them stand too near. Night horses were tied to the bed wagon for the boys to have ready to go on night guards.

On the desert, much of the time, they had to haul water in barrels for domestic use. They butchered their beef on the range, had dutch oven baking powder biscuits, fried potatoes, some canned vegetables, dry beans and prunes. Sometimes for dessert, they had rice and raisins cooked together – "Bear sign", they called it, and they had syrup.

The S Cross cowboys and other cowboys of the Western Slope wore chaps, boots made to order, spurs and Stetson hats with brims that didn't curl up on the sides like they do today. He carried a saddle slicker to keep him and his saddle dry, reaching to his feet. He had a lariat held fast to his saddle with a rope-strap, and he had a "piggin string" – and a short small cotton rope, much softer than a lariat – used to tie the two front legs and one hind leg of a calf together after it was thrown to be branded. Most of the boys in those days wore good leather gloves, carefully chosen with regard to the seams, smoked Bull Durham, and rolled their own. They played poker and Black Jack, and ran cattle that had gone wild on the range – renegades, they were called – and branded the mavericks when they could catch them.

This old-time cowboy knew how to use his saddle turned upside down for a pillow, and spread his chaps and saddle blanket for a bed to lie on. He often carried a six-shooter, and use it perhaps to turn a stampede, or to kill a rattlesnake. Real cowboys didn't go 'round shooting up people and places, a long time ago. He carried his change of clothes, either spread flat in his bed between the blanket and the tarp, and slept on them – or, he crammed them into a flour sack and rolled it in his bedroll. No suitcases went on a round-up.

Not all round-ups were done with wagons, but sometimes with pack horses, or they rode from the summer camps and bunched the cattle to brand the calves. They didn't use airplanes to hunt the strays, but rather followed tracks and sign. Some of the boys became so proficient, they could tell how many days old a cow track was, as well as pick up a track even in pine needles where scarcely an imprint was made.

Cowboy's horses' names were interesting. Some at the S Cross corrals were: Fox, Peg, Crackers, Rocky Mountain Joe, Anger-eye, Rimrock, Brother-in-law, Parrot and Poker. Neither did other cowboy language always mean what it said. A sleeper was not a sleepy guy, but a calf that was earmarked but not branded. A slick was an unbranded animal with no earmark as was a maverick. When a fellow working for another cattle owner was riding with the wagon, he was paid to be "repping," for instance. He was repping for the Lazy Ys when he rode with the S Cross wagon. A bronc-twister didn't twist the bronc as often as the bronc twisted him. He was a man qualified to break and train horses (mostly for cow horses) and who did this work as a full time job. He was employed by the big cattle outfits, or by horse-raisers at their ranches. He was called on, too, to try to make a cow horse out of a spoiled horse or an outlaw; one who bucked too many cowboys off.

While Mrs. Mock's comments on bronc-busting are absolutely valid, there were variations according to Franz Muhr:

> We were on the Flying W Ranch at the tail end of the spring round-up in 1918. Ote Osborn had his car at the ranch and every evening, as soon as the work was over, he and Si Nearing would tell some of the boys what horses they wanted to ride the next day; ask them to catch the horses the next morning for them and then they would take off for town.
> This soon got old for the boys who had to stay in camp, so one morning they caught the horses, led them up the creek and tied them behind some brush, then ran a four-year steer in the close pen, put Si's saddle and hackamore on him and put Ote's saddle and bridle on the very end of the arm of the hay derrick.
> When Ote and Si got home from town the next morning, they didn't see their horses and their saddles weren't where they had left them. But with a little help, they soon found their saddles.
> Si had to ride the steer out in the big.corral, while we did all we could to make his ride interesting. Ote was supposed to give the hay derrick a try, but the altitude was a bit high, and it was all he could do to get to his saddle and let it drop. This sure broke the boys of a bad habit for that season.

It was not all fun and games, however. Trail driving was another part of a cowboy's work. Morgan Goss, now living in Grand Junction, recalls an early drive:

The Goss family came to Fruita in 1887 in a covered wagon. We lived in a log cabin with a dirt roof for awhile and then moved over to Cleveland. In 1904, my father bought land west of Fruita where we ran a few cattle in the Big Salt Wash area. When I was seventeen, I started working for Cuddy & Lane who were in the cattle business in the Big Salt Wash Canyon. In the fall, after the weaner round-up, and the calves were weaned, we would deliver 250 to 300 steer calves to John Wilcoxon on Kimble Creek over the old Ute Trail. This Ute Trail goes up the mountain where Salt Wash and East Gulch fork and winds up through the cedars and then up the side of the main mountain on top and down to Kimble Creek.

In the spring of 1908, Bart Owens shipped 600 head of Mexican cattle to Mack, Colorado. After they were unloaded, his crew, Bart and Dode Howel, Arthur Gross, Lee Bennit, Bob Goss, Ed Colthorpe, and Ray Geigil spent three days branding them. They were camped east of Mack and south of the railroad tracks while they did this work. There were about 25 to 30 head of horses in the cavvy, and I was the horse jingler. I believe Al Sayles was the cook. We started out early one morning headed for Blue Mountain, forty miles north of Rangely, Colorado. The route was by way of Salt Creek over Douglas Pass, down Douglas Creek to Rangely, over the White River and then due north to Blue Mountain. We were three weeks on the road, and when night came, that's where we camped – rain or shine. While we were in

Rangely, we laid over one day to let the cattle rest. At that time, there was one store, one boarding house, one saloon in a tent, and a few log cabins in Rangely. Some of the boys found that tent. Some time later, Lee Bennit rode in all lit up and caught a Plymouth Rock hen that was feeding around, and put her in a dutch oven alive. The cook made him wring her neck and dress her out.

When we arrived at the foot of Blue Mountain, we ate supper at four o'clock so we could get up before daylight the next morning and get the drive finished. We didn't get any breakfast until one o'clock that afternoon when we arrived on top.

On the way home, I stopped at the N Bar Ranch and stacked hay for three days; then I rode the 65 miles home in one day.

Jefferson Duckett Dillard was a Texas cowboy who rode in the trail drives of the early West. In 1934, at the age of 74 years, he wrote his memoirs while spending the summer at the JEF summer camp on the Uncompahgre Forest Reserve near Delta, Colorado. In the following sequence, he tells of coming to Western Colorado:

In a few weeks, Mr. R. W. Johnson, who was the President of the San Miguel Cattle Company on the San Miguel River in western Colorado, and who was a manufacturer of surgical supplies in New Brunswick, N.J. (the Red Cross Johnson & Johnson Co. of today) stopped in Pueblo. He had been visiting his ranch on the San Miguel which he and his brother had started about 1883 after the Ute Indians had been moved to the Uintah Reservation. He heard of our Texas cow herd, and as they had a large number of beef steers to sell that fall, they wanted more cows to turn on their range. He telegraphed his general manager to go look the outfit over, and if it suited him to deal for them. It was about the 8th of September, and we were holding the herd just south of Chivington on the plains.

    Mr. C. E. Wetzel, manager of the San Miguel Cattle Co., came out, rode around through the herd for about a half-hour and soon made a deal with Wallace and Harding. He bought all the cattle and horses, and we were to deliver them to Lamar, Colorado.

    Wiley Everett and Buchannon could not sell their cows and were going to take them back south on the Neutral Strip and winter them over there. When Everett heard that Wallace and Harding had sold out, he wrote to me to go to the Neutral Strip and take charge of their cattle as he had to go back home. Buchannon had already returned to Texas. I held a good horse out of the oufit and made plans to take over Everett and Buchannon's outfit as soon as our herd was turned over at Lamar.

    We tallied out the Wallace and Harding cattle for brands as there were several owners, and then grazed leisurely over to the Arkansas River as there were several days before date of delivery. The evening before we were to put them in the Lamar stockyards, we drifted across the river and bedded the cattle in a valley about a mile above the town of Lamar. That night, a fellow came up to the camp leading a pack-horse with his bed and belongings; rode in and unpacked his horse, and after he had his supper, we got to talking with him and found out he had come from the Panhandle of Texas. He said he came across the Neutral Strip and stayed a few days resting up with a Texas outfit who were going to winter there. He said, "It was the worst tore up outfit I ever saw. There had been a killing. One of the cowboys had killed another and had pulled out. The owners had gone back to Texas. Everything was in an uproar."

I knew immediately that it was the Everett-Buchannon outfit I was to take charge of. I studied good and hard over what I should do, as I knew all of the fellows. I made up my mind that I would be taking on a lot of trouble, and as I had not made any promises to go, I decided to go with the San Miguel Company, as they had asked me to help ship the cattle to the Western Slope of Colorado. I planned to do so, as I could go to Pueblo with them and return to Texas via the Santa Fe Railraod.

I had never been west of the Continental Divide, though I had seen Pike's Peak several times. That Divide bothered me as the stars have always done. Many a time while laying in my blankets, I have looked up at the stars, restless, couldn't go to sleep, and watched the faithful old Big Dipper swinging around the North Star and wondered what was on the other side. Saw Pike's Peak and wondered what was on the other side of it. So just to see the country west of the Continental Divide, I turned my horse to the fellow who had the trail mules and wagon and hit the caboose behind those Texas cattle to Pueblo, Colorado. There we transferred from the Santa Fe to the narrow guage Denver and Rio Grande. The Pueblo Stockyards then were where the depot is now. Forty-seven years have passed since we took those three narrow guage trains from Pueblo to the Roubidean where we jumped them out of the narrow guage stock cars. We had come by Salida, Gunnison, Black Canyon, Grand Canyon, Marshall Pass to Montrose and Delta. We ate dinner there while we were waiting for the train ahead of us to unload at the Roubidean. Ed Wetzel and I were with the last train.

We laid over in Pueblo one day and while there, I went to the Gallup Saddle Shop and bought a Gallup Saddle. My old Texas saddle had had many a Texas steer tied to the pommel. It was an iron fork tree and had been made by August Zinke, saddle-maker at Llano, Texas. Mr. Wetzel hired two cowboys in Pueblo to come over on the Western Slope to work for his outfit. One of them had no saddle, so he took my old one. Ed Wetzel had brought two of his cowboys over to help ship over the Divide, and when they rode out to the herd while we were in Lamar, I got to talking with one of them and found he was Andy Middlemist, borther of Bob Middlemist, I had ridden round-up with on the plains in 1886. Andy and I have always been good friends, though nearly fifty years have passed since then. We are old men now and hardly ever meet anymore. He lives in Denver and has raised a fine family. We were partners in a bunch of cattle years afterward, and I bought his interest when he went back to Deer Trail east of Denver.

Well, this country was all new to me. Coming through the Grand and Black Canyons over Marshall Pass, I felt well paid for my trip over to the west side of the Rockies. What a story I'd have to tell them Llano fellows.

It would take several books to write all that history, but before I stop, I want to tell you about getting those big old Texas longhorn cattle onto that mountain range, the likes of which they'd never seen before.

Our train pulled down to the Roubidean, and we got them and

the other trains unloaded and grazed around in the sagebrush flat where it is all farms now. Ike Hight and Bob Brewster, two of the San Miguel cowboys had brought down horses from their summer camp to meet the shipment and help take them on the range. I took my saddle and other effects off the caboose and put my saddle on a club (San Miguel Co. horse brand) horse and bed on another. After visiting awhile with some who had come to see the cattle – as it was quite a sight to see that big herd of longhorns that had walked and stampeded all the way from Texas and had ridden a train over the Continental Divide – I got on my horse and joined the herd.

We drifted the herd out of the Creek bottom and on to the flat where our big corral is now and gathered them up to night herd. After we had ridden around them a few times, they were bedded down and ready to rest as it had been a hard trip in those narrow guage cars. We rode over to the shack which had a cook stove, a rawhide bunk, cupboard, table, some dishes. Two of the boys were cooking supper. All the fellows but two on herd saddled their night horses as did I. I got a plate and filled it up and started to eat, but had both ears open to catch all the conversations. There was talk about summer camp, summer range and winter range which was all Greek to me. I soon learned that they had to put the cattle up on Uncompahgre Plateau for the summer months to protect the winter range on the foothills below. I was saying nothing and taking orders, as I had lost my say automatically when I got on the train at Lamar.

All over the hills the feed was fine white sage and native grasses which cattle seem to like better than the plain's grasses. Horses were no trouble, as Texas horses are broke to stay close around the wagon and camp. At breakfast, they talked about going up the Escalante. I wondered what that could be, though I asked no questions. We day-herded around winter camp the first day, as the cattle were tired and bruised from shipping with some crippled.

The next morning, we started the herd toward the Escalante, grazing them along, until all had breakfast and changed mounts. Ike and another fellow packed up the beds and outfit and got ahead of thé cattle with the horses. We drifted along over the old Negro Gulch. It was a very good Ute trail then. As we got to where the trail went off into the canyon, the herd was beginning to get dry and were strung out for a half-mile. I was riding on the side and began to notice the fellows ahead and the cattle disappear, as it seemed, into a hole. I trotted up to see where they were going, and there they were stringing down into the canyon and drinking from the creek in the bottom. I chuckled to myself and thought, "What sort of cowmen would even think of putting cattle in a place like that and call it, cattle range." That was my first view of the Escalante Canyon, Dry Mesa, etc. which for so many years was to be winter range for the JEF, my own outfit.

Well, we got them down on the creek. I stuck my face in the water and filled up on as fine water as I ever drank, and I was sure dry. Part of us went to the camp where the two boys ahead of the herd was cooking dinner. The cattle grazed, and we had dinner and started to drift up the creek. Right away, it was clear that the old Texas cows had rebelled and did not want to go up that canyon any farther. They would run up the bluffs over the big flat rocks any and everywhere but up the canyon. We crossed the creek ten or twelve times, before we got to a place to night herd. I had been climbing up bluffs and trying to keep the cattle going up the creek, most of the time on foot. I thought I had never heard as much cussing and swearing before, and I never had. I can see Ed Wetzel now with his bald head shining and calling them cattle all kinds of Texas renegades. I thought he and his foreman could find more cuss words to use than I had ever heard in all my days of trailing.

We got them rounded up under the bluff about dark and had come only two and a half miles all afternoon. I had something to eat at the camp, saddled my night-horse and rolled in my bed with my horse tied to a cottonwood tree close by the bed. I had hardly gotten to sleep when I heard a long echo rolling down the canyon, cussing and hollering. I jumped on my horse and got up to the cattle as quick as possible. Some fellow was up on the bluff with about two-hundred head that had gone around the bluff and crawled out on a bench. He couldn't make them come back to the bunch. I got up there and helped him get them back to the bunch and quieted down again. I finally went back to my bed, and it seemed but a few minutes until I was awakened to go on herd.

We got to going the next morning early and to the nine of us, Ed added a rancher who lived in the canyon to help. He had a dog and without that dog, I'm sure we would never have gotten those cattle through the tall willows, as we couldn't see a cow ten feet away. Along in the afternoon, we got to the Alkali Beds. The Texas cows had been drinking soft water and without salt since we left the Arkansas River, so they went after that alkali as if they were licking salt. We worked for several hours getting them by the Alkali Beds. It was dark when they were all rounded up for the night.

They left me, and one of the Pueblo wooden cowboys to hold the cattle, and the others went to camp to catch up night horses and eat supper. I sure thought they intended to leave us to hold them cattle all night. It was nine o'clock before anyone came to relieve us, and I was beginning to get hot under the collar. I sure thought they were playing a joke on me, and was thinking very seriously of breaking my relationship with my newly acquired outfit in the morning. Finally, the relief came, and we stumbled around in the dark trying to find where they had made camp, and finally about ready to go back to the herd when someone hollered way up the creek. We got there, had a little to eat, and it was very little, as not much was left. I lay down, turned things over in my mind and concluded that I was out for experience more than for what I was making, and as I didn't expect to be with the outfit but a short time, I could tolerate anything for a while.

The next morning, we drifted on up the Creek and held up in a big sagebrush flat and grazed until the herd was filled. That flat is where the Musser Ranch is now. John Musser had a cabin down on the creek, and corral and a garden. The first night in the canyon, we nightherded under the bluff where the corral is on the Brent Ranch, now Oscar Huffington's peach orchard.

The pack outfit went ahead of the cattle, and we drifted on up through the sagebrush and pinons through what was the Bob Smith Ranch and is now, Calhoun's. We went up the right-hand canyon to where the Ute Trail went up on the Kelso Point. When we got the last ones up that trail, the sun was just going down. They took the pack outfit up to a cabin, and I rode up, got off my horse, and walked up to the door. It was the first time I ever saw R. S. Kelso. This was his summer camp, and he was frying venison steak. He had canned corn, biscuits, syrup, coffee. I thought that deer meat was the finest I ever had. After that, I was in a much better humor.

Next day, we started drifting up the bench. There was fine grass. My feet, as I rode along, dragged through the grass which had all gone to seed. Cattle were full and seemed to want to travel. It looked as if they had taken on new life. It was all open country with little scrub oaks and now and then a grove of thick aspen. Several lakes of water were there. Kelso saddled up to help us. We drifted up to a big open space about where lower Calhoun corral is now, and rounded up. We had fifty head of old long-horned Texas bulls to trim up and dehorn. Then they strung the herd out and cut them about in half. Half the crew took the lead bunch over to where the Club beef pasture is now and turned them loose. The rest of us took the other half across to Long Point. A good, plain Ute trail ran across to Long Point, and the bunch grass was belly deep to our horses all over the country.

The San Miguel Cattle Co. had brought in three herds before this one. They had about a hundred and fifty saddle horses, all sleek and fat. I rode up on top of a ridge. The cattle were fat, and there was fine feed everywhere. Deer were getting up and trotting around, and the country was beautiful. There were springs everywhere, fat cattle, fine horses, fine water, deer and bear. I had come to stay several weeks. It was three years before I returned to sell my property in Texas. Then I came back, and the Uncompahgre has been summer paradise for an old trail-driver, his children and his grand-children.

One job not on the regular list of cowboy duties was hunting down wild cattle which had taken refuge in out-of-the-way places. These bovine hideouts were usually located in rough mountainous terrain, and riding on such a round-up was risky business; going into the brush after an old renegade steer could make an old-time pigsticking hunt seem tame. Certainly, it was no place for a greenhorn.

First off, it took a horse that could outdodge his own shadow. In full chase, he might jump sharply to the right to avoid a rock or a tree. The next jump could be abruptly back to the left; the whole maneuver being like a corkscrew leap. It was a ride to get the blood up and make the short hairs at the back of the neck feel like coarse bristles an inch long. According to Bill Raber of Kannah Creek, it took a renegade horse to handle the job in the rough brush country under the west rim of Grand Mesa. His brush horse, Smokey, qualified as one of the best.

It is interesting to note that as late as 1940, there were wild cattle in the Grand Mesa rim country. In the early forties, Forest Service and BLM officials advised Kannah Creek ranchers that range permits in that area were going to be cut, unless the wild cattle were removed.

Walt Anderson and Bill Raber were two ranchers who decided to go in after the renegades. They were joined by Crafts Black, Jack Wadlow, Bus Click, and Lawrence Mash, but it still took six winters to get them all. The men would stay out for days at a time, sleeping in tents, and eating Walt Anderson's Wells Gulch Stew. Mr Anderson comments on the results:

It was a rough time. We got about 100 head out alive and about

25 dead. Some of those brutes weighed a good 1500 pounds on the hoof and would dress out 800 pounds of meat. Putting a rope on some of the big ones was a hairy bit of business. We spoiled some good horses on those hunts.

It has been said that cowboys could see the funny side of most situations, but they always tried to bring things into balance in everyday relationships. If, for example, a cowhand was rawhided by one of his friends, he might wait a long time to even the score all in one bounce.

One of the places open to friction had to do with a man's riding ability. There was an old saying in cow country that, "there never was a horse that couldn't be rode and never a rider that couldn't be throwed." While it was generally admitted there was nothing to be ashamed of in being thrown by a good bucker, most riders did their best to stay on as a matter of personal pride. Shorty Gross was known as a man who could ride hell out of anything that wore hair. Ed Young, boss of the Flying W was one of those who waited impatiently to see Shorty get tossed on his ear. Sooner or later, an incident had to come.

Says Short:

It happened at round-up at the Flying W holding ground near the mouth of the canyon. I had just changed mounts and tossed my saddle on a tough ol' horse that was still a bit rank. I was just swinging up when Ed came alongside and spurred my horse to make him buck. As soon as I got him settled down, I turned and loped back toward

Ed. He was wearing a big oversized knit sweater, and I grabbed the bottom of it and quick-like pulled it up over his head. Then I took a turn around my saddle horn with the end of that sweater, and Ed's head and arms just kind of leaned my way. I sunk spurs to my horse and started down the canyon on a dead run. Ed had no choice but to come along. The first half-mile, we were neck to neck, and Ed was cussin' and threatening to kill me. By the end of a mile, he had changed his tune and promised never to rawhide me again. I knew damn well he didn't mean it, so I took him all the way down to the line fence, before I turned him loose.

"It was," Short concludes with a perfectly straight face, "one helluva horse race!"

*   *   *

DISPATCH

1884
Grand Junction, Colorado

In March the first effort was made toward organizing a company to build a toll road through the canyon on Grand River to connect with the Garfield County road down the Grand at the county line. A company was formed consisting of Henry R. Rhone, Dr. W. A. E. DeBeque, E. D. Bonton, J. W. Bolden, Edwin Price and others, and a survey made. The estimate made, however, of the cost of construction discouraged several of the members; so the organization informally disbanded. Mr. Rhone never entertained a doubt but that the road could be built, and that the road would be of inestimable benefit to Grand Junction. He therefore organized another company, and almost single-handed commenced the construction of the Roan Creek Toll Road.

CHAPTER FOUR

THE HOME PLACE

There's always room for company
Round our table any day.
And if they really want to,
We've got room for them to stay.

Leone Hamilton

The image of a little home in the West has, over the years, become an integral part of American folklore. To many, it is a legend with practical overtones of style and status. To them, it can mean privacy, isolation, or a house with a specific form of architecture. To those who lived it, however, the legend means more — much more than that. For in the broadest sense of the word — home is not in any particular spot on this earth; it is a special place in the mind.

Certainly, architectural style and form had little meaning in the early-day West where people were required to build shelter from materials at hand. Nan Blain — pioneer school teacher in Mesa County had this to say about early buildings in the Grand Valley:

> Our first school in Grand Junction was held in a little log building at what was then the extreme east end of Colorado Avenue. The one hotel – also a log building with roof and floor of earth – stood near the west end of the same street; and between those two, were all the business houses in town, except two which were on Main Street.
>
> There were three stores and seven saloons, a barber shop, a butcher shop and a bakery; one hotel, and one restaurant; also one drug store.
>
> The school house, like all the others, had a floor of earth, and roof of the same. Those dirt roofed cabins were the very best of residences for the early settlers in Grand Valley, where the heat was intense, because there was no vegetation whatever, except along the river. Hence, the sun beat down intensely upon the barren adobe, reflecting his rays, so that at midday,. during the summer of 1882, the thermometer sometimes registered as high as 112°F in the shade – the only shade in this city being upon the side of her cabins, opposite the sun. Hence, the cool interior of those earth-covered cabins was very comfortable.

Miss Blain, who is probably better remembered as, Nannie Blain Underhill, had this to say about attitudes and conditions in outlying areas:

> In the beginning, nearly everybody was discouraged and homesick, wishing for a chance to sell their possessions; they only wanted enough money to get away. I knew of one ranch being sold for $75. Doubtless any ranch in Grand Valley could have been purchased then

for $500. City lots were held at $15 to $25 each, but none were being sold.

Building practices changed rapidly in Grand Junction with the coming of a saw mill and a brick yard, but out in the country, things remained primitive for some time. A new arrival named, Whiting, tells of conditions on a ranch near Fruita about 1890:

> The ranch house was a combination of shanty and dugout. Dan Dine, who owned the ranch, had dug a hole about 10 x 12 feet in the side of a small hill, made a front and roof of logs, covered this with brush and the brush with clay dirt to keep out the rain. There were many people at that time living in similar huts. At a later date, he had built a board shed in front of this dugout about 10 x 12 feet. I thought I had lived in some poor abodes before, but this was the worst of all. I found my new partner had rented the ranch on "Tick," and had gone in debt for horses, harness, wagons, and farming implements. The storekeepers were trusting him for seed and supplies, until he could get returns from the ranch. However, so many ranchers had made big money the summer before, he convinced me it would turn out good, so I agreed to go halves with him. Besides ourselves, we had a hired man, and the three of us batched, taking turns cooking with the agreement that anyone who found fault with the grub must do the cooking. We had to use the water from the ditch for cooking and drinking, with more or less bugs and pollywogs in it. The water was mud color, making it difficult to see the bugs,

so sometimes they would be in the cooking. One of us would discover them and say, "There are a log of bugs in this – but I love stewed bugs."

Times were obviously rough in the 1890's.

But regardless of the bugs and primitive conditions, a great many of the early settlers clung to the land. The frontier formula required a man to hang tight; and the hard pulse of America still had a powerful beat. Progress might be slow, but it had to come. All it took was time, determination, a lot of hard work, and a dream.

R. C. Brown of Fruita had such a dream, and Maude I. Brown tells of it:

After three years of business career, the chance came that Ross had waited for so long. The chance to buy a small bunch of cattle, a camp, range for the cattle and the brand. He was lucky in finding a buyer for the business, so he sold the store and house and bought this outfit. It was a small beginning, but it was a start, and at last the dream began to be a reality when he became owner of the Jerry Mc Carthy outfit in 1909.

This outfit was located on the south side of Douglas Pass – at the foot of the pass and 35 miles from Fruita. It was not too isolated, as it was on the main road over Douglas Pass. The road was not much more than an improved trail. Frequently a wagon or horsebackers came over the pass. He had neighbors – Lee Ashleys lived about a mile above in one canyon, and Al Sayles about 1½ miles below in another. The men all worked together.

Ross first moved to camp in the spring of 1910. With his wife and little son, Evert, they started out from Fruita in a spring wagon quite heavily loaded. In spite of poor roads, everything went quite well until about three miles from camp a dirt slide had blocked the road. By shoveling, a way was opened to get over the slide. But the horses were tired, and one was a little balky, so he refused to cooperate which hindered the efforts of the other one when he tried to pull. No amount of coaxing or pursuading could induce him to change his mind or to try. After all efforts failed, Ross unhitched the team, put the willing horse on the end of the tongue, gave him the signal to go, and he pulled the outfit over the slide quite successfully. By doing a little road work at a later time, the slide was made passable, and future trouble at this place was eliminated.

The family lived that summer in the McCarthy cabin; a small one about 12 x 14 feet. There was a bed in one corner, a stove in another, a door in another, a small window and a table on one side, and a cupboard in the other corner. Small as it was, they managed. They entertained neighbors and cowboys and often a wagon or horsebackers from across the pass would stop for a rest, chat, and sometimes stayed for a meal or overnight. As the family spent their summers at camp, it was soon decided they needed more room. So, Ross planned a larger one-room cabin built of logs gotten from the mountainsides. Most of the time, he worked alone so things progressed rather slowly, but when it was ready for occupancy, it boasted a screen door, screened windows, a board floor, and also a porch on front. As finished lumber had to be hauled from Fruita, it took three or four days to get a wagonload. However, Jim Rector had a sawmill on the north side of Douglas Pass where rough lumber could be obtained, which helped. This, too, was a difficult task driving a big wagon over a very poor road over a steep pass and amounting to a trip of ten miles. A few years later, an adjoining room was added to the house which was a little larger than the first. Then a bunk house was built to accommodate hired help or visitors who often came up for a weekend or a holdiay.

While the camp had a spring of cold water emerging at the foot of a large rock, it was mineral water, very hard, and not good for cooking or drinking. There was a good spring about a mile up the canyon, however, from which Ross hauled drinking water. Then he decided to build a cistern. In the winter when the snow was deep, he would make a trip to camp and fill the cistern with snow. About two fillings would make plenty of good water to last during the time spent at camp. Later, after the roads were improved, Ross had a big tank of water hauled from Fruita each spring which saved him that hard winter trip.

The spring water was run through a box, built in a spring house and which was used as a refrigerator. It was a very good substitute. With no gas or electricity or ice available, the spring house with this box of cold running water was almost indispensable. Also, the spring water was run in a large water trough just outside the yard fence. The cattle would come a long ways just to drink from this trough. Often in the evenings, the deer would come from the mountainsides to drink from it, and occasionally, someone who really liked the taste of this water would take a jugful home to enjoy later for medicinal purposes.

In 1913, Al Sayles decided to sell his outfit. There were few good campsites around that part of the country. If a newcomer were to buy it, it would be possible to bring in a larger herd and crowd the range. The old-timers did not like that. Mose Burkitt was living with the Ashleys and was a good rider, just waiting for an opportunity to find a place of his own. He and Ross decided to buy the Sayles outfit and work as partners which proved quite successful. In 1914, Lee Ashley's health failed, and he also decided to sell. Ross and Mose bought his place also. The Ashley camp was the better of the two, so Mose decided to fix it up and live there as he had recently taken a new bride.

Before going to town for some repairs, he went up to the camp to check on some things and found a big landslide had come down the canyon in the night and wrecked the cabin beyond repair. So, they fixed up the Sayles cabin and Mose moved his family there. The men worked as partners for several years, when they decided to dissolve their partnership. Ross took the Ashley place; Mose, the Sayles. They continued working together, until in 1928 when Mose sold out to the Muhr brothers, and Mose moved to Ridgeway.

The winter of 1919 - 20 was a very severe one. It started snowing the day before Thanksgiving and continued for three days. This snow laid on the ground until spring, together with other snows which fell during the winter months. The snow was so deep over the desert, it was impossible for the cattle to graze and almost impossible for the cattlemen to gather the cattle to get them to feed. The loss was heavy, and the work was hard. But as always, spring eventually came. The snow melted, and the desert began to get green and hope returned.

The roundup in the spring was a tiresome time, generally lasting about six weeks, until they had the cattle gathered from the desert; this included eastern Utah and nearby mountains. They delivered them to their owners, or back on their own summer range. When this was over, there was generally a period of rest and relaxation. Then, there were waterholes to clean and inspect, salt to pack out, and more calves to brand and see to it that the cattle were located on the better parts of the range. The cattlemen had to do a big part of their roadwork, so as soon as they were settled in their camps, they checked the condition of the roads and made the necessary improvements.

Progress is ever on the move. An idea was born to make the Rangely country and the Grand Valley more accessible to each other. The counties cooperated at improving the road from Loma to the foot of Douglas Pass, making it so much better that cars were now able to go over this part of the road. Ross bought his firt car – an Overland – in 1915, which proved a big advantage in his trips to and from camp. Three cattlemen living on the north side of the pass had cars and would drive as far as the Brown Camp, being met there by wagons to take them the rest of the way home. Their cars might sit out for several weeks, before they would use them again. So, Ross built a shed containing three stalls which would shelter the cars from the weather. Eventually, an automobile road was extended over the pass and on down to Rangely.

The cabin door was never locked at camp, and provisions were left so that a hungry cowboy or passerby could always find something to eat. Often, Ross came home to find someone there, taking advantage of this opportunity. Sometimes, getting home late at night, he would find his bed occupied, and he would sleep elsewhere. One *rule he had for camp was, "Always wash your dishes and fill the woodbox," which was always carried out. Later, after the road was improved and more travelers came by, they were not so considerate, and what they could not eat, they took along with them. He had to discontinue leaving the cupboards filled, as it was not there when needed. This proved very inconvenient, both to himself and to neighboring cowboys who happened to be riding by.*

One can readily see that the story of the West is the story of individual effort against incredible odds. It is the story of building on faith and on dreams. It is the story of progress by a determined people. It is a story told in terms of the individual; but in the end, each story is, indeed, an integral part of the whole. As we proceed, the binding thread of individual effort becomes ever more apparent.

Mose Burkitt comments on early housing and other hazards of the day:

Ethel McTaggart and I were married June 20, 1912, at Glenwood Springs, Colorado. Our first "home on the range" was a one-room cabin with dirt roof and cement floor, one window and door. Our first night there, a mouse lost his footing on the ridge pole and fell on Ethel's side of the bed and got tangled up in her hair. Right there, I would have lost my cook, if it hadn't been such a long walk back to town. We had a large "Fred Mantey" umbrella that we stood up in the middle of the table, or bed (which ever we were using) to keep the muddy water from dripping on us when it rained.

About this time, I had my first experience in borrowing money.

I signed a one-year note at the First Bank of Fruita for $100 and got a deposit slip for $88.00, 12% interest in advance. That money sure lasted well. I paid it back in eight months. They treated me better after that.

James Rector — as told by Ruby Rector Kirby:

In April, 1899, James William Rector married Myrtle Rosa McNew of Lamar, Missouri and brought her to live at the "Brick Ranch" at Rangely. Jim Rector was interested and instrumental in the development of both oil and gilsonite in the Rangely country.

In 1887, during the Indian troubles, Jim and a cowboy, Bill Terry, were on a calf-branding trip that took them down White River to the mouth of Evacuation Creek where they camped for the night on Wagon Hound Flat. While making camp, they found themselves surrounded on all sides by Indians, who were on their way to reinforce Colorow's band of warriors being hotly pursued down White River by the Colorado Militia. Jim and Bill didn't even unpack their beds, but spent an anxious and sleepless night.

At the crack of dawn, a much painted Indian, whom Mr. Rector later learned was, "Crippled Tom," a good friend and the one who had kept the Indians from molesting the cowboys the night before, came out of the willows and conducted Jim and Bill several miles up Evacuation Creek. The Indian's parting remarks were, "Maybe so big fight today, Americans and Indians."

On this trip, Mr. Rector picked up a large lump of what he thought was unusually shiny coal, put it on his pack horse, carried *it to camp and threw some of it into the fireplace to see how it would burn. It began to ooze, and soon the smoke drove the men from the cabin. He sent some samples out to get assayed, but little was then known of Gilsonite. Rector staked three claims, and after keeping them several years, sold the claims for $500 apiece. One of the claims was the Rector Mine near Dragon, Utah, which when mined out produced over a million-dollars worth of Gilsonite.*

Sid Pace – Grand Junction, Colorado

Our first ranch in the area of the LaSal Mountains of southeastern Utah was in Castle Valley which is three miles south of the Colorado River and twenty miles east of Moab, Utah. Our summer range was in the LaSal Mountains.

Two of the first cattle companies to use the LaSal Mountains on the north and east side were the Pittsburg Cattle Company, financed by eastern capital and the Lester Taylor outfit. This was in the early 1880's. Since the only boundaries were natural ones, there were many disagreements over range rights and cattle rustlers were everywhere.

Uncle Sid, my father's brother, worked for both the Pittsburg Cattle Co. and Taylors. He took part of his pay in cows, and when he had a hundred head, he persuaded my father, John E. Pace to move from Payson, Utah to Castle Valley where they would establish a cattle ranch with summer range in the LaSal Mountains.

So, in 1891, my father traded his home in Payson for a bunch of two-year-old heifers which he and Uncle Sid drove to Castle Valley, a distance of about 210 miles. They bought the filings on a ranch there from Mart Fish.

When my mother came to the ranch, they rode horseback from Moab over Matt Martin Point on the west side of the valley. My older sister, Ireta, a baby, was pinned to a pillow across the saddle horn in front of mother. My older brother, Lynn, about two years old, rode behind father. They had to come over the rim of the valley down a very steep trail.

I was born July 30, 1893 in Castle Valley. I had two sisters younger than I, and a brother. One of my sisters died at the age of five with scarlet fever. I went to a school close to the ranch in Lower Castle Valley. There was also a school in Upper Castle Valley at Castleton. I graduated from the eighth grade in 1908. I then went to school one year in Provo, Utah and one year in Logan, Utah. That was the end of my education. My folks wanted me to finish high school, but I decided I had gone long enough.

At the two school houses in Castle Valley, we had lots of dances. Besides the ranchers living in Castleton, there were quite a few miners who mined in the LaSal Mountains. We went to the dances on horseback, or in a buggy, and usually danced all night with refreshments at midnight. The younger children were put to bed on the tops of the desks which had been pushed back.

From the time I was eleven years old, I spent my summers riding with Uncle Sid. After I quit school, most of my time was spent cowboying.

In the fall of 1908, there was three feet of snow which fell in October in the LaSals. The cowboys were just beginning to gather the weaners. They had a hard time getting the cattle and sheep off the mountain and had to break trails to them with work horses. The summer of 1912, Uncle Sid sent his son, Reece, and me to Pinon Mesa to ride with the S Cross outfit, a large cattle operation owned by the Sieber Cattle Co. John Mock was the foreman. He had two brothers working there, Ira and Boots. The remainder of the crew was Charlie Glass (a negro), Emp Davis and John Sieber (a son of the owner), and a cook. Reece decided to go on to Grand Junction for a little vacation, leaving me with the cowboys. We were camped at a place on the east side of Pinon Mesa called, Circle Pasture, when we were hit one night by a cloudburst and hard wind. Another boy and I had gone to bed, but the rest of the cowboys were playing poker. A hard gust of wind knocked our big tent down, and there was a flood in the wash nearby. We scrambled around in the dark, dragging our beds from under the tent and trying to find a level place to put them down. I stayed, until the ride was finished, but we didn't find any of our cattle.

Our headquarters in the LaSal Mountains was Sally's Hollow, and a bunkhouse was built there in 1902 and is still used. After I quit school, my brother, Lynn, and I had a chance to buy thirty head of cows from a rancher who was selling out. They paid for themselves in three years. At that time, we owned a ranch at Rock Creek which is on the Dolores River where drainage from the LaSal Mountains empties into the river. We wintered our cattle south of the river between Rock Creek and the north rim of Paradox Valley.

Around 1915, we bought the land and cattle owned by Bill Doak and Lee Kirk which was the Sinbad and Kirk's Basin property. Kirk's Basin is six miles north of Sally's Hollow. By then, we had formed a family corporation named, Pace Brothers Co. In those years, we sold our steers as yearlings and delivered in June at Bedrock in Paradox Valley to buyers who would take them to summer range on the Lone Cone. In the fall, we gathered our fat dry cows and other cattle to be sold and drove them to Cisco, Utah, a six-day trip, and shipped them to Denver or Kansas City.

In September, 1920, Lucile Hansen came from northern Utah to teach school in Castle Valley, and we were married in the summer of 1922.

In the late summer of 1929, my brother Lynn died, and since he was the business manager of our outfit, it was a blow to us, especially since we were hit by a severe depression. As a result, we lost our Colorado property and five sections of our Utah land. By that time, my father was in poor health; Reece had left; Uncle Sid had drowned, and it was left to my brother-in-law, Bert Buchanan, and I took over the outfit and managed it. In about ten years, we were back on our feet and doing well. But several years later, Bert died, so Ireta and I divided the outfit. She and her son, Buck, took the Castle Valley ranch, and Lucille and I took the mountain land. We divided the cattle and bought out my father's interest. We didn't raise enough feed at Kirk's Basin to winter all our cattle, so I bought hay and pasture in Grand Junction and fed part of them there. So, we moved from Moab to Grand Junciton, where we had been living in the winters to send our children to school.

Several years after this, we had a chance to buy the Sinbad ranch again.

In 1955, our son, Sidney, decided to come back to the ranch, after being in college and in the service. We formed a family partnership in 1962, and called it, Pace Ranches. Now, Sidney manages the ranches and the business. In the summer and fall, I do what I can to help — fixing fences and riding. My wife and I still spend our summers at Sally's Hollow as we always have.

Catherine H. Moore — Grand Junction, Colorado

Not much is known of this area before 1880, except the fact that the Ute Indians were here. Among the first settlers was my grandfather, Charles Sieber. He was a native of Germany and came to Colorado in 1862. My grandmother's parents came from New York with a covered wagon train in 1857 and set up a stage station on Cherry Creek, 35 miles from Denver. My grandfather Sieber was the stage driver from there to Pueblo. The Thatcher brothers, Mahlon and John, ran the stage station, store, and bank in Pueblo. My grandparents were married in 1869 and moved to Wet Mountain Valley and went into the cattle business. When Colorado was admitted to the Union as a state in 1876, Grandpa Sieber was elected to the first state legislature. In 1882, he came to Mesa County looking for more range. He decided on what is now known as, Glade Park and Pinon Mesa. In 1885, he moved his family to Grand Junction. By that time, they had eight children; four more were born in Grand Junction. The older girls were sent to St. Marys of the Wasatch in Salt Lake City, Utah for their education.

Mr. Sieber brought 10,000 head of cattle to the Glade Park area and went into partnership with Mr. Hudson in a retail meat market in

Grand Junction. The Siebers then moved to Fruita onto a ranch with orchards. They contained all kinds of fruit and berries. The location was on the east side of the Monument Road out of Fruita and extended from the railroad tracks to where the Fruita bridge is now. They irrigated and raised hay and grain.

Grandpa Sieber insisted that all his daughters be taught everything connected with homemaking, and hired a woman by the name of Ida Saxbury for that purpose. Grandma had her hands full with the younger children. One died in infancy. Six girls and Mrs. Saxbury canned fruit, jellies, smoked ham, canned chickens, geese and ducks, smoked bacon, made lard and cheese, even wine and cider. My mother has told me that besides the family being provided for, they kept all the cowboys supplied with everything except flour, coffee, sugar, etc. At that time, there were thirty cowboys. By 1900, some of the older girls were married and gone, and the family moved back to Grand Junction.

In 1896, they closed out their partnership. In 1897, the Sieber Cattle Co. was formed by Sieber and Johon and Maholon Thatcher. Mr. Sieber, as half-owner, was president and general manager of this company. By this time, Mr. Sieber had acquired large ranches on Little Dolores Creek and Coats Creek and Pinon Mesa.

Around 1913, the S Cross Cattle Company due to homesteaders, sheep and cattle thieves went out of business. The cattle were shipped, and the ranches were sold to some eastern people by the name of, Shaw & Armstrong. Their plan was to bring the water from Pinon Mesa and irrigate all of Big Park. They did start a ditch on Pinon, but for some reason, the plan fell through. Then, they sold the *former Sieber Ranches to O.S. Wright, who kept one ranch and sold the rest of the land to different parties. Mr. Wright kept the Upper Ranch on the Little Dolores. He owned it for many years and leased to several different people: Claybaugh and Simpson, Dunnans, Harold Stevens, and finally to Ted Hammer who wound up buying it. This is the ranch we bought in 1963 from my cousin, Anna Hammer, and then sold part of it to my sister and her husband, John Collier.*

The Fifth Street Bridge in Grand Junction was the first bridge across the Colorado River. Before that was built, John Gorden, grandfather of Georgie Kruckenburg and Dorothy Mahoney, ran a ferry about where the Grand Avenue Bridge is now. After the Fifth Street Bridge and the Gunnison Bridge were built, the settlers in this area made what was called then the Blue Hill Road. It is now called, Jacob's Ladder Road. Jacob's Ladder Road was the road from Little Park onto Pinon Mesa by way of Monument Springs. The first road up was a toll road built by John Gorden and came up on Little Park back of where the east entrance ranger station is now.

In 1906, or thereabouts, the Fruita pipeline was started. At the request of Fruita, the government withdrew from homestead entry onto Pinon Mesa – an area three miles wide and four miles long. This area is now known as the Fruita Reserve, and there Fruita has their reservoirs which supply the town water. Before this, there was no road out of Fruita to Glade Park. They bridged the Colorado River and made a road through what is now the Colorado National Monument. It was known as the Fruita Dugway, and was a son-of-a-gun. It was possible for teams to get across it, and in those days, people were satisfied with any road they could get a team and wagon over.

Charlie DuVall built the first dry farm homestead cabin on Big Park in 1907. It was south and east of the Glade Park Store. The next was Sam Douglass. His old cabin still stands on the M.H. Lawrence property, south across the road from the store.

In 1910, Jennie France started the store and post office on Big Park and called the post office, Glade Park. This was a small three-room shack. It changed hands several times, until M. H. Lawrence bought it in 1923. A few years later, he built a large store which he improved from time to time. Now, this community is served with a modern store, and the old hitching rail has been replaced by a filling station. The mail stage came three times a week, which it still does; however, there is a difference now. In those days, it was a four to five hour trip from Glade Park Post Office to Grand Junction. Now, it takes about 30 minutes. Jennie McKenzie was the first stage driver.

By now, the whole country was being fenced, wells dug, ponds made here and there, sagebrush grubbed the hard way with a grubbing hoe. Families tried to make a living by dry-farming. A few made it, but mostly, they were coming and going for many years. Those who did stay, acquired stock and became prosperous people. Some of the first dry farmers were Frank Thompson, Guy Murphy, Williams, the Leslies, Redds, Woods, Parish, Jefferson, Bert Charles, Hensley, DuVall, and many others.

In 1912, the schools were started. There were seven at one time: Little Park, Pipeline, West End, Sleeper, Road Canyon, Coats Creek, and Woodruff. At that time, it only required three pupils to hold a school. Mrs. Sleeper, Mrs. Thompson, and Mr. Lane were the first school board members, and they held office for several years. The

—104—

school houses were built by the people of the community. Box suppers, dances, and card parties were held to raise money for school supplies. There is only one school here now — Coats Creek School. The other schools were taken over by School District 51 in the early 1950's. A school bus comes to the Glade Park Store and takes the children from there to Grand Junction.

There is only one dry-farmer up here, now, that makes his living solely by dry farming. Floyd Griffee raises beans. The other dry farms have been reseeded to grass and bought up by stockmen for grazing.

John Otto, who worked for many years bringing Monument Canyon into the limelight started a trail over the cliff, and this is now the famous Serpent's Trail, which was started in 1921.

It so happened that there were three men living up here at that time who all were civil engineers. They were Frank Sleeper, Bruce Claybaugh, and O.S. Wright. They got their heads together and figured out a road. They donated all their survey work. Most of the building was done by hand and donated by the people of this area as their share in the expense of acquiring a better and shorter road.

The Trail of the Serpent! It was steep and narrow and twisty, but how glad we were to have it. It was used from 1921 to 1959, when the Park Service Rd. was opened for travel. Part of our country had by this time been taken over by the National Park Service. The old Fruita Dugway, on which so many had toiled up and down with teams, is now a wonderful scenic highway, and people from all countries come to see our natural wonders.

The first automobiles were introduced up here about 1918.

There were always some places at which all passengers had to get out and push or dig. We all expected that, and no one complained. It usually took from two to three hours to make the 25 mile trip from our ranch to the Junction. But we thought it a great improvement over toiling all day long with a team or on horseback.

In years past, stock was driven to market, sometimes taking three or four days. Now, very few people trail. The stock is trucked into the stockyards in an hour or two.

About the time the Serpent's Trail was built, my mother and George Gorden decided it was time to have a telephone. The Grand Junction exchange agreed to let them hook on providing they built their own line. So, the Glade Park Telephone Company was organized at $50.00 a share. Sixteen shares were sold, and with this money, plus donated quakie and cedar posts along with donated labor, the telephone line was built. It was patched with barbed and baling wire, and it was used about 35 years. Then, a new Glade Park Telephone Co. was formed with the intention to improve the line. They did away with crank phones and put in regular telephone wire. As the old line cost each person $50.00 in cash, plus labor, the new line cost each person $750.00 and still our service was poor. Now, the Mountain States Telephone Co. has taken it over. There are about forty phones at a cost of approximately $250.00 per person. We are all waiting to see if the Sunday sightseers will still shoot off the insulators.

Charles Stewart Silzell came to Whitewater, Colorado with his parents in 1892. Several years later, he became involved in a ranching operation in Unaweep Canyon. Effie M. Silzell tells of early days on the Uncompaghre:

> *Charlie was born nine miles southeast of Saguache, Colorado on July 2, 1880. At the age of twelve, he and his older brother Aaron Alexander, twenty-one, his younger brother, William Edward, five, and their parents, Billy and Phenie Silzell moved to Whitewater in the fall of 1892.*
>
> *Earlier that spring, Charlie, Will, and their mother had come on the train to Whitewater to visit her sister, Jennie, who was married to John Ross Pennisten. Uncle Ross had served as Superintendent of Schools in Saguache County, before they moved to Whitewater in 1882. Later on, he was owner of a saw mill on the Uncompahgre Mountain. He also built the old wagon road which went to the saw mill from the Unaweep Canyon and can still be seen going up the south side of the canyon at the Divide. Ross Pennisten is the one who is credited with giving the name of, Whitewater, to the community. Charlie believes his uncle chose the name, because after a rain, the stream became white from the alkali soil washing into it.*
>
> *Charlie, Will, and their mother liked the country at Whitewater very much, so they returned to Saguache in the early fall to help prepare for moving later that year. Charlie's father and Aaron, better known as Allie, moved their wagon and livestock including about twelve head of cows and about twenty head of horses. The rest of the family came by train again.*
>
> *For a few years, they rented a small house in Whitewater owned by Clyde Shropshire. There was a large house across the street, one of*

the better homes in Whitewater, which was owned by Henry Snyder. The Silzells bought both houses and used the larger one as a boarding and rooming house which they named, The Cottage Inn. A few years later, Charlie's father built a large barn across the street and used it for a livery and feed stable. The corrals were already there.

For the most part, stockmen from the surrounding areas made use of the accommodations at shipping time. They came from Whitewater, Purdy and Reeder Mesas, Kannah Creek, Unaweep Canyon, Uncompaghre area, the Club Outfit, Blue Creek, Rock Creek, Gateway, and Fruita. Prices were fifty cents per person for each meal, fifty cents for each person for overnight accommodations, and fifty cents for each horse for overnight stabling, feed and water. Besides the stockmen, they had occasional boarders and roomers from time to time from various walks of life, including school teachers, mail carriers, ore haulers, and others.

Charlie and Will attended the Whitewater school and at the age of fourteen, Charlie became a member of the only church there, the Congregational. Later on, Charlie attended school in Colorado Springs for a time. However, the boarding and rooming arrangements were not good; he became homesick and returned home without finishing his schooling there.

As a teenager, Charlie worked at various jobs on two nearby ranches. One was on the east edge of Whitewater; a peach orchard owned by, Carl Shoreman, a native from Germany. The other ranch was located on the west edge of Whitewater and owned by Mr. & Mrs. William Coffman. The Coffman's had moved here from Saguache ahead of the Silzells. Mrs. Coffman was Ella Virden, before she married Mr. Coffman. On January 13, 1895, Charlie's brother, Allie, married Mrs. Coffman's sister, Louanna Virden. They were married in the Christian Parsonage in Grand Junction by the Rev. Meredeth. Five children were born to this union: George, Minnie (Barnes-Kaufman), Albert, Elsie (Pottorf), and Anne (Hamm).

Charlie made his first trip into the Unaweep Canyon in 1897 when he was seventeen years old. He went by horseback to deliver a Western Union message to Pat Anderson, a rancher who later sold out to Andrew Taylor. There were no telephones out that way then.

In the year of 1899, when Charlie was nineteen years old, he took over the salt hauling job his father had been doing. He delivered salt to various stockmen on the Uncompahgre Mountain, driving four horses. Among those who bought salt were, J. W. Musser, the Utah Colorado Cattle Company, better known as the U.C.C. Outfit, the Club Outfit, and the Smith Brothers, George P. and James H., who were connected with the Mesa County Bank.

Charlie also helped haul material over the Uncompahgre Mountain into Mesa Creek for the building of the flume on the side of the cliffs along and above the Dolores River. This famous flume was started about 1887, between Rock Creek and Uravan, and was built and completed over a period of time. Matt Casto and Charlie Bowman helped build the flume, parts of which can still be seen hanging along the bluff down the river from Uravan. The following information was obtained from the plaque which has been put up in recent years by the Bureau of Land Management marking the flume as a historical site:

"This flume was a six mile long wooden channel constructed in the early 1890's and was designed to carry water to the arid gold bearing sands of Lone Tree Placer. $172,000, twice the estimate, had already been spent. Construction halted after the panic of 1893. Operation was on a limited scale, but was abandoned, because there wasn't enough gold production to pay off."

Unaweep is an Indian name which means, the dividing of the waters. From the Divide, East Creek flows east into the Gunnison River at Whitewater, and West Creek flows west into the Dolores River at Gateway. It has been said that the Unaweep Canyon is the longest canyon in the world with such a dividing of the waters.

About 1905, Andrew Taylor who owned a ranch in the east end of Unaweep Canyon, leased about fifty head of cows with calves at their sides to Allie Silzell and his brother-in-law, Bert Virden. However, Bert was a professional bronc rider, got itchy feet, and withdrew from the partnership arrangement. Allie then took Charlie in as a partner. Charlie had already made up his mind some time before that he wanted to make his living out in the open air, rather than behind a desk.

Allie had already patented one-hundred sixty acres about 1903, which is now part of the James Massey place. At this time, Charlie also took up a homestead adjoining Allie's place and patented one-hundred sixty acres which is also part of the present Jim Massey ranch.

The three Silzell boys — Allie, Charlie, and Will — with their father's financial help bought small bunches of cattle from time to time when the opportunity came up. Eventually, they formed a four-way partnership.

In the spring of 1909, when Charlie was twenty-eight years old, he sold the land he had patented to Allie. In May of that year, he and Will bought the Charles Burg ranch which was located two miles west of Allie's place on West Creek. Mr. Burg had taken up this 320 acres of land under the Desert Act in the 1880's. Not much land was taken up under this act. When Mr. Burg first came into the canyon, he trapped and hunted on what was known later as the Heskett place in the east end of the canyon. Afterwards, he had squatter's rights on the Gill Meadow in the winters of 1881 and 1882. About that time, he was one of the first assessors of Mesa County.

This ranch, which was to be Charlie's home for more than fifty years, was thirty-three miles from Whitewater and at the end of the road at that time. A few years previously in about 1903 or 1904, a wagon had been driven from Gateway up to the Burg ranch to bring out a body even though there was no road. Two men living in the Gateway area had gotten in a squabble, and a Mr. Franklin killed Chris Erney. Erney's body was brought out in the first wagon to ever come from Gateway. They had to cross West Creek sixteen or seventeen times to make it. However, at the time Charlie and Will purchased the Burg ranch, it was considered the end of the road.

About 1919, Charlie decided to have a log house built. He and his nephew, George Silzell, hauled the logs from the Uncompahgre Mountain. Other materials needed were brought from Grand Junction by Ed Martin who was hauling mail and freight from there and Whitewater through the Canyon to Gateway. Lute Willey, who also moved *freight, helped haul materials for the house. The carpenters were Will and a cousin, George Johnson. All the men in the family —even Charlie's father — helped cut the logs. About a year or so later, the neighbors had a housewarming party for Charlie. His parents were there and had been for several months. I attended the party, but Charlie didn't know I was coming. I was a house guest at the time at the Hereford Ranch in the home of Mr. & Mrs. Matt Casto about four miles east of the Silzell ranch.*

On May 31, 1923, Charlie and I were married in Grand Junction by R. H. Forrester, Pastor of the Methodist Episcopal Church. At that time, I was the telephone operator on the Whitewater Exchange for the Mountain States Telephone Co. We had to make careful plans to elude a group of young people in Whitewater who wanted to separate us by taking one of us to Delta and the other to Fruita. Our taxi driver, J. S. Dodds, managed to keep us out of their clutches all evening, and they finally gave up.

We had two children — a daughter, Elsie Mae, and a son, Roy Stewart. They received their education through the eleventh grade in a one-room building called the Summit School. Iva Schoolcraft, sister of Mrs. Percy Sheets of Loma, was their first teacher. Through most of the years, they rode the three and one-quarter miles from our ranch to Summit School on horseback.

During 1943 and 1944, the road was changed from what was known as the nine-mile hill to lower ground along East Creek. Later on, it was paved as was all the rest of the road, a few miles at a time through the canyon to Gateway and on up the river to Uravan. The new paved highway was constructed through our hayfields in the fall of 1958.

This new paved highway is a far cry from the way the roads were when I first went to the Unaweep to make my home. They were especially bad in late winter and early spring when the thaw set in. At this time, they would become almost impassable, except for periods at night when they might become somewhat frozen. It seemed as though it was always during these times that someone in the community would become seriously ill, and it would be necessary to get that person to a doctor or to a hospital in Grand Junction. Many times, it would never have been accomplished without the help from good neighbors.

Marketing of livestock is done now by trucks, but years ago, all cattle were driven to the railroad at Whitewater. It was usually a two day drive from our ranch to Whitewater, a distance of 33 miles. The cowboys, cattle, and saddle horses received overnight accommodations at the east end of the canyon at one of three ranches —the Woodrings, Taylors, or Hesketts.

We had the last telephone on the line, and for many years the closest one to Gateway, a distance of 12 miles. There were no telephones in Gateway. As a result, we shared our telephone with residents of Gateway and vicinity, as well as many other people. Through the years, people of all races came by many different modes of transportation to use our telephone. One time, we even had a helicopter land just outside our yard and two men came in to make a long distance call. In the early years, we delivered many important telephone messages to Gateway from Grand Junction and other areas. When the traffic increased in later years, we were able to send *many of the messages — often by having neighbors up the canyon let us know by phone when a car was coming. Other neighbors in the canyon, especially the James Masseys and the Byrl Castos, also shared their telephones and delivered messages. Most of them came to us as we had the nearest telephone to Gateway.*

During much of our time at the ranch, our mail came from the Whitewater Post Office and was delivered to a box out on the highway on Tuesday and Saturdays. It was part of the charm of living rural. We lived in Unaweep Canyon, got our mail at Whitewater, and voted at Gateway.

Marie Becker Young was born in the high-country mining town of Central City, Colorado. In 1914, her father, Peter, moved the Becker family to a farm on Orchard Mesa near the City of Grand Junction. But life on a fruit farm held no special attraction for a high-spirited girl still in her teens. In the summer of 1915, an opportunity for outside employment came from P. A. Rice who operated a saw mill on Pinon Mesa. It was a new and exciting time for a country girl fresh off the farm, and Marie recalls it vividly:

My new job was keeping house for a young couple from the east who were spending their honeymoon on Pinon Mesa. The young man was the son of my boss, Mr. P. A. Rice, and the honeymoon cottage was a log cabin which was separate from the main house. The newlyweds were very nice to me, and I enjoyed my work. There was a time to go riding during the daytime, and I made new friends as the summer passed. One of the events I remember best was the first summer dance that was held in an outdoor pavillion which had been built on the mountain.

Oh, how I wanted to go to that dance. But, Mr. Rice was very strict, being a preacher and all, and he insisted I could not go unless I had written permission from my father. I promised to send word down the mountain and ask for a note, but my heart was heavy. It would not only take days to get an answer back, but I was not too sure my father would let me go if I asked him.

Now, some of my new friends on the mountain were the Henikers, and they were very sympathetic. Henry Heniker wrote a note giving permission to go to the dance, signed my father's name and delivered it to the Reverend Rice the day before the dance. I don't believe I'd ever been so happy – or so grateful.

The dance was even more fun than I had hoped for. It lasted all night, and I danced every dance. I met a lot of new people that night, and one of them was a good-looking cowboy who also danced every dance. His name was, Lew Young. I thought he was a darn good dancer.

Later, I found out that Lew Young had a homestead on East Creek and ran cattle on Pinon Mesa. He was a widower with four children; Nina, the oldest, handled the household. As the weeks passed, I got to know them all.

Summer finally came to an end, and the honeymoon couple made plans to return to the east. I knew my job would be coming to an end, but I sure did not want to leave that mountain. So, when Lew Young offered me a job as housekeeper to help Nina with the youngsters, I accepted right off.

About the time Marie went to work for the Young family, the war in Europe was bringing change to the range country of the intermountain West. Increased demand for wool, hides and meat began to push livestock prices up. By 1916, there were signs that range cattle would soon be bringing as much as eighty-dollars on the hoof. Then with American involvement just around the corner, the various government agencies increased range permits and pushed for greater production. Up on Pinon Mesa, the numbers of cattle and sheep mushroomed, and some ranchers became increasingly concerned about the effects of overstocking. Lew Young began to look for new range. By round-up time in 1916, he had decided to move his herd to the desert country of eastern Utah.

Marie Young remembers the drive:

We started out from Mack with a herd of about 1000 head. In addition to Lew and myself, there were Nina and the three children, John Dowling, Lincoln Click, and a rider from Moab by the name of Woods. We had trouble right at the start.

The old wooden bridge over Mack Wash caved in, and when the cattle stampeded, fifteen head went over the side and were killed outright or trampled to death. My horse spooked in all the confusion, and I was thrown. Needless to say, we did not cover much ground that first day.

The rest of the trip was just plain hard work. We headed west on a trail that would be near to the present route of U.S. 6-50. I remember water was scarce, and we were tired and dirty from eating dust for the better part of two weeks. When we reached the range

Lew had selected, the cattle were allowed to scatter, and we went on into Moab where Lew had bought a house and two acres on the edge of town.

Once we had settled in, Lew went back on the desert to check the herd. Well, now, wouldn't you know that trouble was still doggin' that cowboy's trail! The herd we had brought to Utah had scattered to kingdom come. Being mountain bred and raised, they were not acclimated to the desert and had headed for high-country. There were HT Bar cows spread out from Green River to Thompson Springs. There was nothing to do but shoo them back to the new range. For the next several months, Lew spend most of his time out riding sign.

In 1917. the cattle had more or less settled in on the desert range; beef prices were high and going higher; and Lew Young decided it was time for romance. Although in later years he always claimed Marie talked him into it, there can be little doubt that Lew, as always, made up his own mind about the matter. In any event, the decision was made to go to Grand Junction where, upon arrival, Marie went out to the farm to get her father's blessing.

Said Peter Becker, "You're a domfool."

Once a father's prerogatives had been properly exercised, the wedding took place at home as planned with flowers and cake in abundance and only a slight hitch when it was found that Lew had left the ring at the jewelers.

After the ceremony, Lew surprised his bride by taking her out to practice driving in a brand new 1917 Buick touring car. It was the first experience with an automobile for either of them, so they decided to learn together; Lew steered, while Marie shifted gears.

Says Marie:

> The next day, we started back to Moab, the back seat loaded with groceries and supplies. We did fine, until we reached Cottonwood Wash. Now there were no bridges in Utah at that time, and creeks and streams had to be forded. In spite of my objections, Lew decided we didn't need to shift gears at Cottonwood, and sure enough, the engine killed in mid-stream. There we were, caught in the quicksand in the middle of a muddy wash.
>
> Now high-heeled boots are not made for walking, and Lew was about to wade ashore to set a signal fire, when we heard the sound of a automobile coming up behind us. It was a wedding party, including the preacher, headed for the Cunningham ranch where Catherine Jones and Wallace Cunningham were waiting to get married.
>
> Well, they had to get us out of the way, before they could cross over, so the wedding waited while everyone pushed and shoved. It took a long time, because that Buick was buried to the axles. The men got down in the mud, and even the preacher rolled up his pants legs, took off his shoes and socks, and helped push. After what seemed to be hours, the Buick was out of the mud, and the other car safely across the wash. Lew had just put his boots back on and brushed himself off, when he decided to go over and thank the others for pushing us out. As though they were one man, the entire crew picked Lew up bodily and laughing fit to kill, tossed him head first back into the muddy wash.
>
> All in all, it was a grand day, even if Catherine did have her

wedding delayed.

During the next year, the war did indeed bring $80.00 cattle, but stockmen in the border country were plagued by drought, hard winters and an unnatural phenomenon having to do with the mysterious disappearance of cattle. One situation seemed to feed on another. Bad range conditions caused the cattle drift, and scattered cattle were more susceptible to the "long rope." Lew Young spent more and more time in the saddle, but the HT Bar herd suffered a steady decrease. The breaking point was reached during the winter of 1919-20. The snow came early and stayed on most of the winter; it was two feet deep on the desert from the Grand Valley to Green River. Cattle drifted with the storm, stalled in the deep snow, milled about and starved. It was estimated there were 2300 head in and about the town of Fruita during this period where they invaded woodsheds, outhouses and back porches in search of shelter and food. And all across the winter range, cattle, sheep, and wild life were dying by the thousands.

When the weather broke, the losses were found to be staggering. Hay was in short supply, and prices went sky-high. In eastern Utah, train loads of hay were shipped in, but before they arrived, Lew Young had lost sixty head in the feedlots at Moab.

Marie Young recalls the time:

> *I knew we were in a mell-of-a-hess! On this day, Lew came back to the house - shoved that hat back on his head and said, "By God, Sis, if you can sell this place, we'll go back to Colorado."*

Well, boy howdy! I can tell you, it didn't take me long to sell that place and get packed up. We loaded most everything in wagons, but I decided to ship the piano by rail. Wouldn't you know - they dropped that piano while they were loading it. The damage was pretty bad, but I had it sent to Fruita anyway. I knew I'd get it fixed some day.

Lew brought us back to Fruita and then headed right out to see how many cattle he could bring in. Nina, bless her, spent a lot of time riding with her father. We had a little house in Fruita that Lew had bought some years before, so we had a roof, but not much more. I knew we would need new range, so I went out to see Lew's brother, Ed, who had bought the Flying W spread and was moving his operation to that new range over in the Bookcliffs. Ed just said to move our stock up to his old range on Pinon Mesa.

Now the work really began. How that old cowboy took all that riding, I'll never know. Our cattle were scattered from Green River to the Arches and back to Thompson Springs. He found a few as far away as Dead Horse Point. It took all summer to bring in what was left of the herd. What a job it was! Lew would bring in a bunch from the desert, and we would push them up on Pinon while he rode back to Utah. But now, we faced a new problem. Those old cows were now acclimated to the desert and wanted to go back where they came from. Luckily, Lew's brother, Will, drifted in about mid-summer, and between the two of us, we kept the herd on the mountain.

It was a trying time. We were broke, had no range of our own and barely 300 head left to start over with. But when I looked up at that old mountain, I knew we were home. And I knew we would *make it.*

Marie Young was home, at last. She knew she was home, because an inner feeling told her it was so. Perhaps, it was a sense of belonging to the land that made it so special. Certainly, it is true that architectural style and form had little meaning in the early-West where people were required to build shelter from materials at hand. For in the broadest sense of the word - home is not in any particular structure; it is a special place in the mind.

*   *   *

CHAPTER FIVE

THE LADY OF THE HOUSE

*Give her of the fruit of
her hands; And let her own
works praise her in the gates.* *

It has been said that in all of life, nothing is quite so relaxing to the soul as an old-time country-style gabfest. Certainly, this was true in yesterday's West where the art of leisure was honed to a fine edge; the very nature of ranch life set the pattern. For in this time when most get-togethers were treated as special occasions, people knew the value of simple things - like sitting and talking an afternoon away. And if neighborliness was the key, storytelling was the treasure. The endless stream of stories came from daily happenings having to do with such things as cowboy work, cow nature, horse nature, human nature. They were usually meaty stories told by people who spoke a classic idiom which was filled with salty expressions and touched with the flavor of woodsmoke; the best of them were hum-

*Proverbs - 31

orous tales which grew and grew with the telling. Humor was basic for the simple reason that cowboys liked to laugh. Sometimes, they laughed over trifles, out of pure high spirits. Or, they saw another meaning unintelligible to outsiders as in the old story about a couple of back-country cowhands watching a circus parade for the first time in their lives. "Wonder what's the idea?" said one.

"Don't rightly know," said the other. Then drawing on his knowledge of cow critters added with a chuckle, "They must be goin' to water."

Subtle or pure corn, there can be little doubt the laughter it generated was good medicine. It was a safety valve to let off pent-up steam. It was a way to keep from being too sorry for oneself for all the hard work and loneliness. And it was part of society. For no one loved the get-togethers - the rangeland humor - the tall tales - the laughter - more than the lady of the house.

Ranch life was not all one big round of laughs, however. Perhaps, the reason leisure was valued so highly was because it happened so rarely. At any rate, hard work was the normal order of the day for a ranch wife in those old days of self-sufficiency. This was especially true in the spring just before leaving for summer camp in the mountains.

The following story by Mrs. Enola Mock paints a poignant graphic picture of such a time:

> The cool shade of the big cottonwood trees and the green lawn spread all around invited Mrs. Thomas to come and relax a bit. But, no, there was no time, for there was much to do before

they would leave for their summer camp in the mountains in the next few days.

Around her, stacked against the walls and in the available corners of the kitchen were open boxes and flour sacks, receiving the supplies for the summer. Everything from needles, thimble and thread, and plenty of patches, to vanilla for cakes, and the girl's old rag dolls must be packed - for once you left in May, you did not come back to town until September in time for school.

Millie Thomas was a small woman, short of stature and neat in her gray calico dress with a full skirt that reached to her ankles. A gingham apron was tied around her waist. As she paused in the center of the room, she took a mental inventory: here was the box for the drugs - not too many, but in sufficient supply. There was Ayer's Sarsaparilla, a blood purifier, and Jaynes Vermifuge (a must for worms). Yes, children in those days had worms, and so did adults, too: several kinds of worms, large round ones you got from drinking polluted water or eating raw vegetables before they were washed. Then, there were pin or thread worms which caused intolerable itching, so when a child ground his teeth at night and was restless, it was a sure sign of worms. She had a full bottle of castor oil and Jaynes Laxative Pills, turpentine and camphor for several uses besides mixing with hot grease to make a chest poultice for colds. And there were some old pieces of old woolen underwear to soak in the grease; also some folded white cotton rags, clean and ready to tear into strips for bandages, so when a finger was cut or a toe stubbed, a piece could be wrapped around and tied with a string. No, no bandaids! Antiseptics? Oh, a drop of turpentine, perhaps, but usually soap and water did the trick. Arm and Hammer's Baking Soda was good for burns and indigestion, and that was about all they needed. Viruses, vitamins, and various drugs and diseases along with the marvelous array of cosmetics to make you beautiful were unheard of then. Sometimes, there was a bottle of glycerine and rose water on the shelf.

The children's clothes, too old or outgrown to wear to school next fall, were stuffed into flour sacks, along with Millie's oldest dresses and George's shirts that needed patches. A pile of old shoes tied in pairs with strings or buttoned together lay waiting in the corner.

She glanced at the clock, ticking away on the shelf. 8:30, it said, and the fire had died down in the kitchen stove, so the water in the tea kettle was getting too cold to wash the dishes. From the woodbox nearby, she picked up several pieces of wood, raised the lid with the stove-hook, and put them in.

Her's was not an electric or gas range with a glass oven above, nor was it a micro-wave unit of today, nor a big home-comfort range with its high warming oven that came later. Rather, her cook stove was a square flat-topped affair of cast iron with the oven door decorated with a raised design, an opening on the side down under. It has a hearth in front which extended under the firebox that was a receptacle for the ashes. A door that had an open and close draft to regulate the burning of the fire and consequently the heat, opened across the hearth. The stove which had to be blacked and polished every now and then, stood on four legs and continued on up a black stove pipe that vanished in the wall or ceiling.

Her cabinets were tall wooden cupboards, sometimes called "safes", which stood against the white-washed walls, and there were open shelves for storage, too. Her floor was laid with wide, smooth boards, scrubbed white and clean – minus linoleum. The kitchen chairs might have perforated wooden backs and seats or slat backs which all were solid wood with no veneer. Her parlor chairs might have wicker seats. Now, the chairs stood at all angles around the breakfast table, just left as they had been shoved back after the meal. She must get busy!

As she turned, she picked up a coat or two which the children had tossed aside, and hung them on some nails driven in the wall behind the door. Then, she put the wash boiler on the stove and filled it with pails of water drawn from the cistern outside. The week's washing had to be done today – it was Monday.

When the dishes were finished, and by the time she got the bench in off the porch and had placed two tubs on it, then arranging two chairs to hold a third tub for the rinse water with blueing added, the water in the wash boiler would be warm enough to start the first tub. Filling the boiler again, she added a dash of lye to break the hard water, she then skimmed it before chipping some soap from a bar into it. No detergents. She boiled the white clothes in this water, after she had rubbed out the dirt on the washboard. As they boiled, she punched them down and stirred them about with a clothes stick which she also used to lift them from the boiler into the tub of sudsing water. Now, the clothes stick might have been made of about 28 inches sawed off an old mopstick with its rounded end. The other end had a hand hold of about five inches made square by cutting a small slice from two opposite sides. She began her day's task — which would not be finished until late afternoon when the last pair of black cotton stockings was hung on the clothes line outside.

Later in the week, these same tubs would be packed with groceries and needed articles to be hauled in the wagon to the mountains: vinegar in a brown earthen jug, Dr. Price's Cream Baking Powder (full weight and most perfect, the label read.) Lyonns XXXX (four X) Coffee, or Archichles Coffee in the bean, Baker's Breakfast Cocoa and green tea to be brewed, Arm & Hammers Baking Soda, and yeast. The hand coffee mill could be set in the middle of the tub, and this list packed around it. The coal-oil lamp and several glass chimneys would be put in one of the tubs, too, but not the lantern. It would be left out to be used on the way. On Saturday night, Monday's lowly wash tub became the family bath tub, set on the floor by the kitchen stove.

The stone jar churn with its wooden dasher, could set most anyplace in the wagon where it wouldn't get broken. A couple of old Montgomery Ward catalogs would be used for the summer's supply of toilet tissue and would be packed around the churn. She had Cashmere Bouquet (the richest and most lasting of all toilet soaps by Colgate and Company) was packed along with a few magazines, such as the Chautauquan and Delineator to read and a cotton salt sack containing some fancy work. And, she hadn't forgotten grandpa's Tar Soap for washing hair.

George had gone up to camp this last week with a load of the *heavy groceries, such as sacks of flour, sugar, and a fifty-pound can or two of lard, along with some bedding rolled in a tarp. We had taken potatoes and the garden seeds to be planted, before he returned. While there, he would set up the tents by stretching them on the frames and walls of peeled "quakie" poles and sweep off the wide board floors. He would throw out the rats' nests, so safely built up on the corners of the tent frames, and perhaps help the ground hog move from his sheltered winter abode under the tent floor. As for the mice that scurried everywhere from under the canvas-covered table, benches and cupboards – well – Millie and the girls could clean up their mess with plenty of hot water, soap and a scrub brush. But – he must fix the horse pasture fence, before he left; the winter snows always broke it down, and the deer helped by jumping over and through it.*

With almost rhythmic action, as she rubbed the dirty clothes on the wash board, her thoughts went something like this. "Yes, I put in a couple of cakes of Sapolio, and I think I have plenty of laundry soap to do until we butcher." Concentrated lye and tallow made good laundry soap which she moulded in her oldest bread pans, then cut it when cool into bars. "Enough candles are packed, and George took the coal oil and molasses," her thoughts ran on.

Now, the Thomas family would leave at about four in the afternoon and drive all night to avoid the heat of the desert they had to cross west of Fruita to go to the mountains beyond where lay their summer cattle range. The wagon box was loaded with the boxes, tubs and sacks, and then on top, a place was made with some more bedding for some of the children to ride upon, while the smaller ones rode on mother's lap or down in front of the spring seat where she sat. The rest of the space on top of the load provided a place for a crate of chickens and the cat and her kittens in a box, while the pig, placed in a heavy strong box, was tied at the very end of the wagon on the open tailgate. The milk cows had already been taken up, but the dog waited to go with the family, trotting along under the wagon or following the boys on horseback.

Along toward dusk, they stopped for supper. The brown stone jug of water, wrapped in wet gunny sacks to keep it cool, was set out on the ground. "I'm sure glad I bought new corks for the jugs the other day," Millie said as she knelt and rubbed the cupped palm of her hand appreciatively over the smooth, clean top. "It hasn't leaked a drop," she continued, but no one paid any attention to her.

The children, glad to be off the wagon, were running and playing tag, while George was unloading the food for supper. The boys had dropped the tugs and tied the team to a big greasewood bush and now were tieing their saddle horses to the wagon wheels. Soon, they all sat on the ground and ate, not delaying long, for they wanted to be on their way by dark.

The next day, when they arrived at camp, they would all be too tired to do much. George would turn the horses in the horse pasture, probably he called it the jingle pasture. The boys would put the milk cows in the corral and cut the calves off; a slot would be broken off the box and the cat turned loose, the pig taken down to its pen on the creek. Then, the crate of chickens would be carried to the chicken house which might have been built of willows with a willow and dirt roof. When all the animals were taken care of, some-

-thing easy to fix for supper would be found. The bedding would be rolled out on the tent floors, and they would go to bed – with the mice playing all around.

Mornings came early at the summer camp. A good day's hard work – scrubbing would clean the place for the most part; then the wagon could be unloaded and the groceries packed into the big wooden boxes, mouse-tight with heavy, tight fitting lids. They used these big boxes to sit on for chairs at the table. Clothing was kept in wooden boxes with lids, too. There were no clothes closets. There might be a fair sized quaken aspen tree with several limbs cut off for hooks, set firmly in the ground in one corner of the tent where hats and coats could be hung. That was handy.

There was either a small log spring house built over the clear, cold, bubbling spring which ran on down to irrigate the garden, or the spring might be boxed up and turned into a long, heavy trough. With the cold water running through this, milk, butter and foods in pots, pans and buckets could be set. Everything had to have a lid and probably a rock put on each lid to keep the chipmunks and mice out. It was all the refrigerator to be had and a pretty good one at that.

Not all the cow camps of those days offered only tents for dwellings, but some had one or two-roomed log cabins, or one built of unfinished or rough lumber with the boards running up and down for the walls. Bats were nailed over the cracks to keep the weather out. Pack rats and mice lived in these cabins in the winter, too, but discrimination and segregation was thought to be very decent in those days, so when the people moved in, the intruders were thrown out.

Although these summer camps were a far cry from the fancy summer cottages on Grand Mesa today, they were comfortable with wood-burning heaters and cook stoves. Native trees supplied the fuel – cedar and quaken aspen or the cook stove – not so much pitch, therefore not so much soot. Pinon and pine made a hotter fire and lasted longer in the heater.

In either the tent or the cabins, you found home-made furniture, bedsteads built of smooth-peeled quakie poles, rough lumber tables, cupboards and benches for chairs. Oilcloth covered the table, and where there was a woman, there was the feminine touch with a picture or so cut from some magazine and tacked on the wall. A small rocking chair might be in evidence, but in those days of rough or no roads at all, where only lumber wagons could be used or perhaps only a trail led to the cow camp, pack horses did the freighting. Nothing was transported that wasn't needed. Tin dishes and iron cooking utensils graced the tables and were left at camp in the fall.

Not all the cowmen who wintered in this part of western Colorado ranged so far away in the summer as did the Thomases. Their working schedule was something like this: for example – the Fisher boys, on horseback, drove the milk cows out part way on the desert and left them the evening before. The next morning at daybreak or before the family awakened, a loaded wagon was on the way and traveled all day, while the boys picked up the milk cows and drove them along. They summered in the Douglas Creek and Salt Wash canyons, while the Thomases went to the West Water canyons in eastern Utah.

There was plenty of fun in the mountains in the summer. A cowhorse race might be matched most anytime or most any place where there was room for more than one trail. Neighbors were miles apart. Yet, the whole family would go horseback and spend the day with their friends over the hill at their cow camp. Fourth of July had its picnics where several families gathered to enjoy the holiday. The foresighted parents in later years had some firecrackers for the occasion. If there were small children, they sometimes rode seated on little boxes in panyards on a pack horse. Tied securely, there was no danger when someone led the horse, and it was an easier way to transport the small ones, than to carry them in the saddle in front of you or by letting them hang on astride behind a saddle. But most children rode their own horses, for they learned very early in life to handle a horse and could ride bareback or in a saddle of their own.

In my day, a round-up offered a get-together day. Here would be roping, branding, cutting cattle from the bunch, and sometimes a cowboy showed his skill when a half-broken horse might come undone. Usually, we had a few sandwiches and some black coffee boiled in a can on the branding fire, if there were no camp near that offered a dinner.

Further recreation was found in fishing trips and sometimes an all-night dance. But usually, summertime was busy time. On the wide open range, there were no fences, so cattle strayed afar, and much riding had to be done. Then, there were always "broncs" to break for cow horses.

The cowman's wife would have had no time for bridge clubs, afternoon colored TV shows, or automobile trips to recreation centers, even if they had been known in those days. She scarcely had time for embroidery as a diversion, for she was always mending in her spare time. She made and packed butter in stone jars for winter, and she made laundry soap. When wild berries came on, she and the children found their way to the patches of wild currants, gooseberries, elderberries, choke cherries, service berries (she called them, "sarvice" berries), wild red raspberries and strawberries. She made preserves, jams, jellies, and used some for pies, or to eat fresh with good cow's cream skimmed from a pan. If the cowboys were riding on the range near to camp, then she cooked a big dinner for all the riders. In doing this, she did not enjoy the pampered ease of picking up a package of frozen prepared peas. But, if you please, from the garden plot, she picked a pail of peas and hulled them for the pot. She found a little time to read when she sat down to rest, and the summer passed all too fast with school starting in September.

The cowman's wife on the winter ranch or in town for the winter lived the average life of most other inhabitants of this western country. The houses were much the same with no modern conveniences, but well built, comfortable and inviting with hand-braided rag rugs on the floor in front of a fireplace in the livingroom. A pedal organ with its high ornate top, or a large square piano, was in the parlor that had a wall-to-wall ingrain carpet sometimes laid on a mat of clean loose straw to let the dust through and to make for softer walking. Since vacuum cleaners hadn't been invented then, she swept with a broom, and it was a dusty job, so she usually put on a dust cap which was sometimes made pretty with ruffles, lace and ribbon over her hair.

For winter entertainment in Fruita, there were public dances, a literary society, home talent plays, and family dinners on the holidays where all the relatives came and stayed all day.

Mrs. Thomas, typical of the country woman of her age and era, was of genuine dignity – not of the sophisticated society type, but quiet and unobtrusive. She was efficient and could meet most any occasion, even to shooting and killing the bear that was trying to kill the pig when all the men were gone. Yet, by nature, she was the gentle and genteel woman and mother that befitted her position in life. She earned and commanded the respect of her children and husband, and they loved her for it. She spent time and patience in teaching the children obedience and discipline, and in those days, children did not "talk back" and argue, even though they were born with the same complexities and emotions of the normal child of today. She considered her position as wife and mother as an honorable and necessary place of high esteem and not one to be neglected or to take second place to some outside salaried job. She worked hard and put in long hours with her home and her family, accepting humbly the demands and duties of each day as it came, and – she kept her faith in God.

In 1970, an article written by a Frenchman named, Oliver Blanc, appeared in the French Magazine, Le Chasseur Francais. In the article, Mr. Blanc tells of a visit to the Currier Ranch which is located on Buzzard Creek, one of the upper tributaries of Plateau Creek. As Mr. Blanc relates it: The ranch is, "lost in the mountains" near the small village of Collbran. The article goes on to tell of how the ranch is operated by Mrs. Tom Currier and her sons, Charleton and Franklin. It delves into the economics of modern-day ranching for the most part, but at one point, Mr. Blanc makes the following observation: (translated from the French) — roughly.

> "But the cowboys over there are not all dead yet. As we saw in the Western pictures and magazines, literatures and so on. In the history of Indian killing, the saloons in the old days with some bad guys around. Certainly, the thought now is to take the best care of the livestock that is possible."

The Currier ranch of today consists of some 8000 acres which can handle 1500 head of livestock. It is a mechanized efficient operation, and the headquarter buildings are comfortable and picturesque. It was not always so. Chastine Currier tells of the early days:

> *Our home was a log cabin of one room, hewn out of quakies grown on the place, (door chinked with pieces of quakies and daubed with mud and with a rough board floor). The door was out of rough lumber with a two-inch hole in it through which we drew a chain that fastened the door by being hooked over a bent spike. There were two barn hinges on which the door swung, two barn windows which slid between grooves made by 1x1s. The design of the furnishing were in keeping with the cabin — all second-hand; an old dresser, an iron bedstead with a good mattress, and comforters that my mother-in-law pieced; a very old wood range and heater, a mouse-*

proof and rat-proof cupboard (very essential), a table and chairs (very nice) at a cost of $10.00, some new pails, a few dishes, pots and pans, black-handled knives and forks with some silverplated spoons, a washbench, and a woodbox. This was our mountain home over half of the year for seven years. During the winter months, we lived in the valley with Tom's folks while he looked after the cattle for his brothers and father. We didn't have much, but we were both happy and willing to work. We had milk cows specifically for our own daily use, and had to have milk cows for the feeding of calves whose range mothers had either died or else had accidently been weaned from them. The milk that was not used was thrown away when not needed for either purpose. It seemed wasteful, so I, for a period of about twenty-three years, sold cream at Collbran, some sixteen miles distant.

The ranch grew as the years passed by, and the ever-industrious Chastine Currier became involved in many community affairs, including the women's auxiliary of the Cattlemen's Association. In a letter dated March 14, 1975, she tells of promoting "Beef for Father's Day." An excerpt follows:

Naturally I was and am interested not only in the production, but also in the promotion of the sale of our product, and then to serve as a helpmate to the men folk in their arduous tasks. Consequently several of like mind of the women who had gathered at the State Cattlemen's Convention decided to formulate a woman's organization. This was at Alamosa. The wife of the Editor of the Daily

Stockman was elected as our first president. The assembly chose to call the group the Colorado Cattlewomen's Association. I was placed on the constitution and by-laws committee. Later I served two terms as State Treasurer and two terms as State Secretary; still later I organized the first unit in Western Colorado and was elected its President. The name was subsequently changed to Cowbelles both in the state and in the individual units. In the National I was also a charter member and in all of this work gained acquaintance with many wonderful men and women interested in the cattle business, which helped greatly in promoting Beef for Father's Day. No one is an island.

Our menfolk have worked so hard on the ground level as producers, as ranchers, as rangeriders, in the feedlots and with the legislative bodies, and I greatly wished we of the Cowbelles might in some quite distinctive way show their appreciation not only of their labors but also of their thoughtfulness of their families. It was then I began to wonder just what our menfolk appreciated most when relaxing after a day's labor. Was it not the smile on the mother's face and the well cooked meal featuring beef? Why not have a special day for him. Father's Day; that was the day to honor him. Mrs. John Bruce Dodd in 1910 promoted the idea of honoring our fathers, and this too would further honor him. She is a jewel who lives in Spokane, Washington.

I presented it to my own local Cowbelle unit in Collbran, Colorado first. They showed great enthusiasm and urged me to present it to the Western Colorado Council. The executive board of the Council were quite passive toward the idea, so I presented it on the *floor of the assembly who again were quite as enthusiastic as my own unit. Then with some apprehension, I approached some of the National officers. They liked the idea; however, because the idea involved the men, they thought it might be best, for the psychological impact, to be promoted by the Cowbelles. Next, Tom, my late husband, and I started by car over ice and snow to take the thought of Beef for Father's Day to the National meeting at Reno, Nevada. I presented it before the assembly of Cowbelles who were quite apathetic and no motion was made to accept Beef for Father's Day. David Rice, Executive Secretary of the Colorado Cattlemen's Association, and I later conversed and he showed great concern over the near loss of the honorium to men everywhere, so he invited seven of us to his hotel room that evening where after some discussion, a knowledgeable paper was prepared and the next morning it was taken before the National Executive Cowbelle Board where it gained hearty support and was disseminated throughout the nation.*

Chastine Currier's concern about the course of events in the cattle industry led to activities in many areas. She became an accomplished speaker, and for a time contributed to a regular program on KREX, the pioneer radio station in Grand Valley.

In one of her speeches, Mrs. Currier tells of events having to do with the Taylor-Grazing Act:

Some statisticians have shown that the consumption of beef has produced a more vigorous bodily growth in Americans than that of vegative substances alone. A better understanding of these facts needs to be disseminated. Repetition by the lay producer is a must. An English teacher was emphasizing the relevant value of repetition to her class: "Repeat a word eight times, and it becomes yours." A sweet young thing in the back of the room was overheard in an audible whisper, "Fred, Fred, Fred . . . ".

The economy in our country basically depends upon our land. Near at home in Colorado, particularly in the western and northern sections in the 1920's, nomads with their thousands of sheep were ruining our lands by close grazing, leaving nothing save barren soil and sheep tracks. Western Colorado cattlemen realizing the desperate situation did some tall thinking. They formed an organization of cattlemen with an executive board to represent them, with Ferry Carpenter, a practicing lawyer of Hayden, and also a cattleman, elected as chairman. Others were Claud Reese of Rio Blanco, a cattleman, banker; and also State Legislator, Tom Watson of Eagle, Tom Currier (my late husband), all board members. Following the board's decision, Claud Reese, along with Mr. Oldland who was another legislator, formulated a bill and presented it to the State Legislature. It passed, and was known as the Reese-Oldland Bill, which legislated the separating of the government grazing land into units available to resident livestock owners. Because it protected the land, it worked wonders. Instead of the sheep-cattle wars resulting in much bloodshed, it resulted in the salvaging of thousands of acres of grass lands because some cowpunchers thought it through.

In view of the success of this state bill and the execution of it, this board of cattlemen decided that the salvation of the open land of the eleven western states was at hand. They met many times to for-

mulate a knowledgeable paper to effectuate results. Frank Delaney of Glenwood Springs was chosen as their legal council. After the pertinent facts were assembled, the document was presented to Ed Taylor, a Congressman of Glenwood Springs who in turn presented it to Congress which passed the bill which became known as the Taylor-Grazing Act. The President signed it, and it became law in 1934. Ferry Carpenter was appointed the first administrator of the act and served with an elected advisory board in each area. Tom, my late husband, was the first one elected in our particular district and remained in this capacity until his final illness. The land was preserved, more erosion avoided because cattlemen prevailed.

The purpose in mentioning my husband's name as a member of the Western Colorado Cattlemen's Board is the fact that we were partners in business from the first of our marriage and also the fact that he preferred to have me with him when he travelled to far-away places alone, so I generally accompanied him. Though not a member of the board, the men would let me sit in on their sessions. At least at one time, they invited several other men to be present in their deliberations. I did not wish to be the only woman present in such a large group of men, so I prepared to leave. Mr. Carpenter asked me to wait; I did. He and Mr. Reese then procured a comfortable chair, placed it on the stage of the Rifle schoolroom where the meeting was being held, invited me to sit in it, then drew the stage curtain; again I was present, but not with the group. I thus became aware many times of the proceedings without voice or vote.

God bless the ecologists, the preservationists, the Sierra Club, the vacationers and others of like mind. They are trying, but often their thoughts are more visionary than down to earth. They say that the cattlemen preserved the land and forage for selfish reasons. It was preserved. They drew the chestnuts out of the fire for others as well as themselves. The land is in far better condition in most areas than it was in the 1920's, and it is needed for future utilization. The earth was made for utilization as well as for beauty. It is claimed that only one-tenth of one percent of our population make use of our wilderness areas, but one-hundred percent make use of the food produced on our land.

Lucile Hansen grew up on a dry-land farm in northern Utah near the small Mormon community of Beaver Dam. After attending Brigham Young College in Logan, Utah and a summer term at U.A.C., she became a schoolteacher. She taught school briefly at Randolph, and then took over a school at Sage Creek in northern Utah. About 1920, she decided to look to the south and in the following sequence, she tells of coming to Castle Valley, Utah where she met her cowboy:

> *Having had enough cold weather, I sent applications to several counties in southern Utah and was assigned to another one-teacher school in Castle Valley, Grand County. It was harder to leave mother this time, as we had the length of the state between us instead of 60 or 70 miles.*
>
> *Mother went to Salt Lake with me, and I got on the train there to go to Cisco which was the nearest railroad point to Castle Valley. It was evening when I got on the train, and I reached Cisco*

about midnight. I was told there was a hotel of sorts there, so I got a room. The next morning at daylight, I got up and looked out the window, and my heart sank. As far as I could see was a desolate desert, so different from the rolling hills, green fields and snow-capped mountains of northern Utah. I was tempted to take the next train back to Salt Lake. I found out that the thrice-weekly stage would be leaving that morning for Castle Valley and that there was another passenger, Sidney D. Pace. So, I met "Uncle Sid," my future husband's uncle. The "stage" was an old truck. We had twelve miles of desert, then came to the Colorado River and followed the beautiful, rugged canyon of the river for about seventeen miles. The road was narrow and rocky, and in many places high dugways directly next to the river. Three miles after we left the river, and six hours of hot dusty traveling with several flat tires that had to be repaired and pumped up, we suddenly saw Castle Valley. It is a gorgeous valley, almost surrounded by red sandstone rimrock with the beautiful LaSal Mountains to the south, and interesting pinacles and red sandstone monuments. Two of the most spectacular were the "Priest and Nuns" on the east side of the valley, and "Lady Skirts" on the north— very descriptive names. Nestled in the north end of the valley was a ranch with green fields and trees in pleasing contrast to surrounding red hills and bluffs. This was my destination!

I was received most kindly by John and Ann Pace, who, with Uncle Sid, were the owners of the ranch. Sometime during the 1880s, Uncle Sid had come to this part of Utah from Payson, Utah, and worked for one of the early cattle companies in the LaSal Mountains.

He liked the country, saw its possibilities, and persuaded his brother, John, to help establish a cattle ranch in the area. John sold his home in Payson and used the money to buy heifers; then, he and Sid drove these, with a few other cattle and horses they had accumulated, to Castle Valley. They went on the train to Thompson and traveled the forty miles from there to Moab on the stage. Since there were no roads into Castle Valley, they rode horseback over the mesas between Moab and Castle Valley and went down a sheer precipitous trail, down the rimrock and bluff into Castle Valley. What wagons and machinery they had to have were brought in the same way, but had to be taken apart and carried by pack mule down the trail. It wasn't many years until a road was established between Cisco and the Colorado River. Then they could get their supplies and groceries once a year from Grand Junction, Colorado, and load them on boats or rafts and float them down the river to be unloaded near the ranch. Then, eventually, the Dewey Bridge was built and the road made down the river, so freighting was much easier. It was sometime after this, before the road was built on down the river to Moab.

The Pace Ranch was as nearly as self-sufficient as it could be. They ground their own cornmeal and wholewheat flour, had their own honey, butter, bacon, hams, etc. I am sure the first years there were hard for Ann Pace, but she was a capable, hardworking girl, a marvelous cook, and had a happy, sunny disposition. Everyone who knew her loved, admired and respected her. John was efficient in his work, too, more quick-tempered, but fair and just, and very hospitable. He was genial with an endless fund of experiences and stories which he told very effectively. He was well-liked, too.

During the winter of 1890-91, Ann went to Payson, where Ireta was born. But two years later, when Sid was born, she stayed in Castle Valley. One of her neighbors, and Alta Fish, an even earlier settler than the Paces, helped her. She and her husband, Mort, and family lived in Castleton at the head of Castle Valley. Zella was also born in Castle Valley in March, 1899. Another daughter, LaSal, was born in June, 1905. The winter she was five years old, she had scarlet fever and died. It was a tragic time for Ann and John. They couldn't get a doctor — the nearest one was in Moab. They buried her on the ranch. It was an experience Ann never got over. The youngest child, Jack, was born in Payson in July, 1912.

At the time I went to Castle Valley to teach school, there was a large comfortable ranch house and also a small store. They sold a few staples to neighboring ranches and were able to get many things wholesale for themselves.

Pace Brothers Corporation had been formed in 1914 and consisted of Sidney D. and John and Ann; Lynn and his wife, Annie; Sid; Ireta and her husband, Bert Buchanan; Zella and her husband, Carl Gilbert; also Reece, Uncle Sid's son, and his wife, Blanch. John and Lynn and their children lived in Castle Valley, Ireta and Bert lived in Sinbad, Colorado, and Reece and Blanche in Rock Creek, Colorado. They also owned considerable land in the LaSal Mountains and had a summer camp there — Sally's Hollow — where Reece and Blanche, Sid and Uncle Sid stayed in the summer. Sid and Uncle Sid spent their winters in Castle Valley, except when they were at one of the other ranches riding. They had also acquired Kirk's Basin which is six miles north of Sally's Hollow; they later developed it into a hay ranch. By the time I went there, Reece and Blanche stayed at Rock Creek the year round, and Zella and Carl lived at Sally's Hollow and moved to Castle Valley for the winter.

But to go back to me – the first night I was there, I was surprised at the number of people for supper. There were three or four hired men besides the family. It looks like with such pleasant surroundings, good food, and nice people, I would have been happy there, but I felt like I would die of homesickness the first six weeks. It was all so different than anything I had ever known. I could hardly eat, and cried when I went to bed every night. There were no young people, except some of the hired men, and nothing to do on weekends.

By the last of October, it had all changed. Zella, a year older than I, moved down from the mountains, and I got acquainted with the girl who taught in Castleton, and I was happy and had lots of fun the two years I taught there.

Lynn and Annie, who had been at Sally's Hollow, where Lynn was running their sawmill, came back, and I moved from the big ranch house to stay with them and their three daughters in their small house just across the creek from the schoolhouse. Dorothy was 9, Lucile 7, and Dixie 2. I also had Jack in my school. He was 8. Ireta's and Bert's oldest son David, 6, went to school there two months and then went back to Sinbad.

The cowboys brought some cattle down in October on their way to Cisco to ship them so the evening they were there, they all came over to see the new "school marm." I had heard about Sid, also heard he was engaged to a girl who had taught there two years before. She was a friend of the family. Sid told me much later that after seeing me the first time, he thought I was a nice, attractive girl, but hardly the type he would "fall for." I felt much the same about him.

I had a horse to ride whenever I wanted one, and Zella and I frequently rode with Sid and Carl. There were dances every two or three weeks at the schoolhouse in Castle Valley, or the one in Castleton. Zella, Carl, Sid and I would go horseback to Castleton – Zella and I with our "nice" dresses tied on behind the saddle (we rode in divided riding skirts). Lynn and Annie and their family rode in the buckboard, and John and Ann sometimes on horseback, sometimes in the buggy. They always took cakes. We usually danced all night, and when the children got tired, they were put to bed in corners on benches, or any available space. At midnight, we had cake and coffee. Lynn played the violin and was always one of the musicians for the dance. It was so much fun.

In the spring, which came early, there were picnics, fishing on the river, horseback rides and trips with the cattle. When school was out that first year, Zella invited me to come back early before school started and visit them at Sally's Hollow. I loved Sally's Hollow! It has been a life-long attachment.

Not long after I came back, Sid and I became engaged. He and the other girl had broken their engagement by mutual consent, during the summer. It was a happy winter with activities much like the year before, except the Castleton school had been closed. I missed Katharine Sullivan, the girl who had taught there the year before who was from Collbran, Colorado.

In the spring, May, Zella and I went with the cowboys to take a bunch of calves to Cisco to the railroad. At the end of the second day, two of the calves had not been able to keep up, so the next morning, the others went on with the rest of the herd, and Sid and I started back to the ranch with the two calves. We got them as far as Professor Valley, then left them. It was a beautiful day, and we had a lovely time together on that long ride. Just why it was such a perfect day, I have never decided, but it has always stood out in my memories.

When school was out, Sid took me to Grand Junction to catch the train. It was hard to say goodbye, but it was just for two months. We were married in the courthouse in Logan on July 21, 1922, in a simple ceremony with LaReve and Frank as our only attendents. We spent three or four days in Salt Lake at the Hotel Utah and then went to Cisco. Heavy rains had washed out part of the road between Cisco and Dewey, so we were marooned in Cisco for two days – of all places. Over the years, we were teased about spending part of our honeymoon in Cisco.

Rose Pritchard Goss recalls the hazards of early trails:

My brother, Frank Pritchard, and I took up claims on Grand Mesa and built cabins just north of what now is the shelter house. How well we remember when trails were broken through grass waist-high, when man did not let his cattle over-graze the land.

The Lands End trail was steep and rough. Teams and wagons were left at the R. T. Anderson ranch, and we proceeded on horseback on the trail which led to the top. The trail for about five miles *was so steep, all riders were forced to walk and hold to the horses tail and try to stay on the upper side of the horse, so as to keep from getting hit by rocks from the horses climbing, and also to be able to keep up. Every little while, the horses would stop for a breath. The trail was so steep, we were afraid the horses would go over backwards with the rider, and several pack horses did go over backwards. Mrs. Gertrude Anderson Krowns pack horse did fall with a heavy pack.*

While living on the claim, I cooked by campfire and a dutch oven and hauled water from a spring and slept in a pup tent. My brother and another man slept under tarps. One time, my sister, Irene, went with us, and we walked to the edge of the mountain overlooking Palisade and the valley, and when dark came, the lights of the town shown. That night, we got lost going back to the partially-built cabins. After about four hours, we came to the fenceline, and I knew my way, as I had ridden there before and had observed a small hill which we had ridden down which led to the road to the cabin.

Although the Utes had been moved to the Uintah reservation in the Territory of Utah in 1881, many of the frontier ranches had contact with the Indians all through the development years. The Utes in small groups or invidiuals families moved about quite freely and often stopped at remote ranch houses for a visit. While the callers usually just wanted food, many of the ranch wives were apprehensive. Frequently they were alone at the time of the visit, and the memory of the Meeker uprising died slowly in this part of the intermountain West. Although reactions to the unsolicited visits varied with the individual, the events were usually peaceful. One of those who traveled about was Chipeta, widow of Chief Ouray. Ouray was known as the white man's friend, and old Chipeta did much over the years to dispel the old fears. It is said, she lived to be well over one hundred years.

Ethel Stanifird tells of eating a meal with Chipeta:

>My folks were Nathan and Katherine Turner, and they trailed their cows in over the mountains in the early days. After I married Jake Stanifird, we lived over in the Uintah country for several years near-by old Chipeta. One day she asked me to eat with her. She had butchered some sheep, but said she was to old to cook the meat, but then added, "You've still got to eat with me."
>
>My brother, Charles, was a great friend of the Indians, so I decided I'd better sit down at the table with her. Chipeta opened a can of tomatoes, and we also had biscuits and a bowl of sugar. We only had one spoon between us, so we dipped in with that one spoon and ate sugar and tomatoes. I nibbled part of my biscuit, and then hid the other part in my dress. The old squaw didn't pay any attention to me while we were eating. After she had finished, however, she went in her trunk and got a lot of old pictures of her and Ouray. She seemed to be very proud of the old chief. I have often thought I should have asked her for something as a remembrance of the occasion, but I didn't think about it then. I've often thought it was quite an honor to eat with old Chipeta. She was one-hundred years old at the time.

Ruby Rector Kirby also comments on the Indians:

My family history dates back to 1885 when my father, J. W. Rector, brought the first trail herd of Texas cattle that ever came into the Douglas Creek country. He had first taken the herd into Wyoming and then decided to bring it on into the Douglas Creek country.

I was born at Rangely, Colorado and my age isn't a secret. I was born in 1902. I grew up in the Rangely country, until 1910 when my family moved to Grand Junction where I attended school. I went to high school there and then on to Western State College. I married Albert Kirby in 1938. When we decided we were going to be permanently in the cattle business; first we had what was the old Cross ranch, which was my dad's ranch and had been in the family for some 65 years. We later acquired ground around this country, and then purchased what used to be the old Adams ranch on West Creek.

In the early days, the Ute Indians were very numerous in the Douglas Creek country and always welcomed visitors in our home. Whenever any of us kids arrived on the scene, the very first people to see us were Indians. In fact, the Indians came to see us when my brother, Richard, was born, and they brought him the three-day measles.

Ellen White Kilby on an incident in Rangely:

I was John White's bride of just three months when we went over Douglas Pass with a pack outfit. No road. When we got over Douglas Pass, there was a little cabin where we rested awhile, and then we went about sixteen or eighteen miles down the canyon and stayed the night. The next day, I rode in the mess wagon with the cooks. We camped down on the river that night near Rangely and stayed in a tepee. I spent my first summer at Rangely boarding out. My husband made arrangements for me to stay during the summer, because he was foreman for a big cow outfit. When we went over there, it was soon after that Meeker Massacre, and the people were stirred up.

In later years, the Indians often came up Spring Creek above Rangely with their dogs, kids, and horses to kill deer. One year the game warden decided they were killing too many deer, so he went down and told them to move out. They got into a battle, shot at each other, and the Indians run him out of the canyon and down to the river. They shot his horse out from under him, and he got down in a deep wash and finally hid under a fence surrounding an alfalfa field close to the river. They didn't find him, but the next day a neighbor that lived across the river from us came along and asked me to go on to Rangely with them. It was about four miles, and when we got into Rangely, there were a lot of Indians without any squaws walking up and down with their guns. I was well acquainted with the store man, so I went in and said, "What is going on?" He told me about the warden, and then said the Indians were talking about people trying to keep them back on the reservation. They wanted to hunt in their old places off the reservation, and that is what they were mad about.

When we went back down to where I lived, there was a regular city of Indians, tepees, and everything, down along the river.

There I was alone with my three babies and pretty frightened. But when the neighbor from across the river said I could go over and stay with them, I said, "Well, if they are going to kill us, you couldn't protect us, so I will stay right here at home." I spent a sleepless night, but the next morning the Indian camp had all been moved away. They had gone away and hadn't bothered anyone.

I had been so frightened over this Indian trouble that I sent word out to my husband on the range where he was most of the time. When he came home, he said that he had seen more Indians up there than we had around Rangely. He told me to write a note next time so he would have set instructions about what to do. In later years, I got so I wasn't afraid of Indians at all.

Catherine Moore relates an incident involving her grandmother on Glade Park:

As I have said before, the Indians were here when my grandfathers came. It was also quite a hideout for outlaws. People never asked a stranger his name. If he wanted work, they hired him. Some stayed and became respected stockmen. The going wage in those days was $20.00 a month and board, of course, and $30.00 for the foremen. The Indians gave no trouble, except to make pests of themselves by riding in every few days and demanding a meal.

Grandmother Sleeper came from New England, and great was her consternation one day when all alone in camp to see ten Indians ride in. They all got off their horses and crowded into the cabin. They wanted bread. She told them she had none. So, they said they would wait while she made some. Now, grandmother was a very resourceful woman and not timid. So she provided the biscuits, but for the liquid, she used coal oil. They ate the biscuits, but they never bothered her again.

Minta Gerry of Rangely, remembers the Indians coming to the family home on Douglas Creek:

>My mother did a lot of sewing, and she often made buckskin gloves and other garments from deer and elk hides. The Utes often stopped at our ranch, and when they showed up, would usually walk right in without knocking and ask for food. It always made mother nervous when they did this.
>
>One day, mother was making a dress for herself when an Indian couple walked in the door. They watched her for awhile, and then demanded that she make a dress for the Indian woman. Mother told them she would sew it, if they would furnish the material. Several days later, they came back with yards and yards of white calico. They waited all day while mother made a Mother Hubbard, which the woman sported proudly over her regular clothes. The Indian man then insisted that something be made for him as well. They stayed over another day while mother made him a white calico shirt. This pleased him very much, and both of the Indians were very friendly after that. They would bring hides to the ranch, and mother was not so afraid of them just dropping in anymore.

Nina Turner Gavin recalls another kind of housekeeping chore:

My dad, J. D. Turner, better known as, Uncle Jim, trailed cattle from Missouri in 1877 to Huerfano County. From there, he trailed cattle again over to Utah near Westwater in 1885. About 1896, he and my uncle and a Mr. Fletcher bought the Flying W Ranch. It was known then as the Goslin Sheep Ranch. We moved to the ranch in 1896, and I think nearly all cowhands in this part of the country either worked for dad or with him during the years we were out there. I remember many of them. There was Burns Fisher up Hay Canyon, and Mr. and Mrs. Skelly were up Hay Canyon at that time, and up Trail Canyon were the Mose Burkitts, the Lee Ashleys, and the Al Sales.

I often think of how hard it was to keep house in those early days. I don't know how my mother ever managed to cook for so many hired men. There were no conveniences at all. The only water available came from wells or springs. She had to wash by hand on a scrub board and had to carry the water. I remember how the men always helped to carry water.

In 1917, my husband, Doc Gavin, and my brother, Ernest, bought out Fred Mantey. They held the ranch for two years, and in 1919, they sold it to Dale Mitchell and Ed Young. My husband then bought a place on Cow Creek at Ridgway, and we kept that until 1945.

Very often, the cattle business was only a part of an overall venture which kept an entire family occupied. Mrs. Gertrude F. Mogensen tells of a family meat-packing operation:

I came to the valley from Kansas in a covered wagon in the year 1890 with my parents, Mr. & Mrs. George M. Porter, and three brothers, now known as Dr. R. B. Porter, William M. Porter, and Dr. M. J. Porter. Our route over the mountain was by way of Monarch Pass, fording streams, and occasionally crossing by ferryboat.

I married J. M. Mogensen, an immigrant from Denmark, who had been attracted to the area as a promising locality. He started here as a farmer and orchardist. Late frosts soon halted the fruit business, so livestock and farming took our attention.

One son, Porter Mogensen, was interested in cattle, so we bought an interest in the Franz Muhr operation in the Douglas Pass area, later buying out the Muhr interest and adding adjoining areas and desert grazing land.

Having learned something of the meat-packing business in Denmark, where he apprenticed to a butcher, Mr. Mogensen started a small packing plant and operated it for some years. One son, M. L. Mogensen, proved to be an efficient butcher, and the younger son, H. F. Mogensen adapted his talents to all phases of the operation: farmer, stockman, and butcher.

The poor quality of mixed cattle delivered to the slaughter house prompted Mr. Mogensen to start raising registered Hereford cattle. Selling registered sires to the stockmen soon produced a much better quality animal for slaughter.

Our business seemed to be a family affair, making use of efforts of sons, daughters, Petrea and Elena, and daughter-in-law, Anna, Porter's widow.

I feel a history of the area would not be complete without mention of my brother, Dr. R. B. Porter's venture in cattle business. While short lived, due to an unsatisfactory partnership and the burdens of his medical practice, he made the venture into a business that was of secondary interest to him. Many of his best friends were cattle people whom he dearly loved.

While there can be little doubt that pioneer women were extremely hardy and contributed a great deal to the overall effort, it should probably be acknowledged at this point that every once in a while the stiff upper lip trembled, and the lady of the house just had to give way to a feminine impulse — or two. One can imagine tears shed, situations cussed, husbands nagged, and just plain all-around bitchiness.

Marie Young found a special way to vent her frustrations as she recounts here:

After we came back from Utah, Lew kept watching for a chance to pick up some new range of our own. He finally found it over on Dry Fork in the Books. We bought the improvements Bart Ownes had made on the old Nearing place for $1500. This included fences, corrals, and an old log house. Later, when that area was opened, we filed for rights to the land. This became our summer camp, and over the years, we added to the ranch through purchases and range permits.

Now after the war, cattle had dropped to $20.00 on the hoof, and things were so tight a silver dollar looked as big as a cart wheel. Once we went out to camp in the summer, we were likely to stay put the entire season. I remember one summer in particular when things got to me a bit more than usual. The long summer days seemed to blend one into another, and it was a continous round of baking bread, cooking meals, churning and washing clothes. Lew was out riding the rims most of the time, and I was alone with kids more than a woman should be.

A person just couldn't pick up and go to town in those days. First of all, it cost money, and also because it was an all-day trip. In order to get to Grand Junction from our place on Dry Fork, we had to drive to DeBeque, and then all the way over through the Blue Stone country to near Collbran and down Plateau Creek. In addition to the long round-about way, the roads were usually rough, and it took much longer to cover the distance than it does now.

We still had our Buick, but Lew had it parked in a shed some distance down the road, since we did not use it for weeks at a time. On this day, I had gone down to the shed thinking how nice it would be to get away for awhile. I found the rats had gotten into the seats and strewn the cotton stuffing around. The rats would be taken care of with strychnine in cornmeal at a later date, but that did not help at the time. Somehow, I felt all hemmed in.

Up near the corrals, several bulls were bellowing, and I noticed several more of the big fellows coming in from a back pasture. Although they were separated, both bunches seemed to be on the fight, and I couldn't help thinking they were all as tired of being cooped up as I was. Suddenly, I was down at the corrals opening the gates and letting all those old bulls get together. Then I climbed up on a corral pole to watch the fun. Boy howdy, did they ever *carry on!* They bellowed and pawed the dirt and then charged at each other. It was pretty gory, but finally the biggest and strongest bull won out, and the others turned tail. My, it had been exciting!

Then, just as I was about to get down to close the gates, I looked up, and there was Lew sitting on his horse and watching me. Those blue eyes kind of snapped, and he shoved that old hat back on his head before getting down. I couldn't tell whether he was trying to control his anger or keep from laughing. He was quiet for a moment, but then he said, "Sis, I've just got a good notion to get you a crooked stick and send you down the canyon."

I guess I was fired, but it all blew over, and somehow I felt much better for the rest of that long summer. And I was always sure those old bulls enjoyed it all as much as I did.

*   *   *

DISPATCH

November, 1882
Grand Junction, Colorado

The General Election passed off quietly with a majority in favor of the local Republican ticket. It was on the day of election that a perceptible earthquake shock was felt through the valley, and, indeed, through the entire state. A party camped on Douglas Creek stated that they saw huge rocks tumble down the mountainside during this shock, and afterwards saw large volumes of smoke, with a sulphurious smell, emerge from crevices newly opened in the ground.

CHAPTER SIX

THE WOOLY BOOGERS

Now I ain't goin' to moralize
Or give no sage advice;
When a man burns his fingers in the fire,
He ain't goin' to try it twice.

In the movies — when a cowboy goes to town - his first stop is always the front-street saloon where he orders a double shot of redeye. In no time at all, he has challenged somebody to a fight and fired twice at the mirror over the bar, shattering it. Once outside, he shoots out the lights or rides up and down the street pumping lead into anything that moves. This image of the gunslinging West which has become so firmly established over the years is, at the very least, an exaggeration. For while such incidents very likely did occur, they were not standard procedure. Certainly much of the confusion surrounding the romantic gunfighter era is the result of distortion in movies and television shows, in books and magazines. In the following sequence, some of the oldtimers speak of cowboys and guns.

Shorty Gross:

"Guns were a natural part of a cowhand's equipment, and only a few didn't carry them. There has been a lot of talk on how cowhands used their guns to shoot up people every chance they got. That was actually a rare thing. The attitude of cowboys toward shooting was that it was a good thing to know how to do, because it might get you out of a tight fix sometime. I've often shot up a box of cartridges as I rode along, aiming at cans and rabbits. I never was one for strapping a gun to my hip, though."

Franz Muhr:

"The main reason for carrying a gun was the lonesomeness of the country and the need to take care of yourself in case of accidents. Almost anybody on the range could shoot a little, and some would practice a lot and get to be an expert. But the so-called two-gun man was a rare specimen and lived mostly in books. A lot of the boys carried a gun in an inside shoulder holster, but I always liked mine in the pocket of my chaps."

But old-time cattlemen were like a certain species of tree or plant that could grow in a crack on solid rock; they had been ages in the barrel, filled with an unshakeable stubbornness and baptized with independence; and they could be unpredictable. Sometimes they erupted with astonishing suddenness when a certain situation provided the trigger. These eruptions could be with a gun or other means.

Byron Smith of Grand Junction remembers an incident that included Charley Glass:

> "I rode with Charley Glass for a number of years. He always carried his gun in a shoulder holster. It was an automatic — 32 or 38 calibre, and Charley knew how to use it.
>
> The first time I saw Charley was one evening when he came riding into my camp over in eastern Utah. It was about 1917, and I was working for Oscar Turner out on that Cottonwood range. At any rate, Charley came riding in about sundown, and I told him to light and eat. He said Oscar had just hired him and had sent him down to me. Well, sir, my family came from the south, and I wasn't too sure about this new development. I sized Charley up while we ate, and he fit the bill. He was neat, soft-spoken and willing to help around camp. We were together quite a lot after that.
>
> I remember one time in particular when we were taking a little herd into the yards at Cisco. We got in a mile or so ahead of a bunch of sheep, and when Charley rode up to open the gate, a Basque herder was blocking the gate. This "Basco" was waving a rifle and just wasn't going to move. I could see Charley siding in, and I figures he was getting ready to go for that shoulder holster.
>
> I decided to take a hand and shook out my rope and loped in from the side. My loop dropped over the "Basco", and I spurred

my horse and dragged him over two sets of railroad tracks quicker than you can say, scat. I sure broke that old boy to lead in one quick lesson."

It was some time after this that Charley had his legendary shootout with a herder named, Felix Jesui. The confrontation came about, according to legend, because sheepmen repeatedly crossed a line established by the State of Utah to keep nomad sheep herds under control. In spite of the fact that the sheep had been quarantined, the Basques continued to trespass across the line.

According to newspaper accounts at the time, the herder was found shot through the head and still holding a cocked .30 calibre rifle containing one empty shell. Charley Glass was arraigned in Moab, Utah, and charged with second-degree murder. He pleaded self-defense.

At the trial, Charley said he had warned the Basque to go back over the line, and turned to leave when the other man shot at him with a rifle. Charley then drew his pistol from the shoulder holster, whirled and fired several times. One of the shots penetrated the herder's brain. The jury reached a verdict of acquittal on the first ballot, and the legend of Charley Glass began.

While this most famous of the borderland incidents was settled with an automatic pistol carried in a shoulder holster, many men on the frontier preferred to use a rifle.

Kenneth Young of Glade Park comments on the Winchester as a weapon.

"Joe Pace was still active up on Glade Park when I was growing up. He always used a Winchester and shot from the hip. I remember one time when he leveled off at a pack of killer dogs and dropped three of them at seventy yards with three shots. Another time, some of the boys were kidding him about shooting from the hip with a rifle, and he responded by keeping a tin can jumping until he emptied his gun.

My dad (Lafe Young) was another one who always used a rifle. He carried it in a saddle scabbard on the right side with the butt to the rear. When he stepped off the saddle, he could bring it with him in one slick motion. I guess dad got into a lot of scrapes in the old days, and sometimes he would tell us about them. One tale had to do with the time he was working in a cow camp over in the White River country near Meeker. One day, he got into a hassel with another puncher, and the guy went for his gun. Dad was shot in the buttock as he stepped down, but he hit the other man square. Since he was new to the country, he was afraid to go back to camp, so he headed for home. He rode about twenty miles with that hunk of lead in his tail and finally decided he had to get it out. He stopped and built a fire, and then started to cut that bullet out himself. He used a shaving mirror to see his behind, and he'd dig awhile, and then pass out. He finally got the slug and then cauterized the wound with his knife. How he rode home with a wounded tail, I will never know. Dad always called it the time he got his ass shot off. He was sure a tough old bird."

It is unlikely that anyone in the border country would dispute the fact that all of the Young brothers were tough old birds. Whatever the term used, however, it is clear they were, at one and the same time, true individualists and close-knit as a family unit.

Lottie (Young) Weldon of Fruita comments on the ties between Lew, Lafe, and Ed Young:

> "They were really close, but I guess the best way to describe them is to say, they were characters. They were very much alike in many ways, and yet each one was different. This always came out when they took a nip. Someone once said: one fights, one laughs, one sings, and they all drink out of the same bottle. I just don't understand it.
>
> My dad (Ed Young) was a man of changing moods, but he always got a lot of fun out of life. I remember one time when he was riding in a parade in Grand Junction and decided it was moving too slow. He pulled out of line with a whoop and rode his horse up the steps and into the courthouse.
>
> Dad was really a good rider, and he was a wonderful shot with a handgun. Very often out at the ranch, he would put up a row of tin cans and then ride by at a gallop and shoot them off the fence posts. I always thought he was the greatest shot in the world."

Kenneth Young recalls an incident when the brothers got into a barroom brawl with several strangers, and the fight ended up out on the sidewalk:

> "They were all in pretty bad shape, but still pounding away at each other when Uncle Ed turned to dad (Lafe) and shouted through swollen lips, "We're sure fightin' sonsabitches, ain't we, Lafe?"
>
> Dad stopped for a moment like he was thinking about it and finally drawled, "Yeah, I guess we are! But, tell me, Ed — just who in the hell did we ever whip?"

As we proceed, it becomes ever more obvious that most stories of the past are touched by the brush of personal viewpoint. This does not negate the original portrait in any way, since a certain amount of shading can, by emphasizing shadows, bring out the highlights previously unseen. It is here in the area of shaded portraits, of course, that we reach the shadowy world of dreams.

It seems clear that in almost everyone's life there comes a time of wistful speculation known as daydreaming. In these dreams, we are able to indulge in fantasy — to be someone else, to leap out of every-day life and into another skin, another life. This other self has a shadowy, ideal life of its own. Daydreams of possibility enlarge the mind. They haunt the conscious intellect and stimulate the notion of self-renewal through thoughts of dreams popping into reality. In the end, however, the whole mechanism of daydreams, of another-self, usually depends upon fantasy remaining fantasy. The exception, if there is one, is in the realm of discovery. With this thought in mind, we return again to our theme.

Stories of the West, whether on film or in print, have always found an audience. It is in the Western that the American discovers himself again as one of the descendants of a people who knew how to face life with courage and independence, who were prepared to die for what they believed in. For many, the Western represents adventure and idealism, achievement, optimism for the future, justice, the opportunity to excel as an individual. The West stands out above the push-button, set-routine world most of us live in; in the mind it is pristine and pure, strong and brave, the beautiful land. Under such circumstances there can be little wonder as to why it has been the particular function of the Western to provide a vehicle for our dreams; a storyteller especially tuned to that function was a man named, Grey.

Zane Grey has to be considered the most effective producer of Western stories in the history of publishing. In his lifetime, Grey wrote fifty-six novels of the West. One of them — **Riders Of The Purple Sage,** (considered by many to be his best) has sold more than 1,200,000 copies in hardcover alone. By the time he reached the peak of his popularity in 1925, Grey had been in the top-ten on the bestseller lists nine times. Over the years, his books literally sold by the millions, and they still sell in reprint editions today. Most of the stories were made into motion pictures — many of them several times. If ever a writer hit the eyes, the hearts, the minds of the general public, it was this man. And if ever a major writer was ignored or downgraded by professional critics and other highbrows in his chosen profession, it was this man whose stories of the wonders of the West brought pleasure to millions of readers worldwide.

The criticism of Grey's writing began with his earliest books and increased in direct proportion to his popularity. From high in their ivory towers, the nitpickers launched poisonous attacks on each new success, condemning the format, ridiculing the dialogue and wondered aloud why the public continued to read such rubbish. In spite of the barbs, Grey continued to produce one hit book after another and somehow, it appears, he managed to get all that loot to the bank. History does not record whether he managed a chuckle or two in the process. There is a point to all of this, of course. On one hand it shows, quite clearly, that people can be (and usually are) different in thought, action and capability. On the other, it demonstrates more or less conclusively that no matter how diligent one may be, no matter how successful one may become, there will always be someone ready to say, "You should have done it my way." Whether it's sour grapes, the spirit of competition, or just plain oneryness, makes little difference. At the very end — it's the way of things. But as can happen with rules of this kind, there are exceptions.

If ever a person was stamped with the mark of the frontier, that man was Gary Cooper. He was the Westerner, America's link with its outdoor past. The image he projected from the screen was the personification of a man anchored in the old ethic. No one opposed. No one sniped. No one objected. Everyone loved "Coop" — even the goddam critics. In his time, he built an image which could not be debunked. The name stood as a symbol of trust, of confidence; he was the honorable American. As the legend formed, he not only became an integral part of our national heritage, but in the minds of many, the sum total of what a genuine man should be. How did such a thing come about? Why such universal appeal?

Cooper was born in Helena, Montana on May 7, 1901. His father,

Charles Cooper, was a Montana State Supreme Court Justice and although the family lived in Helena, they also operated a good-sized ranch property near the Big Belt Mountains some forty miles from town. It was a working spread, and a young Gary Cooper learned the rudiments of ranch life at first hand.

During schooling at Wesleyan College in Bozeman, Montana and later at Iowa's Grinnell College, Cooper took several art courses, leading to an interest in and knack for drawing cartoons. Some of his early cartoons and caricatures appeared in the Helena newspaper and thus encouraged, young Cooper went to Los Angeles in hope of becoming a full-time cartoonist. The big city newspapers were not ready for his talent. It was now that the Montana background came to the rescue.

In 1925, Hollywood, California was in a final phase of consolidating its position as the film capital of the world. Motion pictures, although still silent, were getting more sophisticated in their storytelling, and the public reaction was being recorded at the ticket office. The movies took one to a never-never land of adventure and romance uncomplicated by thought. They provided more than rousing entertainment, more than escape; for once the lights dimmed and the theatre darkened, the silver screen gave a visible promise of what might be. And eighty-million each week were liking it.

Westerns at this time were getting set for their biggest boom of the silent period. Dominating the scene, head and shoulders above the rest, were two men — Tom Mix, the actor, and Zane Grey, the writer. Into this hot-bed of activity stepped young Cooper to begin his moton picture career as an extra and stunt man. His ability as a horseman opened the door, and the climb was swift. Although the list is not complete, records show that in 1925 Cooper appeared in four top-flight Westerns — 1) **The Thundering Herd,** from a story by Zane Grey, produced by Paramount Pictures and starring Jack Holt — 2) **Wild Horse Mesa,** again-written by Grey and starring Jack Holt — 3) **The Vanishing American,** from the novel by Grey, produced by Paramount and starring Richard Dix — 4) **The Lucky Horseshoe,** produced by Fox Pictures and starring Tom Mix. The Mix picture apparently had an outsized affect on young Cooper's decision to continue on in the movies. When told that Mix received $17,500 a week for his film heroics, Coop said, "I figured I could do that kind of acting, too."

Thus began the climb to motion picture stardom, to the top of the heap.

In 1926, the bit part of Abe Lee in, **The Winning of Barbara Worth.**

In 1927, the title role lead in Zane Grey's, **Nevada.**

In 1928, the leading male role in Lilac Time opposite Colleen Moore.

Then in 1929, came an event that would set the image of Gary Cooper for all time. In his first all-talking picture, Coop played the title role in Owen Wister's classic story, **The Virginian.** In a scene depicting a card game in a local saloon, the villain, Trampas, played by Walter Huston, snarls at the Virginian, "Bet, you sonovabitch".

Without a change of expression, Cooper draws his gun, places it on the table and leans forward ever so slightly to say, "When you call me that, smile!"

Now it must be remembered that this was 1929, at a time when motion pictures were just starting to talk. The impact of this scene on the movie-going public was dramatic and instantaneous. Those words the Virginian spoke to Trampas became a catchphrase; they were repeated at parties, printed in the papers, used by kids in their Wild West games and by comedians on the radio. "When you call me that, smile", caught the fancy of the nation, and Gary Cooper became the Westerner. It was an image that would stick throughout his career, a career that lasted more than thirty years; and for sixteen of those years, Cooper was one of the top-ten moneymakers in the film industry.

Some of his pictures were classics: **The Lives of a Bengal Lancer; Mr. Deeds Goes To Town; The Westerner; Sergeant York; The Pride Of The Yankees; High Noon.**

Others were classic Cooper: **The Plainsman; Saratoga Trunk; Springfield Rifle; Vera Cruz;** and perhaps best of all, **Friendly Persuasion.**

The image he projected from the screen was the personification of the ideal American; he was Gary Cooper — the Westerner.

Another actor stamped with the mark of the old frontier was cowboy star, Buck Jones. Like Cooper, Buck projected sincerity, and sure, simple honesty. Somehow you knew that here was a man who would overcome adversity regardless of the situation or the odds against him. This was the genuine article.

Buck Jones started in show business with the famous 101 Ranch in Oklahoma. Like many show riders of the period, he ended up in

Hollywood shortly after World War I looking for a piece of the action. He found it with Fox Films in a Tom Mix Western. By the early twenties Jones was a Western star in his own right. All through this decade of the silents, his films struck a happy balance between the fast-paced daredevil action provided by Tom Mix and the rugged realism of Bill Hart. And by the time sound came in, Buck was ready for the transition.

In the early thirties, many of the greats of the silent era (including Tom Mix) found the move to pictures that talked extremely difficult. But the man named, Jones, moved into the new medium with scarcely a ripple. His pictures took on a fresh new luster, and now the name of Buck Jones was listed as the top money-making Western Film star by the Motion Picture Herald. A fine actor, Buck appealed to kids and adults alike. Several of his pictures made for Columbia Pictures in the early thirties (notably one called, **White Eagle)** had strong adult themes, and although produced on a B-picture budget could undoubtedly have held their own in first-run houses. It was generally suspected as time passed that Buck would have liked to have made a definitive Western — one which could be listed with "greats" — but it was not to be. He continued to be the man in the "white hat" until the final call.

The time was 1942. America was at war, and Buck Jones was out selling war bonds for Uncle Sam. One night during a giant rally held at the Coconut Grove night club in Boston, Massachusetts, fire broke out backstage. The place was jammed; so overcrowded, some said, that the exits were blocked, and panic took over. Although Buck got out safely, it was learned later that he re-entered the burning building three times in an effort to drag panic-stricken victims to safety. On his final entry, he failed to return. The man in the white hat who loved people was a hero to the end. Greater love — hath no man!

It should probably be noted here that the present chapter is not intended to be a comprehensive study of the Western. No effort has been made to chart or rate the contributions of the many participants involved. The purpose is pure and simple to show an orderly progression in the image of the "Western Character" and its influence on American attitudes. It is an influence which has been substantial over the years and on both sides of the fence. Cowboy star, Tim Holt, was one of those who believed completely in the value of that influence.

Tim Holt grew up in the Hollywood atmosphere of movie-making. His father was actor, Jack Holt, one of the silent greats who successfully made the transition to talking pictures. In the mid-thirties, Tim attended the Culver Military Academy in Indiana, where in addition to the regular accepted activities, he was to learn the finer points of horsemanship. It was training which stood him in good stead over the years. For here was a man who understood and valued the old traditions and showed it throughout his life.

Tim Holt's acting career followed a pattern which when examined is almost unbelievable. That pattern began in the late thirties when after parts in several films, he was cast as the cavalry officer in John Ford's, **Stagecoach.** This Western epic was a milestone picture that not only made John Wayne a super-star, but attracted special attention to every member of the cast. Tim immediately took on a series of action Westerns for RKO.

In the early forties, Tim landed a key part in Orson Welles', **The Magnificent Ambersons.** Although the cast included such high-powered performers as Joseph Cotton, Agnes Moorhead and Anne Baxter, many people (including this writer) believed that young Mr. Holt had stolen the picture. Still, it was back to the boots and saddles.

After his discharge from the Air Force in 1946, Tim was cast in the role of Virgil Earp in John Ford's, **My Darling Clementine.** Others in the cast were Victor Mature, Henry Fonda, Walter Brennan and Ward Bond. It was a major picture. This was the big-time. But Tim Holt went back to his western series at RKO.

In 1948, John Huston made a picture which must be considered as one of the "greats" of all time. It was, **The Treasure of Sierra Madre,** starring Humphrey Bogart, Walter Huston — and Tim Holt. Once again, it was a key role in the big-time. And then, once again, it was back to RKO and that white hat.

The time of the series Western for movie theatre release came to an end in the early fifties with the advent of television. It marked the end of an era. For the record, it should be noted that the Tim Holt Westerns at RKO continued to be a fast-paced, quality product in the old tradition right up to the final moment. It is equally clear that a very determined man intended to wind it all up doing exactly the thing he loved best. In later years, Tim became involved with a rodeo operation, television and ranching in Oklahoma. In all of this activity, however, the old cowboy ties were apparent, and until his death in 1973, he never lost his deep-felt feelings for the old Western values.

In the following sequence, Mrs. Tim Holt of Harrah, Oklahoma, comments on values shared with this remarkable man:

"In one of the last interviews given before his death, my Tim expressed concern about the lack of heroes, "The guys in the white hats," as they used to be referred to on the screen, to whom children could look up to and emulate in their games of make-believe as well as their daily lives. Upon his death, we received hundreds of letters from people who were his fans and loved his movies. Almost to the letter, each one said the same thing. He had been their hero when they needed someone — how much influence he had on their lives — how pleased they were with their lives now and wished their children had someone as they did in their childhood. Many told how they had thought of him over the years, and spoke of how many times they wanted to express their thanks. Now, due to his untimely death, it was too late, but they wanted to let his family know they cared. It was all very sad and heart-warming at one and the same time.

For my money, the American cowboy has always played an important part in this country's heritage. And they are not through yet. Recently, I attended a reunion of veteran cowboys and their families known as, "The Wild Bunch," who get together during the National Final Rodeo held annually in Oklahoma City. They were honoring Yakima Canutt at this time, and as I looked around and saw Joel McCrea and Frances Dee sitting there, I couldn't help thinking of all the friends who were so kind to Tim during his illness. I couldn't begin to name them all: John Wayne, Ben Johnson, Roy Rogers and Dale Evans, Chill Wills, The Careys (Olive and Harry).

The next night I attended a banquet at the National Cowboy Hall of Fame honoring the new champions, and from where I sit, there isn't much change. They are daily gaining more recognition across this great country, and I am convinced that one day we will again have our heroes. Whether on the ranch, on the screen, or in the rodeo arena, they are still the kindest, nicest, most polite, most handsome and beautiful people in the world. And to think that in my teens, I would not even date a boy who wore cowboy boots; they sure have made a believer out of me."

The hold of the old frontier ethic on the average American has confounded sophisticates and a generous assortment of professional critics for several decades now, and it's likely to do so for many more years to come. It is a "thing" difficult to put a finger on in some ways; and yet so clearly definable in others. To some of us who have bellied-up for a closer look, it is tied tightly to that American phenomenon known as diversity, and perhaps even more closely to that elusive something called, spirit. In any event, it all seemed to jell in the Western character as presented over the years by John Wayne.

The big Duke was an outspoken man, and yet despite his blunt "tell-it-like-it-is" exterior, he was universally admired in this country. Continuing in pictures well past his prime, this acknowledged conservative symbol of the frontier ethic consistently remained a top-draw at the movie box office, and national polls regularly placed him on a list of, **The Ten Most Admired Men In America.** Newsmen, talk-show hosts, and other enlightened experts pondered the Wayne paradox at great length, and most developed profound theories on the matter. Few, however, got down to any real understanding of the Western ethic; nor did they consider that key word, professionalism.

John Wayne was a symbol. The men he portrayed were above moral forces; they perceived immediately, without a moment's hesitation what was right and hence what had to be done. And at the moment of decision, we, the viewers, became involved in the action. The other self took on a shadowy, ideal life of its own. Now, we too could make decisions without a moment's hesitation. For all his toughness, Mr. Wayne was supremely comforting.

Professionalism can probably best be shown by example. But before proceeding, it may be in order to make an observation. It is simply this: no correlation between the successful films of any given period can be pushed too far; there is always a vast diversity of talent among the actors, a vast diversity of taste among the viewers, and an element of chance in the whole process. Some movies seem to belong in another era; **True Grit** was one that did.

In this picture (which won an Academy Award for the Duke in 1969), Wayne plays a cantankerous and aging deputy marshal who likes to embibe in the sauce. At one point, he actually topples from his horse after taking a snort too many. Some big-city critics said the picture was a parody, that Wayne was kidding his own career. Sad, for they missed the point by a country-mile.

John Wayne was a professional. By 1969, he had been making pictures for forty years. In a true sense of the words — he knew how. Nowhere is this better demonstrated than in the key scene near the climax of **True Grit** when he confronts three mounted outlaws in an open meadow and calls on them to surrender. The leader refuses with an insulting remark about a "one-eyed fat man". In a fury, Wayne makes ready to charge as he shouts, "Fill your hand — you sunuvabitch!" With that, the one-eyed fat man puts the reins in his teeth, sinks spurs to his horse, and with revolver in his left hand and Winchester in his right heads straight at his opponents. It was one of the finest (and surely the most thrilling) Western action sequences ever put on film. At the scene's end, the bad men have bitten the dust, and Wayne is pinned under his dying horse. "Beau", he grouses, "you've never let me down before."

A parody? Not hardly! It is a scene out of the past; one that might have been. For there have always been men willing to charge against any odds. And there will always be men like this. Proof positive: on February 2, 1983, at an American checkpoint in Beirut, one of President Reagan's Marines stopped an Israeli tank with his pistol.

As we wind this chapter down, it is ever more obvious that stories of the past can be touched by the brush of personal viewpoint. This does not negate the original portrait in any way, since a certain amount of shading can, by emphasizing the shadows, bring out the highlights previously unseen.

Howard Brouse of Kannah Creek, comments on Joe Pace:

"I was just a boy of fourteen when I went to work for Joe Pace. If I had to sum up old Joe in one word, it would be — onery.

Maybe it was because I was so much younger that I remember him this way, but I do know there was little give in him.

I never saw him do much shooting, but I do know he wasn't much good with a handgun. The fact is that he usually shied away from shooting at all. Whenever he butchered a beef at the ranch, he would hand me his .45 and tell me to kill it. I usually got up close, so I wouldn't miss, but always wondered why he had me do the shooting. I thought I had the answer one day when a porcupine got into the horse corral. Old Joe rested the barrel on a fence rail and emptied the gun at that porky. Didn't hit him once. It could be that his eyesight was failing, but he never gave any other sign of it."

But neither guns nor words were involved in the following incident as told by Shorty Gross:

"It happened out in the Cottonwood country over in Utah. The boys had been "worrying" some sheep camps, and those old "Bascos" were pretty jumpy. One group decided to move to higher ground one night and set up near a Pinon tree. First thing they did was cut off the branches and then the top. When they got it all cleaned up, they set a brand new tent over the stump, parked the wagon a little way off and set up camp.

Early the next morning, Byron Smith and an ol' boy named, Tomlinson, were out lookin' around and spotted that bright new tent just sittin' there sparkling in the sun.

Well, sir they decided right on the spot to do a bit of raw-

hiding in order to break that new tent in proper. First thing they did was to tie their ropes together so's they could cut a big swath. Then they each tied fast to the saddlehorn and took off across the flat on a dead run. When the rope hit that tent — I tell you —there was cowboys and horses scattered all over that sheep camp. Those old "Basco's" were hiding up in the brush all the while, and they must have kept laughin' for at least a week."

It does appear at this point that parallels are at best an invitation to thought. For just as it is a law of science that energy cannot be created or destroyed, so it is a law of nature that no two people are exactly alike. Nature has, for example, seen to it that all fingerprints are different. The difference may be slight, but it does — always — exist. This individualism obviously carries over into thought processes and personal viewpoints as well. The strength of American ingenuity has always been rooted in the idea that each individual has a right to a seperate viewpoint. In the end, therefore, it does seem clear that the real significance of any opinion lies in the fact that somebody holds it.

*   *   *

DISPATCH

July, 1884
Grand Junction, Colorado

The war between the D&RG RR and the western extension took place during the latter part of June, and the first part of July. All of the rolling stock that came into Grand Junction from the west was captured and sent to Whitewater, and on July 3rd, a construction train was sent west with orders to take up the rails near the state line. This war, along with the high waters of the Gunnison, cut off communications both from the east and west for two weeks.

The high water did considerable damage to many of the ranches along the river banks in the Grand Valley. In some cases, many acres of choice lands were detached from the ranches to become a part of the river bed.

CHAPTER SEVEN

CHUCKS ON

Oh, it's bacon and beans most every day,
And I'd as soon be eatin' prairie hay."

Once, someone with a warped sense of humor started a rumor. Then, nourished at the exaggerated swollen breasts of time, the libel grew into legend. Little old ladies repeated each story as grandpa and Uncle Jake told incredible tales of fierce-tempered cow-camp cooks. Maiden Aunt Gussie decided to find the truth of the matter for once and all and went straight to the horse's mouth. "Not so," said Shorty Gross, "an' I consider myself a genuine expert on the subject of cooks."

Once tuned in to the matter, Short warmed to the subject. "Now, old cooky," he went on, "was a very important member of the crew. On a roundup or with a trail drive, he might have to work pretty nearly any and all hours. He had to get up by four in the morning, at least, so to have breakfast ready before the day's work began. His work was done with equipment that was none too good, and half the time, he was short of wood or other fuel for his fire. Some hairbrained puncher or other stray critter was always kickin' dust in the food he was preparing, and ants got in his biscuit dough. But even so, he usually got paid more than anybody else in the outfit, except the foreman, and since he always got seconds, his life had to be a happy one. In fact," Short cocked his head a bit and looked sideways out of half-closed lids, "a bad-tempered cook would probably been such a surprise to everybody, that no cowhand I knew would have survived the shock."

Now, one must admit that ol' Short's yarn is strongly on the order of a tall tale, but then, as Franz Muhr always says, "No one is perfect." At any rate, cranky or not, a good cow-country cook was generally appreciated, and he certainly had his work cut out for him. The staple range diet was fried beef, hot biscuits, thick gravy, and coffee with corn syrup for sweetening. Vegetables, if available, came from a can. Raisins were usually on hand, and sometimes a cook would mix up a tasty bread pudding. On roundup, beef was often killed right out on the range. Immediately, after the animal was dressed, all the insides were cut up — liver, heart, brains, etc., and stewed. Cowboys called the mixture "sonuvabitch stew", but if ladies were present, it was simply referred to as, son-of-a-gun.

The regulation hot biscuits on the range were of the sourdough variety. Sourdough was a potent leavening agent produced by mixing a paste of flour and water in a good-sized jar and allowing it to ferment. The process could be induced by placing the mixture just close enough to a campfire for the heat to sour it. To use – one simply added the sourdough to a pan half-full of flour, added a pinch of salt and soda, and then kneaded the mixture until it was the right consistency for baking. First-class biscuits were high, light and good. Most cowboys claimed that after six or a dozen as an appetizer, a man could really dig into a regular meal.

Now, all of this stuff about sourdough jugs and sonuvabitch stew was fine out on the range, but back at the ranch or up in summer camp, women became involved, and things were apt to be different. For in a time when breakfast was a meal, the lady of the house always set a good table. Mealtime was the high point of the day's happenings on most frontier ranches, and when company came, it was generally a fun time. It is in this context that we now turn to a listing of oldtime food recipes and certain potions and other remedies good for man or beast.

Although it is our firm intention at this point to generate a chuckle or two, it should be remembered that we are, in the main, speaking of a time before refrigeration, individual packaging, aerosol cans and other supermarket conveniences. This was a time, for example, when it was absolutely necessary to know how:

TO MAKE TOUGH MEAT TENDER

Put the meat into an earthen bowl with enough cold water and vinegar, equally mixed, to half cover it; add plenty of pepper to keep off the flies, a carrot, a turnip, and a small onion sliced, a stalk of celery, a root of parsley, a blade of mace, ten cloves, an inch of cinnamon, and a few bits of lemon peel. Turn the meat several times daily in the pickle, for a week, and then cook like beef a la mode, first browning it with half a cup of flour; then add the pickle and enough boiling water to make a good gravy; season it palatibly, and simmer the meat in it for about three hours while keeping it covered. Strain the scraps of vegetable from the gravy before serving both hot, with plain potatoes, or any preferred vegetable.

Or to preserve it:

BEEF SALTED OR CORNED RED

Cut up ¼ of beef. For each 100 lbs., take ½ peck of coarse salt, ¼ lb of saltpeter, the same weight of saleratus, and a quart of molasses, or 2 lbs. of coarse brown sugar. Mace, cloves and allspice may be added for spiced beef.

Stew some of the salt in the bottom of a pickle-tub or barrel; then put in a layer of meat; stew this with salt; then add another layer of meat, and salt meat alternately, until all is used. Let it remain one night. Dissolve the saleratus and saltpeter in a little warm water, and put it to the molasses or sugar; then put it over the meat, add water enough to cover, lay a board on it to keep it under the brine. The meat is fit for use after ten days. This recipe is for winter beef. Rather more salt may be used in warm weather. Towards spring, take the brine from the meat, make it boiling hot, skim it clear, and when it is cooled, return it to the meat.

In the days of self-sufficiency, the average ranch wife was a very practical person. And while she usually had her own pet file of recipes, home remedies and household tips, she was always on the lookout for more. So, she swapped with her neighbors and relatives, and cut clippings from newspapers, periodicals, and the Farmers Almanac. Much of this information was practical and down to earth; potions and remedies invariably called for ingredients or materials which were close at hand or readily available. And some of it had to do with finer things in life. We list some of the best at random:

TABLE ETIQUETTE

Napkins should never be starched. On taking seat at the table, the napkin should be unfolded and placed across the knees. It is considered bad custom to tuck it under the chin, or fasten it in the button hole of the vest. At home, fold your napkin when you are done with it, and place it in the napkin ring. If visiting, leave it unfolded beside your plate. If gloves are worn, they are withdrawn and placed across the knees with the napkin over them. Avoid unnecessary noises with the knife and fork, and especially with the mouth, such as loud sipping, smacking of lips, or heavy breathing. The lips should be kept closed as much as possible.

BED BUG EXTERMINATOR

1 qt. gasoline
5 or 6 moth balls
Dissolve moth balls in gasoline

Mrs. Laura Osborn

WORLD'S BEST SODA BISCUITS

2 cups flour
2 t. baking powder
1 t. salt
½ t. soda

2 large rounding T. lard
1 Cup sour milk – Clabber, and three days old – not under that time for age.

This makes my soft dough and takes ½ cup of flour to roll out when these ingredients have been lightly mixed together. Roll out about as thin as one's finger. Cut very evenly, and place carefully – not touching – on a cooky tin. Then mop all over with butter and bake in a piping hot oven and serve in a white napkin. These are crisp, dainty, light biscuits which will tempt any man on earth to eat a round dozen.

Mrs. Laura Osborn

HEAD CHEESE

Scald head of the animal and scrape off all hair thoroughly. Boil and remove the eyes. Leave tongue and snout and cook for two to three hours. Add some vinegar to the cooking water. After cooking, peel meat off the bone. Grind ears and all to a fine consistency.

Nettie S. Knight

GALL STONES

Cut three grapefruit up and put in pitcher of water. Let stand 24 hours and drink no other kind of water.

Mrs. Laura Osborn

HOW TO KILL FLIES

To clean rooms of flies, carbolic acid may be used as follows: Heat a shovel or any similar article and drop thereon 20 drops of carbolic acid. The vapor kills the flies.

Mrs. Laura Osborn

LIVER SAUSAGE

Turn casings inside out and wash thoroughly. Let soak overnight in vinegar water. Then, two more washings, until thoroughly clean in preparation for stuffing. Cut casings in 15 inch lengths and tie one end with ordinary string. Use dowel to turn casing to right side. Prepare liver by boiling one hour in a copper wash boiler. Grind fine the liver and season with finely ground bacon for flavor. Stuff casings and secure with string. Hang in smoke house for three weeks. Delicious!

Mrs. Harry Knight

OATMEAL COOKIES

1 c. sugar	*2 c. Albers Quick Oats*
2 c. sifted flour	*1 c. raisins*
1 t. salt	*2 eggs*
1 t. soda	*1 t. vanilla*
1 t. cinnamon	*3/4 c. melted shortening*
½ t. nutmeg	*½ c. sweet milk or buttermilk*

Method: *Sift flour, sugar, salt, soda, cinnamon and nutmeg into bowl. Add Albers oats and raisins. Beat eggs, add melted shortening and vanilla. Add to dry ingredients and beat well. Drop by spoonsful on slightly greased baking pan. Bake in a moderate oven 350° – 15 to 18 minutes.*

Mattie E. Mitchell

BOILED GINGER COOKIES

2 c. sugar	1 c. boiling water
1 c. shortening	1 T. ginger
1 c. sorghum	1 T. soda
Pinch of salt	

Bring sugar, molasses and shortening to good boil. Then add soda and ginger in boiling water. Mix, stir well, cool. Add flour to make stiff dough. Roll, cut, bake.

Ruth Goss

Mrs. Goss also has an excellent recipe for a special kind of pie (sweet potatoe). At one time, however, it got her into an awkward situation. She calls it, Her Most Embarrassing Moment:

> It was bean harvest time, and I had to prepare dinner for two men – our hired man, Stout, and a neighbor, Harold Peterson. The bean field was side by side with the garden. I went to the garden to dig some sweet potatoes for dinner. The hired man came over to dig them for me, and Harold said he had never seen sweet potatoes growing, so he came over too. When the sandy soil was loosened, one could take hold of the vine and pull up the potatoes. There was always some quite small ones, and often we saved them and cooked them and made, "pumpkin" pie. This time, I wasn't about to make pies, so I picked off the larger ones and threw the rest – vine and all – over the fence to the cows. The hired man said, "Aren't you going to save them and make some pies?"
>
> In answering without thinking, I said, "Let the cows make the pies." I never said another word, but got my potatoes and headed

for the house right now.

GERMAN LETTUCE SALAD

Chop leaf lettuce into small pieces. Add ½ cup pure cream and pour over lettuce. Add ½ cup sugar, and keep cool in the cellar until ready to serve.

Nettie S. Knight

EXCELLENT CURE FOR PORK

For 100 lbs of meat use:

3 pints of salt	3 T. black pepper
1 pint of brown sugar	1 scant T. of saltpetre dissolved in ½ pint of warm water

Mix all together; rub on meat; repeat in seven days. Let lie 14 days in all before smoking.

Charles Silzell

SOAP

3 lbs soap grease	1 can lye
3 gallons water (soft)	

Put lye and grease in 3 qts. of water in enamel or iron kettle and boil until it threatens to boil over. Add rest of water and boil until it looks like strained honey. If you like, add a cup of borax and 2 ozs. ammonia.

Charles Silzell

SHEEP HERDERS OR COWPOKE'S PIE
(Sweet and Simple)

After the dessertless meal, place a slice of white bread upon a plate. Cover the bread with milk or cream and allow the moisture to soak into the bread. Then cover the bread with syrup.

Effie Silzell

COVERED WAGON EVERLASTING COOKIES
(A Pioneer Recipe)

2 cups sugar	3/4 cup milk
1 cup butter or lard	2 eggs
2 T. baking powder	

Cream butter and sugar, add two eggs without beating, milk, 2 teaspoons vanilla, and enough flour to make a soft dough. Roll thin, sprinkle a little sugar over the top, cut out and bake in a quick oven. (A pioneer is said to have made a barrel full of these cookies, which were eaten during a covered wagon trip from Virginia to Colorado.

Effie Silzell

BLOOD PURIFIER

Clover tea is a fine blood purifier, drank freely, removing pimples and whitening the skin. It is also a sleep inducing draught, its efficiency in early states of cancer is unquestioned.

Effie Silzell

SPRAIN REMEDY

Take the white of two eggs and put into a cup; stir with a lump of alum the size of an English walnut, until it jellies. Saturate a cloth and apply to the sprain, changing it for a fresh one as often as it becomes hot and dry. Keep the limb in a raised or horizontal position.

Effie Silzell

BREAD PIE

1 unbaked pie crust	½ cup sugar
1 pint milk - Into it add	2 T. flour
2½ slices bread	cinnamon to taste
(soak until soft)	

Mix well. Pour into crust. Bake until knife blade comes out clean — about 40 minutes at 325° or longer.

Effie Silzell

TO REMOVE LODGMENT IN THROAT

When a child swallows anything that lodges in the throat, lift it suddenly by the wrists. It will cause the little one to scream and cough, and the object will generally be dislodged at once.

Effie Silzell

A ROYAL ROAD TO BEAUTY

Breathe deeply, bathe daily — think joy, not sorrow — eat wisely, and never speak unkindly.

Effie Silzell

BUTTER PIE

1 cup sugar *1 T. flour*
Pinch of salt *Butter – size of an egg*
1 ½ cups scalded milk *1 t. vanilla*

Sift sugar, flour, and salt together. Blend with butter; then stir in slightly beaten egg. Stir in hot milk, a little at a time until smooth. Pour in unbaked 8-inch pie shell. Bake at 425° for ten minutes; reduce heat to 300° and bake until knife inserted in center comes out clean.

Effie Silzell

HOW TO KEEP WELL

Don't sleep in a draught.

Don't go to bed with cold feet

Don't stand over hot air registers.

Don't eat what you do not need, just to save it.

Don't try to get cool too quickly after exercising.

Don't sleep in a room without ventilation of some kind.

Don't stuff a cold, lest you should be next obliged to starve a fever.

Don't sit in a damp or chilly room without a fire.

Don't try to get along without flannel underclothing in winter.

Effie Silzell

SUNSTROKE

Sunstroke is prevented by wearing a silk handkerchief in the crown of the hat, or green leaves, or a wet cloth of any kind. During an attack, warm water should be instantly poured on the head, or rags dipped in water and renewed every minute.

Effie Silzell

OLD TIME CURE FOR PNEUMONIA

Take six large onions or ten of medium size. Chop them fine and place in large skillet over the fire; add vinegar and rye meal to make a thick paste. Let simmer from five to ten minutes. Put it in a cotton bag large enough to cover the lungs, and apply it to the chest as hot as the patient can bear. When this cools, apply another. Heat and apply the poultices, until perspiration starts freely from the chest. In a few hours, the patient will be out of danger.

HOW TO STUPEFY FLIES

To clear a room quickly where there are many flies, burn pyrethrum powder in the room. This stupefies the flies. Then, they may be swept up and burned.

Mrs. Laura Osborn

RHEUMATISM REMEDY

3 c. of spinach	*¼ c. of parsley*
3 c. of celery	*3 c. of carrots*

Add 2 quarts of water and simmer ten minutes. Drink 2 or 3 glasses 2 or 3 times a day. Can season with celery salt.

Mrs. Laura Osborn

BROWN SUGAR PIE

2 c. brown sugar	*4 egg yokes*
2 T. butter	*vanilla*
3 T. flour	*4 egg whites for top*

Mix 2 cups of milk or water with the mixture and cook. Bake shell and fill. Enough for two pies.

Mrs. Laura Osborn

HAIR TONIC

1 oz. Castor oil   2 oz. Bay Rum
2 oz. French Brandy

Can be scented with rosemary or rosegeranium.

In the days of self-sufficiency, flour came in a special large-size container. This container had several practical uses. Mrs. Nettie Knight of Grand Junction, tells of one of them:

> When I was a girl growing up near Collbran, the only packaged flour in Western Colorado was called, "Pride of the Plateau." My mother used flour sacks for many purposes – pillowcases, sheets, aprons, tea towels, ironing board covers, petticoats and undergarments. It was difficult to remove printing from the sack cloth, and she had to boil them with one teaspoon of lye in the water in an attempt to get rid of the markings. It only lessened the intensity, and it was necessary to turn the sacks inside out, before using. A schoolmate of mine named, Jeanetta Wilson, had a pair of bloomers made by her mother which had not been treated at all. This proved to be a great source of embarrassment to her. For it seemed that everytime Jeanetta Wilson stooped over, across the bloomer bottom area were flashed the words, "Pride of the Plateau."

TOILET TIPS AND CARE

Hands: The use of kid gloves help preserve the softness of the hands. Cleanliness and sprinkling with orrisroot counteracts excessive perspiration. Warts are removed by soaking the hands

Nose: *in warm water for a half-hour, and then paring away the white and insensible surface.*

Nose: *Excessive wiping, snuffing and blowing – especially in children – deforms the nose and should only be done when necessary for cleanliness. A nose turned to one side caused by wiping in one direction may be cured by using the handkerchief with the other hand, or by wearing occasionally an instrument surgeons employ for that purpose. Large, fleshy noses are reduced by wearing at night a contrivance which compresses the artery that supplies the nose. Red noses become so by exposure to heat or the sun, by alcoholic drinks, or by a debility of the blood vessels of the skin. The latter cause is removed by gentle friction and cold bathing of the feet.*

Hair: *Cold sage tea makes an excellent hair wash. A penny's worth of borax and ½ pint olive oil, mixed with 1 pt. boiling water; the borax and oil should be first mixed and then the boiling water poured over them. Bottle when cool and apply with a flannel cloth.*

PIMPLES

These are caused by a disordered condition of the stomach and must be corrected. Cosmetics are usually injurious. Correct your diet.

WRINKLES

To 1 oz. white wax and 2 ozs. strained honey, add 2 ozs. juice of lily bulbs; melt and mix and apply once or twice a day.

FRECKLES

Place some finely grated horseradish in a dish of buttermilk and let stand overnight. Strain and apply the wash night and morning. Or, dissolve as much sugar as possible in the juice of one lemon. Apply with a camel's hair brush several times daily.

COMPLEXION

To one pint whiskey, add one oz. powdered benzoin gum. Put a little in the water in wash bowl and bathe face; allow it to dry without wiping. Perfectly harmless.

SUNBURN

To a cake of brown soap scraped to a powder, add 1 oz. lemon juice and 1 oz. cologne water. Mix well and form into cakes. Also removes tan and prevents the hands from chapping.

CHILBLAINS

After soaking the feet for about 15 minutes in warm water, place a pair of rubbers on the feet without stockings and go to bed.

CORNS

A piece of lemon or a cranberry mashed and bound on the corn will remove it readily. Or, cut a hole in the center of a piece of soft leather. Upon retiring for the night, bind this on the toe with the hole over the corn. In the hole, put a paste of soda and soap; bind a thick cloth over this, and wash off in the morning. Repeat until removed.

TOOTH POWDER

To six parts prepared chalk, add one part fine old Windsor soap. Pulverize thoroughly.

HOUSEHOLD HINTS

Disposition of dishwater and soapsuds: *Pour the same about the roots of currant and raspberry bushes, young trees, etc.*

To keep off mosquitoes: *Rub exposed parts with kerosene. The odor is not noticed after a few minutes, and children especially are much relieved by its use.*

Moths in carpets: *Persons troubled with carpet moths may get rid of them by scrubbing the floor with strong hot salt and water before laying the carpet, and sprinkling the carpet with salt once a week before sweeping.*

To make shoes waterproof: *Dissolve some beeswax, adding a little sweet oil to thin it. Before the shoes have been worn, warm the soles and pour the wax on with a spoon. Hold the shoe to the fire and continue the operation as long as the leather will absorb the wax.*

To remove berry stains: *Hold over burning sulphur.*

How to sweep carpet: *Tea leaves, salt, sawdust and Indian meal are recommended, but an even better procedure is: Keep all grocers' paper and druggists' wrappings which are not covered with printing and just before sweeping, tear up some paper bags and put them to soak in a basin of warm water; wring them out to nearly dry and tear up into small bits all over the floor. Sprinkle the carpet quite generously. You should be surprised to see how each scrap of paper becomes covered with dust especially if you wash your broom occa-*

sionally in a pail of water. Care should be taken that paper and broom are not too wet; otherwise, there will be a wet spot in the carpet where the dust will settle doubly. A little experience will show you how dry to wring the paper and how many shakes are necessary to remove the superfluous water from the broom. A second sweeping with the paper will remove every particle of dust, leaving but little accumulation on the furniture.

A SURE CURE FOR PNEUMONIA

Saturate a ball of cotton as large as a 1-inch marble with spirits of alcohol. Add three drops of chloroform to each ball of cotton. Place it between the patient's teeth. Let patient inhale the fumes for 15 minutes; then rest 15 minutes or longer, if needed. Then inhale again 15 minutes and repeat the operation as directed 24 times.

Now, one must admit that under ordinary circumstances, it would be most difficult to top a sure cure for pneumonia. This is obviously the place to stop. Upon review and reflection, however, it was decided the chapter would not be complete without some reference to the importance of water in day-to-day living on the frontier.

Early-day ranching operations usually centered on a water supply, whether it was a clear stream, a spring, lake, pond, or buffalo wallow. For working convenience, most of the watering places had corrals built around them. The cowboys at this stage of the work would keep the corral gate closed, until a bunch of cattle came in to water. Then, they would let them in and check the herd for unbranded calves. They branded as needed, repeating the operation as each group came in, until they were sure all stock watering regularly at this point were branded. Then, they would pull up stakes and go on to the next watering hole and repeat the process. In the spring, cattle often sought relief from swarms of heel flies in bog holes where they could stand in deep mud. Very often, they bogged down and were trapped. For this reason, riders patrolled the miry areas to pull cattle to dry ground. It was a fact of life that after the average range critter had been pulled out by main strength and "tailed up", it would invariably charge its rescuer, or head straight for the bog from which it had been extracted.

In spite of the modern-day TV versions of work life on the range, most of the old-time riders did not carry a canteen on their saddle horn. Some way or another, an experienced man could usually make it to water. According to one oldtimer, stockmen seldom had to make a dry camp. "Of course," he added, "the water we found wasn't always crystal clear. In fact, we sometimes had to chew it pretty thoroughly before swallowing, and it sometimes tasted anything but sweet. And sometimes our bandanas were used for straining out the wigglers, but if it wuz wet — it wuz water."

Regardless of the wigglers, it is clear that history followed the water courses. If it wuz wet — man put it to use. Water has always been the key to existence in the West. Today, there are some who suggest it costs more, in terms of energy, to produce a barrel of water than the barrel contains. It's an old can of worms, and one that can be refuted with another quick look to the past. The following example is tied tightly to strength of character and the stomach to commit.

In 1900, a man named Butler, hit paydirt near a spring called, Tonopah, on an arid hump of real estate in southwestern Nevada about fifty miles from the California border. Butler and his wife took in two partners to raise a grubstake to sustain them, until the first ore could be mined and hauled to the smelter at Austin. One of the partners contributed a wagon and a team of mules, and the operation began with $25.00 worth of provisions on hand. At a point when their supplies were nearing exhaustion, the first wagonload of ore brought $800 to the empty coffers. The news of the find leaked out, and Tonopah began to grow. Although it was now the Twentieth Century, the new town was not a place of modern conveniences. A tankwagon hauled water four miles from the nearest spring and sold it in town for 25¢ a bucket. Tonopah's only bathtub was located in the backroom of a saloon, and oldtimers swear it had a sign over the door reading:

>   First Chance $1.00
>   Second Chance .... $ .50
>   All others .... $ .25

No doubt about it; it definitely took stomach to be larger than life in the good old days.

*   *   *

DISPATCH

Grand Junction, Colorado
1885

The monotony that had existed since the election was broken by the escape of two horse thieves from the County Jail, on the evening of December 30th. The two men, Fogarty and Price, made an assault on the jailor, H. C. Bucklin, while he was giving them supper. The shackles being removed during this time, Mr. Bucklin was first seized by Fogarty, a powerful man, and while he was struggling with Fogarty, Pierce, the other prisoner, assailed him and with a bottle struck the jailor a violent blow on the head. The blow stunned and blinded him, and before he could recover, the two prisoners had bound and gagged him. They then appropriated Mr. Bucklin's revolver, knife, watch, money, etc., and securing what blankets they required, left the jail. Before leaving, they bathed and bandaged the jailor's head and face.

Soon after their departure, Mr. Bucklin managed to free himself and leave the jail for assistance. He was in a terrible condition, his body bruised, his head cut, and a deep gash made along his cheek. His hands were still shackled, and he was weak and almost blinded by the blood flowing from his wounds. A thorough search was made for the fugitives, but they were not captured until a week afterward, when they were secured on Pinon Mesa by Sherriff Innis and his two deputies, Messrs. Barrett and Spencer.

CHAPTER EIGHT

PROMENADE

All to your places,
Straighten your faces,
Hook up your traces,
And pull west.

It is a natural fact of life that over the years, rural entertainment centered on music and dancing. The popularity of country music and the revival of the old-time country square dance on today's scene attest to the durability of sound old customs. As applied to our narrative: cowboys and their gals liked to dance. It is as simple as that.

Once again, Mrs. Enola Mock paints a vivid picture of a special time:

> On December 27, 1923, the Fruita Cowboys gave their first annual ball at the Armory, as it was then called. Later, it was known as the Fruita Memorial Building, and now it is the City Hall. Since

you were admitted by invitation only, it was not a public dance, nor were the cowboy balls that followed through the years.

These dances have always been anticipated as one of the highlights of the social season, and they were gala affairs. You pressed your prettiest dress carefully, and if it were not pretty enough, you made or bought a new one. Usually a new one was thought necessary.

Men wore their ties and nicest suits. Very few came in cowboy boots, for dancing slippers and soft leather shoes made dancing more graceful. But once in awhile, you were invited to come in your ginghams and overalls, and the dance was less formal then. Now, let's go to the first ball:

We had heard that the committees of cowboys and girls had been planning and decorating for several days, but we were not prepared for the transformation they had made in the usually-bare hall. As we stepped through the door, there was cowboyland in all its glory!

Taken from the Fruita news are notes as written in the Daily Sentinel, December 29, 1923, by Mabel C. Kiefer. First Annual Ball:

"One of the most enjoyable affairs of the season was the Cowboy's Ball given at the Armory on Thursday night. The cowpunchers fully demonstrated their ability as dancers, as well as that of their chosen profession. Red and green festoons and ropes, spruce trees, bells, saddles, chaps, horns and all those things necessary to riders of the purple sage, were very effectively used, while on the stage at the front of the hall, a miniature camp gave a realistic effect. The tepee-tent pitched among the spruce trees, with a glowing camp-

fire in front of it, saddle bags, a saddle and an ax, wood and a dutch oven on the fire, while the cowpuncher peered from out of the tent to see that supper was progressing. New fallen snow covered the ground, and a calf looked on curiously from among the trees. At the camp, so recently located at Alkali Springs, the last water hole was a roughly hewn log through, and a tin can gave promise of liquid refreshment for man and beast. Shaded lights cast a mellow glow over the scene, and grazing placidly over all, was a steer who had evidently pushed his head through a convenient opening to see that all was well, and carried out strictly according to the constitution, bylaws, rules and regulations of the kingdom of cattleland.

Harris orchestra (of Grand Junction) furnished the music, and it is estimated that about 350 were present to enjoy the festivities. Jay Nearing is responsible for the Alkali Springs suggestion.

Among those from Grand Junction in attendance were: Mr. & Mrs. Adolph Rettig, Mr. & Mrs. George Hitchborn, Mr. & Mrs. Ludwig Rettig, Mr. & Mrs. Clarence Edison, Mr. & Mrs. Frank Grant, Mrs. Floyd Turner, Mrs. Lena Cobb, Mrs. J. W. Rector, Mrs. Charles Wallis and Mrt Corcoran, Mr. & Mrs. Lewis Farmer, Roxie Chambers of Whitewater, and Mr. & Mrs. Anderson of Kannah Creek, Mr. & Mrs. Ira Mock, and Mr. & Mrs. Cecil Crispin of the Redlands.

The program of the cowboys' dance deserves special mention, being so full of new and fantastic steps. Some of them were especially dedicated to members of the fraternity – for who among the cowpunchers does not know: Beanie, Tex, Bolliver, Cheesy, Cy, Chick, the Bishop, the Deacon, and the Roaring Bull?

COWBOY'S FIRST ANNUAL BALL

Armory Hall

Fruita, December 27, 1923

DANCE PROGRAM

1. *Roundup Circle*
2. *Howling Hop*
3. *Beanie's Toddle*
   First Extra
4. *Yearling Lope*
5. *Tex's Limp*
6. *Gopher-hole Trip*
   Second Extra
7. *Stampede Tackle*
8. *Cheesy's Special*
9. *Broncho Sidestep*
   Third Extra

10. *Deacon's Strut*
11. *Steer's Lock-Step*
12. *Sagebrush Stumble*
    Fourth Extra
13. *Bishop's Trot*
14. *Bolliver's Gallup*
15. *Chick's Delight*
    Fifth Extra
16. *The Bull's Bellow*
17. *Cy's Slip*
    Sixth Extra
18. *Home Sweet Home*

"As the crowd gathers, the old friends of the range who had not seen each other since the rodeo last fall, perhaps, meet with genial smiles and a slap on the back – a glad, "Howdy, and how are you?", as they exchange bits of the latest news, and the market prices along with the weather and a little gossip thrown in."

Mrs. Mock continues:

As I turn back the pages of time, I think I remember another cowboy ball when the decorations were similar to those described. This time, however, saddles, saddle blankets bright with their reds, lariat ropes, boots and spurs, "all shined up" bridles and chaps –

wooly and bat-winged and stove-pipe, completely hid the railing around the upper balcony. The resident cattlemen's brands decorated the walls, while the restrooms were not forgotten — but perhaps bore placards labeled, "Heifers — Bulls."

The stage at the front of the hall was a bit of the range, where the cowboys had made an open camp after a day's ride. The scene was made real with cedar trees standing round and sage brush and greasewood growing in natural places. Over at the front corner of the stage is a campfire of pinon wood, lighted and ready to put on the dutch ovens and the old black coffee pot. A bed roll or two are in front of the fire to sit on, and a couple of saddles and chaps are thrown nearby. There are tin cups and plates stacked by for supper. Then, glancing back over the picture, you see a real pole fence in the background. There was no snow.

Now, on with the dance and how was the dancing? In the good old days, there was less prancing. Less energy expended than there is today — with decorum we danced, and if we wished to stay, we had: waltzes, two-steps, one steps, fox trots, polkas, the schottiche, the varsonvianna, the square dances or quadrilles, and the lancers which also was a square dance, but was not so called and where each dancer memorized the changes. Then, there were the tag-two-steps, the circle two-steps, and the Rye Waltz. The waltz quadrille was danced using the waltz step all the way through, and never just walked or gliding; so were the quadrilles or square dances danced to 2/4 time by two-stepping through the grand right and left and promenades and changes.

Waltzes especially were to be danced smoothly. It was said that if you could waltz, carrying a glass of water balanced on your head, you were a good waltzer. The moonlight waltz was a favorite, with the lights all turned low, and the sweet, dreamy music played softly. Matching the slow rhythm of your partner's step, perhaps you rested your head on his shoulder as he held you close. Since this was sort of a lover's waltz, you danced with your best boyfriend or beau, or perhaps with one who was seeking your attention. With the Prize Waltz, this situation was different, as the man chose his partner with regard to her waltzing ability, and not necessarily because he especially liked her. This was a contest dance, and as elimination of the poorer waltzers progress, there would be fewer couples on the floor. Then soon, there were only two couples dancing with all eyes of the ballroom on them, until the committee of three made their decision and gave the prize to the couple waltzing best.

A good woman waltzer danced on her toes, never touching the high heels of her slippers to the floor. A man danced more on the soles of his feet. Since the steps were gliding, there was very little sound of moving feet on the polished wax floor. And when the dancers sometimes sang the choruses of some favorite tune, the effect was magic.

Any tag dance explains itself. As the dance began, there were several men on the sidelines around the hall who had purposely chosen no partners. So as couples came dancing by, this one and that one stepped out and tapped a man on the shoulder or tagged him. This was the same as saying, "I'll take your girl, and you go tag another fellow and take his girl. If you were a popular girl, you danced with many partners, before this dance was over, which might be a long one.

A circle two-step differed from an ordinary two-step, as its name implies. You might designate this as a "called dance", for after you had danced a few minutes, the caller sang out, "Everybody join hands and circle to the left," thus forming a large circle that danced around the hall until the caller again called, "Allemande left – then grand right and left," and you kept going, until he called, "Everybody two-step." The circle was then broken into couples dancing away. Whomever was nearest during this dance, several circles were formed, following the same procedure, but seldom ever had one a chance to dance with your original partner. It was fun, but sometimes you got a fellow that was hard to dance with, and you were glad when another circle was called and you got rid of him.

One of my favorite dances was the Rye Waltz with my husband. He loved it. This was a pretty dance with a heel and toe and three glides repeated through the verse of the song, "Coming' Through The Rye;" then, waltzing the chorus.

At all the old-time dances, there was a floor manager who was a combination receptionist, introducing all the strange men to the ladies and also acting as a sergeant-at-arms. If one or two became too exuberant, he escorted them to the door and invited them to leave – which they did. On the other hand, if you were a wall-flower too long, he brought you a partner who asked you for this dance. Ambrose Walsh was an early-day floor manager for many years, and a good one.

Two people who always attended the annual Cowboy Balls were Mr. & Mrs. Jake Goss of Loma. Ruth Goss recalls the several different orchestras that played at the balls over the years:

> In one of the groups, Ernest Swindell was the violinist. He always played the melody while the others, usually two in number, chorded. He never used sheet music, but played from memory. There was perfect rhythm with Mike Fromm, a much loved Fruita saddlemaker and cobbler as his steady. Mike played an electric guitar, and if one of these two played for a dance, the other was always playing with him. The third member was a pianist, and of these, there were several. The first I remember was Mrs. March, and often her son, Forest (Red), played a banjo with them. Then, there was Mrs. John Brubaker, Mrs. Reardon and Mrs. Burgess. On special occasions, other instruments were added as drums, accordians and wind instruments.
>
> At a square dance, callers were as important as the music. For a number of years, my husband, Jake, called from two to four squares in an evening, he never sang the calls, but used a loud, clear swinging tone. He never used too much lingo which might be confusing. Other callers were George Gosnell and Robert Cox.
>
> Each square dance began with: Honor your partners right and left — all join hands and circle to the left. Then, Jake would call one of his favorties: All to your places — straighten your faces — hook up your traces and pull west. Everybody circle — break and swing and promenade home. First couple swing right — back left and a two-hand swing — chase the rabbit — chase the squirrel — chase the pretty

girl around the world. This continued until each man had chased each lady around the world. This was a long one.

One of the fun calls went: First lady out to couple on the right – swing your ma – then your pa – and don't forget Old Arkansaw. On to the next and swing your ma and then your pa – and don't forget Old Arkansaw. By the time a lady or gent has completed the circle, he has been constantly swinging for twelve swings. If you think this doesn't bring on a cheap drunk, try it. A square dance was often finished with the caller saying, "All promenade to you know where and I don't care."

At midnight, it was time for supper. The main part of the meal consisted of real old-fashioned barbecued beef roasted for hours in a pot between heated rocks. Johnny Sieber (Brownie, we all called him), superintended in this culinary art, until later the barbequeing was done by the town bakery in its big ovens. There were several methods of preparing the meat for cooking; one was wrapping it in dough.

These suppers were served on big long tables upstairs in the balcony diningroom and were feasts with plenty of hot coffee in those old days. The invitation to the 28th Annual Ball and Barbeque Supper said: supper, 60¢ per plate. It also said: You and your lady are cordially invited to attend the Fruita Cowboys 28th Annual Ball, Saturday, March 3, 1951 at 9:00 PM, Fruita Memorial Building in Fruita, Colorado – Admission $1.25 – by invitation only. The balls usually lasted until 2 or 3 o'clock in the morning, and even then you were reluctant to go home. But when the orchestra played, "Home Sweet Home," you danced the waltz with your escort and *then said, goodnight, to your friends. It was a delightful time to be alive.*

Very often, it seems, childhood memories are rooted in a Golden Age which existed before evil came into the world. Such memories are, in most cases, of fun and good times, or of a special incident having to do with both; in the rural West, they are likely to include family. For if one thing stands out in this collection of stories, it is the closeness of family relationships in the range country. Certainly, it is clear that in the early-days, fun-time was usually family-time. Children accompanying parents to the old-time dances obviously enjoyed the dressing up and the activities of the ballroom as much as the grownups. One of the most charming of such recollections is an account by Gladys (Young) Hitchborn of Fruita:

We children always looked forward to the dances. The dance hall or schoolroom always seemed to have a special aroma for the occasion, and people smiled a lot, and the kids all had a fresh-scrubbed look. When the music started, everyone would suddenly quiet down, and then for a moment, something like fine electric needles would run up and down your spine. My, it was a dazzling time!

The kids would run and slide along the edge of the dancefloor, and sometimes we girls would dance together in little circles. Then, sooner or later, my dad (Ed Young) would come over and ask us to dance. My uncles would dance with us, too, and I always loved to dance with Uncle Lew. He was such a good dancer.

I'll never forget how special it was when my dad whirled me out across the center of the floor. I felt so grown-up.

In most places in the rural West, the closeness of the family unit was parallelled by a general community spirit. Nowhere was such community togetherness more apparent than on Kannah Creek and the surrounding area. Winifred Raber comments:

When the time came to relax on Kannah Creek, we all shared in the fun. The Cross Bar Cross outfit had a big barn which served as the gathering place for parties and dances. Every year on August 24th, we had a party here to celebrate after round-up time. Everyone came — parents and kids. We danced square dances, polkas, schottische and others. The musicians were all local people and were good players. Many had good singing voices. The one dance that was always the most fun was called, "The Broom Dance," where one holds the broom and mingles amongst the dancers. When the broom person chooses their next partner, the object is to drop the broom with a thud at the feet of their choice, and the partner then takes the broom and repeats the process — a changing-partners type dance.

At all parties of mixed company, the women would provide the food, and there was always plenty for a large crowd. Everyone knew everyone at these parties, and there was always some joker who loved to play practical jokes. They all knew I would not touch spirits of any kind, so at one party, Warren Fifield spiked the water bucket with booze, and then did not rest until my turn to get a drink of water. I took a huge gulp and realized what was in it, and everyone burst out laughing. I've taken a lot of kidding about this incident over the years, but I've managed to survive with my sense of humor intact.

It has been said that nothing goes on forever, and one must admit this is probably true on Kannah Creek. Yet the feeling of the past does linger, so that in this area which had hardly been settled for a full century, there are haunting echoes of antiquity. A person caught up in this slow dream of the past can only agree that it was, indeed, a wonderful time to be alive.

*   *   *

DISPATCH

March, 1885
Grand Junction, Colorado

Last month, gold excitement took place in the White Canyon, Utah, and quite a number of local citizens left for the supposed gold fields. Among those that left on this wild chase for wealth were W. E. Shaffer, J. J. Lumsden, A. P. Cook, John Vaughn, James Hale, W. E. Lunch, Nels Pritchard. Cosgrove and W. A. Gipson from Fruita also took part in the stampede. The party was gone about five weeks and returned with an account of a journey filled with rough and exciting experience. No gold was found.

CHAPTER NINE

A SIDE TRIP

We've reached the border of the state;
Beyond, lies Utah's Castle Gate
That entrance gives to fairy-land
Where Canyon, vale and mountain stand.
— E. Pabor

Gold, it has been said, is where you find it, and there can be little doubt the lure of striking it rich opened the Intermountain West. In 1858, stories of gold in the Colorado mountains triggered a massive gold rush. Wagons by the thousands trekked over the plains bearing signs reading, "Pike's Peak or bust." In the minds of many, Colorado was one vast gold mine, and in places, it was just that. The story was told of a greenhorn who could not decide where to stake his claim, so he threw his hat in the air, sank his pick in the hat — and found a vein which assayed at $600 a ton. From rags to riches at one stroke; such is the stuff of tall stories — and legends. And whether the subject was gold or cattle, horses or men, the tall tales continued to dominate frontier culture.

By 1870, the gold fever had reached to the San Juan country in southern Colorado. The Little Giant gold lode in the Animas district produced ore worth $4000 a ton. The entire area literally swarmed with men determined to hit paydirt; nothing was too remote, and no terrain too rough, for when gold is at stake, no known force can keep men from pursuing it. It is safe to say every inch of the Rocky Mountain country has been covered, and every likely spot probed with a pick during the past one-hundred years. The wilderness seekers of today would be hard put to find an area truly free of the imprint of man; determined men in search of a dream are certain to have been there before them. The mining fever focused national attention on the Rocky Mountains and for several decades investors grubstaked prospectors on trips into the back country in return for a half-interest in whatever they might find. By the end of the century, most every rock in the west had been turned or examined by professional rockhounds or by amateurs searching for the pot at the end of a rainbow. In most cases, the cost of the search far exceeded the return. Still, there can be little doubt the imperial energy of gold opened the west, and who is to say the effort was a total waste of time.

In 1890, a small group of men from western Colorado set out for uncharted regions of southeastern Utah to search for a lost silver mine. One of the riders was, John Frank Sleeper, who kept a diary of the trip. Upon his return, he wrote to his grandparents in New Hampshire to tell of the adventure. The letter is included here, because of its rich and vivid descriptions of the time, the place, and the people involved:

Chiqueta Delores, Colorado
February 23, 1891

Dear Grandfather and Mother,

    We arrived home safe and sound the 18th. The trip was a failure from the day we started. In the first place, Jim Hunter, Thad Duckett and Father are thoroughbred kickers, and Tom says if hell were turned upside down, it would not dump out three lazier men than the Ducketts. Lyman Hayden was a worker, the only one in the layout and Mart Hobbs which makes the total number 8 did not worry much about work. December 5th was the day set to start. We were all ready but thought it best to wait until the 6th to get an early start. Father and I were packed and over there at half past eight. By the time they were ready, it was half past eleven. Then we ate dinner and started at twelve to drive 25 miles. That night, most of the horses came back, and we only moved camp 5 miles on December 7th. Laid over the 8th to dry out the coffee, tobacco, tea, salt, blankets, etc. that were on two of John's horses that tried to swim the Grand and came near to getting drowned. December 9th, we made Little Castle and stopped at Grant's Place. He was not at home. Some of our horses were coughing. They had distemper. The 10th, we went down the Grand River Canyon to Moab, a Mormontown that has the name of the toughest town in Utah. Here we laid over six days as most of our horses were down sick. (December 9th, while going down the River, we ran onto a bunch of mountain sheep. I saw them first, but John got the first shot as his gun was loaded and mine was not. He killed one, and I got a running shot and hit him too far up on the shoulder. Thad and Father chased him for three miles but gave him up.)

While we were in Moab, we ate apples, drank homemade wine, went to one dance, and had a horse race which we won together with $10.00 and an old plug of a horse, which played out on the road and they had to leave him. Moab is as nice a little valley as anyone would care to look at. They can raise anything from peanuts to peaches, corn, apples, and grapes. We picked grapes that had been frozen and dried on the vine. They were fine raisins. A man by the name of Warner owns the finest fruit orchard. He makes lots of wine which brings $2.00 a gallon, sells lots of apples at the ranch at 6¢ a pound. The second day out of Moab, we reached the Hatch Ranch which is a rendezvous house for all of the horse thieves in the country, and they were all on the dodge for some stealing or killing that they had been in. When we came in sight, they sneaked off up in the hills thinking we were officers. Some of their friends who were working for a cow outfit that were camped there went and told them their mistake and directly, they came straggling back one at a time. The next day, we passed Carlisle's Place. He is the largest cattleman in the country. Owns and runs over 30,000 head. Here is where we saw the first signs of Indians and (Thad had a little pain in his stomach).

That night, we camped three miles beyond Carlisle's Place in 6-inches of snow, but lots of grass. Father allowed it was a hell *of a place to camp and showed his disgust by pulling on along to Monticello, four miles further, where he stopped with an old Mormon and his 4th wife.*

From the Blue Mountains to the San Juan River until a few years ago has been a wild country, the only white men that lived there were cattle and horse thieves. Carlisle was the only honest man in the country, and the cattle thieves stole from him and each other. Some of the men got rich, for instance, three years ago one of them bought 30 head and drove them in there, and last year he sold 600 head of beef and steers. Within the last year, the United States officers have made it so hot for the Mormons that have a half-dozen wives that they have had to leave the thickly settled portion of Utah and these wild out of the way places like the Blue Mountain country catch quite a number, and there are now quite a few small towns that have sprung up within the last year.

From Carlisle's Place, we were three days to Bluff City. One camp at South Montizume over at Mustang Springs and then at Bluff. From South Montezume to Bluff, the ride was quite interesting owing to the number of old ruins of ancient cliff dwellings, and Moque Indians. There were few cliff dwellings, most of the ruins were what looked to be stone houses, that is, they were probably stone houses thousands of years ago. But time has left nothing now but a pile of rocks and quantities of broken crockery. In all of our digging, of which we did considerable, we failed to find a whole piece. The size of these old houses were judged to be 12' x 18'. At Bluff, we laid over one day to feed and rest our horses. Here we first saw the noble redman. We had all seen canyon Indians before, but these are noted for the number of white men they have killed. There are 48 white men's bones laying in one pile on the Navajo Reservation, the work of the Navajos.

The Navajos as a rule are good looking. They are straight and slim, skin tight nose and straight, large black eyes, rather large mouth, but good, white even teeth. The squaws are under the average height, but well built, and I saw one in Bluff that was good looking. Their dress is very plain, but with a good blanket is quite showy. Moccasin leggins, calico dress and blanket makes the bill for the squaw. Some of the bucks put on lots of dog. I have seen some with $75.00 worth of silver on themselves and horse in the way of concho buttons, belts, and a bridle that is covered with silver. There were quite a number of other Indians in Bluff, known as the renegade Piute. They are a dirty, treacherous outfit, extremely different from the Navajo. While we were here, and in fact while we were in Indian country, they were not slighted by the rations, as they always happened around at grub time and stayed until they had their fill.

The day we laid over in Bluff, part of us took a little excursion up the San Juan about three miles to look at an old cliff dwelling which was well worth our time. I will try to give you a little more idea of this ruin as it was the best we saw on the trip. Can you imagine a table land about 600 feet high, 300 feet of the top being solid white sandstone and from the base of the sandstone loose rock and earth sloping down to the level river *bottom at an angle of 40 degrees.*

```
                        /‾‾‾‾‾‾‾‾‾‾
                       /   Sand stone
                      /  Loose rock and earth
_____/
     River bottom                          bottom
```

Now imagine a cave 300 feet long, 150 feet deep and 250 feet from the sandstone arch to the earth below. The back of the cave is a semi-circle. The sand stone makes a perfect arch above the earth and the loose rock have a steep slope from the back of the cave to the flat river bottom. In the back of the cave is a bench as a jog in the rock 5 or 6 feet above the base of the sand stone. This bench is 12 feet wide in the widest part, running out at both ends upon this bench are the old ruins. Fourteen rooms in all. The front wall and partitions were about a foot thick, laid up of flat rock and chinked with mud. In this were the imprints of their hands showing all the wrinkles as plain as the day they were put there. (They had a hand the size of a 10 year old with short, stubby fingers.)

Some of the rooms had been two story, but had fallen in. The doors were about 4 feet high at the main entrance. There were footsteps cut into the rock which were worn out an inch or more in places and the whole rock was worn smooth.

While in Bluff, Joe saw an Indian that recognized him. This was thought to be unfortunate, as we were in hopes to get into the nation without the Indians suspecting our business. But now the game was up. And that night we held our meeting to see if we should go across the river, straight to the copper mine, or keep on the north side of the river and try to throw the Indians off. Jim and John were in favor of the former, while the rest of us decided to rely on Joe's judgement. But I feel that Joe's fear of the Indians bore too heavily on his judgement. For he decided that the longest way was the best, so we left Bluff the next morning and went 10 miles down the river and camped on the river bottom. Here was a good set of buildings where a man by the name of Barton kept a trading post. Two years ago the Indians threw a rope on him, dragged him about 100 yards — then shot him, then robbed the store, and the Indian that recognized Joe was one of the party. The next morning while Joe was out after the horses, he saw two moccasin tracks, following them up, he found that there had been two Indians on the bluff over the camp the night before watching our movements. This settled the whole thing in Joe's mind. He said if we cross the river, they would surely run our horses off and perhaps kill the whole outfit. This view of the thing did not increase our courage. Hayden, a man 50 years old, who has spent 30 years prospecting, said that he heard more Indian fighting talk on that trip than he had heard in all his life. Thad, the principal contributor to the Indian talk, was pretty sick as this is the way that fear affects him. His courage went down 50% in Bluff, but now he was bad off, and he tried his best from there to the San Juan to make us all mad so we would turn back, but without success. It was 14 days ride to where we were to cross the river, 50 miles below. Nothing happened worth of note, and as yet, I have said nothing of the object of the trip. But suppose Mother (by the way we got her *letter at Bluff and was glad that she had arrived home safely) has told you that we were going to look for a silver mine. This mine I have every reason to believe exists, but where that is the bother. The Navajos use $50.00 worth of silver to any other tribe's $1.00 and prospectors have found their old smelters and in the slag, they have found chunks of silver worth $3.00 and $4.00. This with the fact that they killed the only white man that ever claimed to have found it is good evidence that they have found the mine, and that it is a good one. Another object of our trip was to locate a copper mine trail, 20 miles from the mine. The next day, Joe and Father went down the river to look out a trail. They found a trail and also a fresh Indian track, where he had crossed the river and walked up the bluff. This Joe said was to cut signs to see if we had gone down the river. The rest of us took but little stock in it, but afterwards proved to be the case, as the Indians themselves acknowledged it. This gave Joe a new idea. He always thought that down the river was the proper approach to the mine, but now he knew it, and as it was impossible to take horses down the river by any trail he knew, the only way left was for four to make a raft and sail down. We agreed that the river was shallow in places and a raft the size needed would not float, but Joe was positive it would, so we spent two days in making the raft and moving the horses onto good food. December 30th, we started on the raft. Hayden, Hunter, Joe and myself. We took grub for six days, one blanket, a rifle with 75 rounds of ammunition. Everything went on smooth for two miles, then we were stuck on a sand bar. Here we put in six hours of hard work* *and went a half a mile further and landed on the opposite side of the river, tore up the raft and took out on foot. About this time, it commenced to rain, and we walked 5 miles and camped under a shelving rock, partially out of the rain. By this time, we begun to realize what kind of an undertaking we had before us. But Joe gave us new courage by saying we were only 5 miles east of Canyon Mesa, our destination, but we traveled all the next day and was then 5 miles from the Mesa, and as far as we could see impossible to get on top, as the Mesa was at least 3,000 feet above the river, with a perpendicular cap of sandstone 600 feet thick on the top. During the day, it cleared off, clear, and cold that night. We decided that one blanket was a poor apology for a bed. The next day at 3:00, we were under the rim rock of the Mesa where we were in hopes to climb to the top. Hunter was the brave man of the party, was not afraid of the whole Indian nation, and could climb over as dangerous a place as any man.*

There were two breaks in the rock, but from the bottom looked quite favorable. Joe tried one of these, and I the other. I went up a couple hundred feet and could go no further and came back. Joe went part way up, came back and thought we might make it. He said if I would go first, he would take my pack up to the worst place and pull them up with ropes. When brave Hunter came to the worst places, his knees shook so that he was in danger of falling off, and I had to pull him up with the ropes as well as the packs. In two hours, we were on top, and that night we walked until dark through 4 inches of snow. That night it was cold. There was but little sleep for anyone, and we were on the tramp long before daylight. We traveled 5 miles up the Mesa and after looking at the country, Joe said we were 15 miles from the point. As our stock of grub was low and one blanket too thin for such cold weather, we decided the trip was a failure and turned back to camp. Joe did not want to go back the way we came, as he said the Indians might be on our trail. But we thought it was best to take our chances than to go 20 miles around. We got to camp the next day, found the boys all well. The day we left on the raft, John said he was sick of Joe's foolish whims and concluded to strike out alone. He took his share of the grub and pulled out. Joe told him the Indians would kill him, and Thad said it was the same as committing suicide. He went about 8 miles from the river, found no wood, water, or grass, remembered that he had no spoon to mix his bread, so he turned back to camp. The next day, he and Father went up about 12 miles to look at the country. January 4 — we held another meeting and decided to go to the copper mine. January 6 — looked over the mine, held another meeting, decided it would take too much valuable time to put in a 10 foot hole with two drills and one pick. Grub was low. Some were in favor of sending for more, and Hunter was "deadly opposed." January 7 — moved camp 3 miles to more feed and water. Held another meeting. Decided to send for grub. Hunter declared his intention of quitting the outfit in the morning. January 8 — Hunter started for home. Hobbs and Joe for Bluff after the grub. They were gone 8 days. During the time we laid around camp, except for a few hours work on the trail. January 16 — the boys got back from Bluff. The 17th — we started for the east Canyon Mesa. Camped there the evening of the 19th, met 4 Indians on the way who were very anxious to know where we were going. That night, 2 rode into camp around 8:00, took supper and stayed all night with us. The next 3 days we spent in prospecting. Found something the boys said was almost pure silver. Hayden, Father and I said there was nothing in it.

John and Joe concluded it was the best thing they had seen yet, thought it best to move camp as it was down the Mesa 8 miles. So, next day we moved camp. Here the Indians called every day. One thing we noticed that everyone would ride clear around the camp, before riding into it. We supposed it was to see how many men had left and which direction they had taken. We prospected four days from the camp. The last day, the Indians ordered the boys back. Hayden, Hobbs, Thad and John were in the party. Thad wanted to go back. John went ahead. He had made up his mind to prospect a portion of east canyon and was not going to let a few Indians scare him out. The Indians packed up the squaws and sent the sheep down the canyon, and then scattered out along the sides of the canyon in the rocks. Thad got played out a number of times, but they could not persuade him to wait until they came back. But when they did turn back, he led the party into camp.

We had so much company from the natives that our provisions were again getting low. Within the last two days, it had snowed about 8 inches. The snow put an end to our prospecting and by a vote of 7-2, we were to pull for home. The Indians showed us the trail off of the mesa. I thought I had seen steep trails, but they were all wagon roads compared to this one. Although we came down without an accident. Two days later, Father and I left the rest of the boys as we wished to come back a different way and not to go across the Blue Mountains, because there were liable to be a lot of snow.

Next morning our horses were gone. Father told me to get breakfast while he went to look for them. He wasn't back by sundown. I was pretty worried all day, but didn't dare leave camp for fear he would come in and find me gone and be worried. Just as the sun was going down, I saw six Indians coming on horseback. I thought "Well, this is it; they have killed Father and now are after me."

They rode up and just looked at me for a minute. Two of them that I recognized and some we had been feeding finally told me they had run our horses off the night before, but Father had found them and would be in camp soon. Then, if we were not gone by sunup next morning, they would kill us. Sure enough, Father came in before they were out of sight. We decided not to wait for morning, we packed up right then and got on our way.

We made our first camp on the San Juan. We were 5 days from there to the Colorado at the place called Dandy Crossing, about 20 miles below the mouth of the Dirty Devil. Here and 18 miles below are the largest gold diggings in the United States at present. Here we expected to find a ferry boat, but there was none in sight, and we had the river to cross. I started in to see how deep it was and kept on until I was across on the other side, *and the water only reached the saddle skirts. Father tied the pack horses together and led them across without wetting a pack.*

We were 3 days from the Colorado to Gaves Valley, 35 miles up the Dirty Devil, where we got hay and grain for our horses. We were 2 days from here to the San Rafael and 5 days from there home. Coming across the Green River, I got one shot 500 yards at an antelope, missed. There were four of them. These with the mountain sheep and 6 deer were the only game that were seen on the trip. The rest of the outfit came in one day behind us. Since we have been back, it has snowed a foot. Had one fair day. This afternoon it has rained. Tonight there is a warm wind and the snow is nearly all gone.

Tell Mother I have not seen any of the neighbors, but I am going down to the Siebers in a day or two, and Jim Jones is sick again. Tom says Mother may expect him and Watch next June. I rode Watch all the way, and he tried to buck today, before we got home.

Love to all,

Frank

Heading west on Interstate 70 in the desert country of eastern Utah, you can see forever. Here and there, the precise outline of a distant peak looms up against the blue sky, but in the main, there is nothing to stop the eye but the far horizon. It's like riding on the rim of the world. But turn south at the Crescent Junction exit, and you soon drop off the edge and enter another world. The change is abrupt. Suddenly it's a brand new world; a fantasy world of red sand slickrock and row upon row of immense stone cliffs stretching to the end of vision. This is canyon country, a land of sandstone and rimrock in living color.

What strikes the Easterner is the emptiness, the utter overpowering void. To the outsider, the place aches for motion, for the sounds of the city. No sound is heard; not a word, not a cry, not a whisper. It is as if some plague beyond comprehension has snuffed out life and left all else intact. Then, suddenly, it IS a brand new world; in the mind of the newcomer, THIS, is virgin territory, acres and acres of it. What to do with such a vast emptiness? Set it aside for posterity? Preserve it?

Preserve it!

Preserve it.

At any moment in time, some currents in the great stream of history are diminishing, and other currents are gaining strength. At any moment, there are things ending; and there are also things beginning, old orders giving way to the new. And the moments continue to move — on and on.

Faster!

Faster!

*   *   *

DISPATCH

1976
Grand Junction, Colorado

TEN MINIMUM REQUIREMENTS FOR RANCHING
OR
WHAT IT TAKES TO BE A CATTLEMAN

1. A wide-brimmed hat, a pair of tight pants and a pair of $200.00 boots.

2. At least 2 head of livestock; preferably 1 male, 1 female.

3. A new, air-conditioned pickup truck with automatic transmission, power steering, trailer hitch, and a punch button radio for listening to football games.

4. A gun rack, for the rear window of the pickup, big enough to hold a walking stick and a rope.

5. Two leopard dogs to ride in the bed of the truck.

6. A $40.00 horse and a $400.00 saddle.

7. A gooseneck trailer, small enough to park in front of the cafe.

8. A place to keep the cows, a little land too poor to grow crops.

9. A spool of barb wire, 3 cedar posts, and a bale of prairie hay to haul around in the truck all the time.

10. Credit at the bank.

Author unknown

CHAPTER TEN

THE WINDS OF CHANGE

Vegetarianism is harmless enough,
Although it is apt to fill a man
with wind and self-righteousness.
— R. Hutchins

The problem was as grave as any America had faced since World War II — a regional dispute of such scope and complexity that it had the potential to transform the U. S. economy, destroy political concensus and undermine traditional lifestyles. From remote back country ranches to corporate boardrooms in cities all across the New West, trouble was brewing. Tempers had reached the boiling point, and from all indications the West was spoiling for a fight. Now at the turn of the year 1980, the great Sagebrush Rebellion was in full swing.

At the issue was the dominant Federal presence in the West, clearly expressed in a Federal land policy which affected every phase of life in the region: timber, minerals, recreation, wilderness, grazing and wildlife. Westerners complained that a Federal government, dominated by Eastern interests, was regulating them to death. Invariably, the Feds responded with new directives straight from Washington, D.C. where nameless legions continued to crank out an endless stream of rules for a nation to live by. Regulations seemed to be the order of the day, and confrontation brewed, visibly, in the Western sun.

Among those hardest hit by the endless, seemingly mindless, regulations had been the Western ranchers. One of the primary reasons had to do with the lay of the land. For unlike Eastern farmland, the West is a checkerboard of private holdings surrounded by Federal lands. Once, not so long ago, this was not a problem, but now in this era of new regulations it was, for the independent rancher, like being caught in a set of giant ever-closing pincers of some creature from outer space. Precident had gone that-a-way, and the third-jerk reaction was to get the back up. To make this reaction clear, it is once again necessary to take a look back in time.

In 1950, the U. S. Forest Service decided to eliminate all grazing under the Grand Mesa rim of Kannah Creek range in the Grand Mesa National Forest. The announcement was accompanied by an estimate that in 1951 and 1952 grazing use on top of the Mesa would be cut approximately 57 percent below the normal number allowed. The decision on Kannah Creek was contained in a letter from Lyle F. Watts, Chief of the Forest Service, to Frank Bradbury, Secretary of the Kannah Creek Stockgrowers Association.

In his letter, Mr. Watts said, "I'm firmly convinced of two things: first, that the topography, soil, and general conditions below the

Mesa top justify closure of that area to grazing with the exception of that portion...to provide for cattle drift to and from the top of the Mesa; and second, that conditions of the Mesa top justify adjustments to a point where the vegetation will be given an opportunity to increase in volume and value for forage and watershed purposes."

Now by any reasonable accounting, these announced reductions were drastic and sudden and not without opposition. Clarence Thornock, Supervisor of the Grand Mesa Forest, made an effort to enlist support for the cutback by inviting local groups on guided tours to the top of the Mesa. In order to understand the significance of such an outing, a short description of the area is in order.

The Grand Mesa is a landmark oasis of cool forested beauty which God in His wisdom saw fit to place at a point overlooking the confluence of the Grand (Colorado) and Gunnison Rivers in extreme western Colorado. The "Mesa" is an immense lava-capped upthrust of tableland containing 368,418 acres of National Forest. According to Forest Service literature, this largest flat-top mountain in the world has more than 300 trout-filled lakes scattered on its top and over its broad flanks, and is home range to more than 10,000 deer, 1500 elk, and 300 black bear. The booklets also state that some 12,000 cattle graze the wild green meadows during the summer months.

There are several roads to the top of Grand Mesa, but the highway to Land's End overlook is by far the most memorable. This unpaved roadway twists like a pretzel as it climbs and bends ever upward in a determined scramble to reach the top. Ragged lava slides mark the last stretch of road just under the rim, and nearby a creek spills over the edge and sends slender columns of sun-silvered water dashing to the rocks below. On top, the panorama from Land's End is so staggering to behold, the mind can scarcely cope with the vision on its monitor. For here on this edge of eternity 10,000 feet above the level of the sea, is the grandest view in the West.

Five-thousand feet below, the Gunnison River probes its green-bordered way toward the junction with the mighty Colorado. It's a long way down! Then, the eye follows a path up and over a massive dark uplift known as the Uncompahgre Plateau and sees a rising, twisting mass of color changing, rockstrewn wilderness sweeping west and south to the visionary ends of the earth. Hidden in its shadowy depths are untold miles of forests, remote ranches, uranium mines, a couple of towns, a national monument, and a unique canyon with two mouths and no head called, Unaweep. In a wider arc from the perfect tip of Lone Cone Peak in the south, past the dark humps of Utah's LaSal Mountains on the western horizon, to the sterile front-folds of the Bookcliff mountain range in the north, there are endless vistas of far-away snow peaks, distant deserts, exciting canyonlands, and a fabulous green velvet patchwork of irrigated farmland marking the course of the mighty Colorado River. Although it has been discovered time and again by an untold number of people, for many, this isolated overlook is an integral part of the wilderness.

And it was to this precise spot that Forest Service officials brought a group of forty school teachers on a sure-fire awe-inspiring outing. Pearl Anderson and Winifred Raber, wives of the two prominent Kannah Creek ranchers, decided to join the group to see what was going on. The story of what followed is related by Mrs. Raber:

We joined the group of teachers while they took in the view from all directions. Finally, one of the Rangers called for quiet and began to point out the various landmarks. Suddenly, he made a grand sweep with his arm off to the right and to the desert below and said, "There below you is a prime example of how overgrazing can ruin the land."

The area he pointed out was not only miles and miles away, but was a high ridge of the desert that had been completely sterile for fifty-thousand years — more or less.

"I'm sure you all noticed the waterfall as we came up," the Forest Service spokesman went on, "and I want you all to know your Forest Service built the reservoir that supplies the water to keep that beautiful steam flowing. We have, in fact, constructed a number of such reservoirs on this end of the mountain."

Pearl could take no more and jumped to her feet.

"Like hell, you have!" she blurted loudly. "Those reservoirs were built by my husband and the other ranchers on Kannah Creek."

Thus did the issue of prior use of the land come to a boil here and in other parts of the West. Would the concept of "first in time —first in right" stand against the forces of bureaucratic pressure? Ranchers all across the intermountain region believed that it would. After all, precident was on their side; early-day history backed the stand.

Anita Clark, Whitewater, Colorado, comments on "prior use" of the land in the Kannah Creek area:

In the early days of Kannah Creek, Purdy Mesa and Reeder Mesa, the area raised tremendous amounts of livestock, both beef and dairy. The ranchers cleared land, built ditches and reservoirs. This was done with a tremendous amount of hard work and dedication. No one really can visualize the hardships and risks they undertook in order for them to realize their hopes and dreams. Shortly after the cattlemen arrived, the homesteaders and farmers followed. Many of these people raised dairy cows and a regular route was made throughout the week to pick up the cream, and usually in the summer months the cows were driven to Grand Mesa and were milked there, by hand, twice a day; then the cream brought down by pack-horses. Frand and Pearl Anderson told of many accounts of this procedure. Other oldtimers who had dairy cows and handled in this manner included the Sam Ashleys, Charles Kerstetters, and a man by the name of Walker.

My father, Walter C. Black, came to the local area from Little Park in 1917. Before that, he lived in Longmont, Colorado, prior to that in Shelby, Alabama. When he and my family came, they lived first in the Hebert house on Hebert Mesa at the foot of the old Beef Trail. He obtained his water from both Spring Camp and Indian Creek. He bought the W. H. Williams ranch in 1919 and that same fall on Thanksgiving Day, a heavy snow fell, so much so they moved to the Ternahan ranch and spent the remainder of the winter with them. There were five of us children: Tom, Crafts, Winifred, Wanda and myself. My dad sold the ranch to my husband, G. Keith Clark, and me in

1953. After that, he lived on Grand Mesa during the summer and ran the reservoir water for the waterusers, until his death in December, 1961.

The Anderson family were true pioneers of the Kannah Creek area. Walter's father, R. T. Anderson, came to Reeder Mesa in July of 1891. On May 2, 1914, Walter Anderson married Elizabeth Click of Appleton, Colorado. In Mrs. Anderson's comments on ranching on Kannah Creek, she tells of the Forest Service range permits and the building of reservoirs on Grand Mesa:

Walter was born on the Anderson Home Ranch, June 21, 1892. He has spent most of his life on Reeder Mesa and North Fork ranching, cowboying and working with sheep which were bought in 1928 and run until 1943. The sheep didn't make us popular with our cattle neighbors, but they saved our bacon. We finally sold the sheep, but kept the cattle business running good commercial Herefords until selling out.

In 1915, Walter L., William H. and Frank E. Anderson took up 640 acre claims under the Taylor Grazing Act on Grand Mesa which they proved up on and added to by purchase of 968 acres. Then, in 1917, Walter and Frank took over the Bolen property.

The Forest Service came to this area about 1905. A man named Barney Duffy, was the first Forest Ranger. When the Forest Service first established grazing permits, over 4000 head of cattle were allowed on the west end of Grand Mesa. In 1917, during World War I, they increased permits to about 5000 head.

It was not until 1948 that the Forest Service began making cuts in permits to about 1500 head.

No sheep were ever permitted on the west end of Grand Mesa Forest. When we had sheep, they were run on deeded and leased land. We had to have special permits to cross the Forest Reserve.

There are twenty reservoirs on the west end of Grand Mesa, and all were filed on and built by local ranchers. The only exception was Carson Lake which was built by the City of Grand Junction, but had been filed on by early settlers. All early work was done by horses, slips and wheel scrapers. This was before heavy equipment was thought of, and when there were no roads, just steep rocky trails. Five of the reservoirs, built by the Andersons, were sold to the City of Grand Junction in 1955. There are seven under the rim reservoirs: Anderson Lake, Juanita, Purdy Mesa, McDonald, Cheeney, Giles and Ennor.

Bill Raber adds several comments on the subjects discussed by Mrs. Anderson:

Our place was the last ranch on the upper end of Kannah Creek, and evidently along the route of the old Ute Indian Trail. When we cleared the land for cultivation, we often plowed up Indian relics and old rock ovens.

The first Forest Ranger that I can remember was a man who looked to be in his early-fifties. He came riding up the road on a good-looking old horse with two leather saddle bags on the back of his saddle which contained all his official papers. He usually stayed at our place overnight as he made his annual round taking grazing permits for the following season. This man was a far cry from the smart-looking boys we have as rangers today.

His chaps were worn and greasy, his britches were patched, and his boots were run over, but for all of that, he was one helluva good guy. He evidently had been an old cowpuncher and had seen the hard side of life. At any rate, he didn't think the cowman was somebody that was in the cow game because he was too dumb to do anything else. Certainly, he didn't think you had to save 70 percent of the grass on a range to avoid overgrazing it.

This was just a few years before the ranchers started building reservoirs on Grand Mesa on a large scale, due partly to the fact that the City of Grand Junction was in the process of building a pipeline out of Kannah Creek to divert 300 cu. inches of water to the city. There were no roads on to the Mesa in those days, and everything had to be packed up by horses and mules over very poor trails. The supplies included groceries for camps, sand cement, lumber, pipes and valves.

There was one person who took a major role in this job of packing, and that was, Frank Bradbury. He lived on the lower end of the Creek, and he would pack up his string of pack horses in the morning and come by our place which was about ten miles up the creek at about 3:00 PM, and sometimes would not get to the top of the mountain until the next morning.

In order to get this reservoir work done each year, we would go up after the first cutting of hay and work until the second *cutting was ready, then come down and put up the hay again, and then go up and work until the weather run us out in the fall.*

Kannah Creek rises in the rugged escarpment of Grand Mesa and drops swiftly off the immense flat-topped mountain headed in a westerly direction to the Gunnison River. To many, the valley area along this rapid-flowing stream has the unique feel of a place set apart. Upstream, the ragged black rim of the Mesa dominates the entire scene. It rises suddenly. There it is before you, a great wall, like the boundary of another world. The sense of isolation is strong.

To the early settler, the region seemed like a catleman's dream come true. High above was a vast tableland of timber, water and upland meadows; one simply had to build an access trail over the rim and construct a few reservoirs up on top to assure summer pasture for all time to come. The tongue-in-cheek term, "simply", is put in proper perspective in the following sequence by Nita Clark:

The Kannah Creek Valley lies to the west of Grand Mesa, with the creek beginning back from the rim of Grand Mesa several miles. Several side creeks come into Kannah Creek, both from the north and the south, before it levels out into the valley below. This gives Kannah Creek a fairly stable natural run of water the year around. Most of these creeks drain man-made reservoirs on top of the mountain, so when the spring run-off is gone, natural springs and reservoir water keep the creeks running. However, in the drought year of 1933 and 1934, there was eight inches of snow on Grand Mesa in April. Therefore, very little run-off water was available for irrigation. According to my dad's (Walter C. Black) diaries, the creek was almost dry in early March, so he or my brothers, Tom or Crafts, would ride into the high country with pack-horses and bring back snow in panniers, to be melted and used for drinking water. The North Fork of Kannah Creek runs north of a high ridge separating the two creeks and then joins Kannah Creek again approximately seven miles before the combined creeks empty into the Gunnison River. The mouth of Kannah Creek is about ten miles south of Whitewater.

Whitewater Creek is farther yet to the north, coming off of Grand Mesa and joining the Gunnison River and paralleling Kannah Creek by several miles separation. The top of Grand Mesa is a spectacular flower garden with many stands of spruce timber and quakie trees. Under the rim, the spruce and quakie soon give way to oak-brush; then to cedar and pinon trees; then, the desert which has a very limited amount of yearly rainfall. Desert vegetation is mostly of sagebrush, yucca with various grasses, shad-scale (breakfast food brush), cactus and bud sage. The area described is approximately 150,000 acres.

Very little is known of the local history before a hundred years ago, when in 1881 and 1882, the Ute Indians were taken from the Kannah Creek and Grand Mesa country. When Fathers Escalante and Dominguez went through the area in 1776, they were south of Kannah Creek by forty miles and yet in 1961, a 17th Century Spanish pewter relief casting was found on Kannah Creek by Thelma Beye of Grand Junction and myself. Rev. John

A. Sierra, S.F., diocesan historian, was consulted, and he sent this piece to Dr. George T. Mills of the Colorado Springs Fine Arts Center. They in turn sent the casting to the curator of the Hispanic Society of America, New York City. It now rests in the Smithsonian Institute. The relic shows the Vision of Constantine. Stephen V. Gransay, curator of arms and armor at the Metropolitan Museum of Art, NYC, wrote: "So far as I can see, this does not have anything to do with armor or horse trappings. It is possible that it may be an applied band from a processional cross." (This quote is from the Southern Colorado Register — Sept. 1, 1961. So, possibly Indians found or stole the piece, and it ultimately found its way to an Indian campsite along Kannah Creek.

Very few signs or traces are left, in evidence of the departed Utes. The most visible is the still partially used Ute Trail, leading from Delta to Mesa, Colorado. It is still very much in evidence in several places. Also, still are found: plowed-up fire pots, teepee rings, teepee poles, arrowheads, matates and mano stones, rock-built game blinds and fire blackened rocks and caves. Until just recently, oak trees were still smooth from leather tannings. The desert area south of Indian Creek and west of Highway 50 is called the Indian Hunting Grounds.

As the Indians were moved out, and even before, cattlemen were moving in with large herds of cattle. From history records passed down from one generation to another, the cattle ran from the Gunnison River to the west, Colorado River to the north and Delta to the south. The cattle roamed the desert country in the winter and followed the snow through the oak-brush and out on top of the Grand Mesa for summer grazing. Two stone chimneys are still standing on Indian Creek, which runs parallel with Kannah Creek about three miles to the south. These chimneys were old camps used by a William Schoolfield who came in the early '80s. He also had a camp on Kannah Creek, and the wire used for his horse corral has grown approximately four inches into oak trees. Schooley Draw or Saddle was named for him in which the Ute Trail ran from Indian Creek to Kannah Creek. Other early cattlemen were John Ternahan, B. F. Lucas, W. L. Farmer, Henry Bolen, who came as early as 1872 and bringing the 7 brand with him, John Sullivan who was one of the earliest ranchers on the Kannah Creek, Daniel Bradbury, Elijah Chambers John Cox, Michael Holland, Willard Honsinger, Emery Riddle, William Spencer, R. T. Anderson, J. J. Raber, Will Van Pelt and a George W. Swain, who raised horses and ran an early dude-ranch. Swain ran the horses both on the desert south of Kannah Creek and on Grand Mesa and never once rode one, always handling them afoot. J. J. Raber obtained the Swain Ranch in 1907. Many of these early day cattle drifted into the Wells Gulch area between Kannah Creek and Delta. They became extremely wild and a very large and interesting chapter could be written about these 'renegades' and the men who eventually caught them. But, recent reports give evidence that there are a handful left.

These early-day cattlemen began the settlement of this little vicinity. First they built trails in order to move the cows from one area to another. Getting these cattle up over the rim of

Grand Mesa was no easy task. One of the earliest of these was the Indian Point Trail, and it was almost impossible to travel even then, but the cows were driven up and down in spite of its hazardous terrain. Finally, this dangerous trail was rebuilt by Fred Simineo and this is the one used yet today. But, there are many bones laying off over the side, indicating the dangers of this trail. The Coal Creek and the Farmer Trails were improved upon by the Forest Service about 1934 and '35 at which time Crafts Black and a Nathan Robb worked on them. The Kannah Creek trail was built by early settlers on the south side of the creek, to help keep cattle from being poisoned by larkspur on the Farmer Trail. The Spring Camp trail to Blue Lake is very old, in fact, the early pioneers cut hay at the Spring Camp Flat and brought it down by use of sleds. This same procedure occurred on the north bench of Kannah Creek under the Shirttail point and forage was also brought down by makeshift sleds. Frank Anderson remembers seeing the old sleds at the head of Dry Fork for many years. John Otto also can be credited with building trails under the rim, one going out over the top near the present Shelter House. When the Land's End Road was built, it was obliterated, but parts of it can still be seen by a sharp eye in several places. Another trail John Otto built is on the north curve of Shirt Tail Point, altho' it is passible only by hands and knees. The rock used and 1" pipe embedded in the lava rock are still visible. The trail approaching the Indian Creek Point from the desert was built by Belt & Van Emmon, two local men. The man by the name of Belt lived in a rock dugout on Indian Creek near Highway 50. This trail was used almost primarily for bringing beef down in the fall, thus it has been referred to for many years as the 'Beef Trail'. The cattlemen built two cedar corrals on Kannah Creek, to aid in handling the cattle. One was about 1½ miles west of the city intake, and the other about 1½ miles west of that. No trace whatsoever is left. Will Purdy, Roxie Chambers and Bill Raber remembers these corrals.

As the pioneers came and settled the country, the mesas, creeks and valleys were given names. Kannah Creek has an Indian name whose meaning has been lost forever. Some say it means 'Cottonwood', while others say it is 'Willow'. Will Purdy, however, says that the cottonwoods on Kannah Creek when his family came were very small. Also, Mr. Purdy said that the proper spelling for Kannah is Kahnah, and old maps use this spelling. The flat mesa south of Kannah Creek is called, Hebert Mesa. It lies directly near the cedars and pinons at the foot of the Belt and Van Emmon Trail. Hebert was a Dr. who lived there in the late '80s and died a very mysterious death. Some reports say suicide, and others say it was murder. One man was accused, and he left the country, but his name remains on a spot under the rim on the Beef Trail, on a local reservoir, and his brand is still used on the creek, by a local rancher. My folks moved the house in 1932 to our place. Very little is left to even show where the house sat, but if one looks closely, the wooden barrels that were buried at the corner of the house to catch rain water, are still there. Irrigation water for this place was from two sources, one ditch coming out of Spring Camp which is the flat bench under the rim, and the other ditch came out of Indian Creek following the old Ute Trail. The cedar post diversion in Indian Creek is still visible, and the original ditch from Spring Camp is still used as the trail to bring cattle out on in the fall.

Farther west of Hebert Mesa, the area is simply South Mesa. South of South Mesa runs Indian Creek, and farther yet is Deer Creek. These two creeks run a very limited amount of spring runoff water. Horse Mountain sets directly between the two creeks and was named for the wild horses that used to run there. At the base of Horse Mountain on Deer Creek is the faint remains of a homestead, owned by a man by the name of Rodgers. He was a promoter and built ditches and cleared some land in the hopes of land development. The story goes that he saw the picture of a model in the Montgomery Ward catalog — he liked her looks and wrote to her, telling her about the wonderful west. She came, they married and had a family. Not too many years ago, one of the sons came through Whitewater asking about the area.

The first store and PO on Kannah Creek still stands on the west end of the Howard Brouse ranch. This was previously owned by Earl Lucas, eldest son of B. F. Lucas. At the time of the store, it was owned by Ira Vincent. Another store on Kannah Creek was at the North Fork — Kannah Creek intersection. It was operated by Carl Farmer, son of W. L. Farmer. At Pride was a store run and owned by Millard Gilbert and every Sunday they made ice-cream for anyone passing that way. This store was approximately half-way up the Farmer Hill which was on the old road to Delta.

Not too long after the Kannah Creek people moved into the area to settle and stay, they realized that irrigation water was paramount. Under extreme adverse conditions, they managed to drag horse-drawn equipment to Grand Mesa by way of primitive trails. They cut trees, built accesses across the creeks, hauled rocks, and cleared out brush in order to get the machinery needed to the reservoir sites. First of all, a cabin was built to house the workers, and someone was hired to care for the workhorses and mules. Bill Raber recalls 'jingling' horses long before daylight in order for the men to have their teams ready for the 10-hour day.

Number 1 Reservoir was the first built with an appropriation date of Aug. 1, 1887. Next was the Scales Lakes 1 & 3, then #8, Chambers, #9, #6, Deep Creek #2, Bolen Anderson and Jacobs, Anderson #1, Anderson #2, Raber-Click, and the Hogchute (Carson Lake) in 1946. The Scales #1 appropriation date 1891, Scales #3 was 1892, Grand Mesa #8 was 1901, Chambers Reservoir was 1903, Grand Mesa #9 was 1904, Grand Mesa #6 was 1904, Deep Creek (formerly called, Carcass Flats) was 1906, Juanita Reservoir was 1911, Bolen, Anderson & Jacobs was 1911, Bolen was 1911, Flowing Park (Sheep Creek) was 1911, Anderson #2 was 1941, Raber-Click, 1939 and Purdy Mesa Reservoir was also about this time. Just recently, Richard Somerville constructed one on Whitewater Creek.

Everyone of these reservoirs were built by local ranchers with private monies and hard work, except the Hogchute and the

Flowing Park Enlargement which was built by the City of Grand Junction. The hardships these men overcame to build these reservoirs is difficult to imagine. After the Land's End road was built and completed in 1935, then power driven equipment was used by the Anderson Bros., Raber Bros., Fred Click and C. V. Hallenbeck. Before the road was built, all sand needed for the valves and for any cement work was packed to the mountain by pack-horses by Frank Bradbury. Someone discovered a thin layer of sand at the Scales Lake vicinity, and Bill Raber would take pack-horses in and gently scoop out handsful and pack it in panniers and back to the reservoir building crew. Mr. Bradbury did all the packing for supplies needed for the crews, and he lived near Highway 50. Many miles from the reservoir sites. He would begin to pack his string of horses and mules and by 11 o'clock AM, he was ready to leave for Grand Mesa. He would ride up Kannah Creek, and by five in the afternoon would reach the City Intake nearly 10 miles up the creek. By nightfall, he would be on Cheever Creek, and here he would unpack all his goods and camp for the night. The next morning he would ride on into camp. Mr. Bradbury was completely and totally reliable which was extremely valuable in this operaton for so many men depended upon him. After a season of using the pack string, many times the animals were turned loose on the desert south of Kannah Creek and many became wild. And, for years, wild horses ran in bunches on Indian and Deer Creek. Some of these horses were captured, broken and ridden by the later cowboys. Frank Lucas had "Midnight" and Earl Lucas had "Maxie", these were caught out of this wild herd and were fine horses.

The cattlemen built cabins not only on the top of the mountain for use in reservoir building, but along various trails and flats under the rim, for use in running their cattle. Several camps were maintained without cabins, such as Spring Camp, south of Kannah Creek and at the spring on the Indian Point Trail. Sullivans had a cabin on Kannah Creek, and 'Sullivans Camp' became a meeting place for riding under the rim.

Walker had a cabin between there and Spring Camp on the trail we called, going around the 'World' when we took cows out of there and on up the Point Trail. Blind Cabin still remains west of Coal Creek, and some say this was the site of a 'still' to make boot-leg whiskey.

The cowboys then built a cabin under the rim near where Kannah Creek comes over the rim, and they named the cabin, the Hog-chute. When the City of Grand Junction built the reservoir there, Howard Brouse took the cabin apart and re-assembled it at his ranch on Purdy Mesa. The Hog-chute was the main headquarters for several years. Then, W. L. Farmer built a cabin at the head of the Deep Creek-Farmer Trail out on top, and this they named, Doves Nest. Keith Clark's mother stayed here in 1901. Lucases built an old cabin south of Kannah Creek out on top, and Ternahan built one under the #1 ridge. These and others have all been destroyed, because of an order sent down by the Forest Service...an eye-sore, they said. Other cabins that met the same fate were the Ashleys, the Cox-Click, Chambers and the old City Camp. The cabins built when the reservoirs were constructed have all been burnt.

After the reservoirs were built, then maintenance problems began. When the reservoirs were filling in the spring, extreme care was taken to prevent water and snow damage to each one. So, Ed Gill was hired to go in on snowshoes to shut all valves and shovel out all wasteways. He was packed in with supplies by packhorses and left totally on his own for about three weeks. He had a pair of snowshoes and from where he camped, he would make the rounds of every reservoir, and this consisted of many miles under adverse and dangerous conditions and extreme hard work. This was long before snowmobiles.

For many years, when cattle were run in large numbers on Grand Mesa, by men by the names of J. B. Claybough, Raber Bros., Lucas family, the Anderson Bros., C. V. Hallenbeck, Cox-Click, Bradburys, Black and Goldsborough, the cows were on the desert until the snow melted enough to let them start up through the oak-brush. No Forest Line Fence existed then, nor County Line Fence between Mesa and Delta counties. The cattle had free run of the country. As the cattle drifted higher in the quakie flats up under the rim, men would move to the mountain for the summer and start riding down from the top every day to gather these half-wild cattle and move them out on top by way of the Coal Creek Trail, the North and South Kannah Creek Trail which joined at the Hog-chute, and came out near the present road. The Point Trail was used when riding the Spring camp country. Much of this time was during WWII, and most of the young men were in the service, so this left the older men and the women to get the job done. Winifred Black Raber, my sister, who married Bill Raber, and my sister, Wanda Sanders and myself, rode under the rim. We thoroughly loved this riding and the country. When the cows were brought out on top, they were left to graze at their free will as no fences were anywhere except at Sheep Creek (Flowing Park). In August of every year, four days were set aside for the round-up, called the Beef Ride, and an annual dance was held on the night of the last day's ride at the cow camp of J. B. Claybough. Bill Raber and Wanda and myself furnished the music, and it was held in the upstairs of the cow camp. A great time was had by all, and people came from several miles to attend. The first day of the Beef-ride was held at 'Layton Stomp' on the northern end of the mountain, and the second day was at the Deep Creek Bunch Grounds near the Anderson Reservoir #2; the third day at the #9 Reservoir Bunch Ground near the Y intersection of the present highway, and the fourth and final day at the Sheep Creek Reservoir. This covered the entire mountain for gathering the cows. After each day's ride, the beef that were cut out to be shipped were taken to the Beef Pasture on the south wing of Grand Mesa and put behind the only fence that was on Grand Mesa which was at Sheep Creek. The beef were then held here until September when they were gathered and brought down the Beef Trail and driven then to Whitewater where they were corralled and put on railroad cars for shipping. The dust from the drive down this Beef Trail could be seen for many miles. Before the Beef Trail was built, the cattle were pointed down over the Williams Basin Ridge and down past Poison Springs, coming out the draw by the present Visitation Monastery.

In the 1930s, the CCC, which was a government project, started a road up Grand Mesa; this road enabled more reservoir development and easier access for all concerned. Both local people and tourists enjoyed this wonderful improvement. It is a very beautiful and scenic road and was even used as a race track for famous racers, such as Louis Unser. The races were first run July 4, 1940 and 1941. This year, 1982, another race was run on August 1st. The men who drove it say it's quite a challenge. It would be for the local ranchers in their pick-ups, that's for sure.

At the Shelter House on top, the original road stayed to the north, passing by Crater View and the Anderson Reservoirs. But in 1967, a new road was built from the Shelter House to the south, passing by Shirt Tail Point, past the trails we used to use bringing cattle out from under the rim, traveling by beautiful and spectacular views of the Kannah Creek basin, and going between the two cabins built by the Lucases and later owned by the Raber Brothers. Near the timber at this spot was the original site of the 'Doves Nest' cabin built by the farmers in the late 1890's.

Today, a few of the original structures and sites of the early days still remain. The home of the Ternahans still stands on Kannah Creek, old rock foundations of homes on Purdy Mesa, old unused ditches running here and there, including the Van Pelt Ditch out of Indian Creek, which is now used for the primitive road into that country. Faint signs of fields that were once fertile, and old grades and fills of the Kannah Creek road that led to the Intake with the two graves alongside. Old and gnarled fruit trees on the Lynch place, the old orchard near the old Purdy home, the tall cedar posts John Ternahan used to keep his elk in on the Elk Glen ranch, remains of fields on North Fork where T. H. Stephens raised corn and alfalfa, the Kannah Creek store and post office, the McDonald Pond on South Mesa which has long been dry, the racetrack where C. V. Hallenbeck trained his race horses, and the foundation of the Purdy Mesa School. Jay Olson still uses the root cellar and cistern John Sullivan built, and the foundation is still visible on South Mesa where Ed Gills lived and packed water in buckets from Kannah Creek or Indian Creek when his small cistern went dry. There is still the faint trace of the grave of the Thompson woman who was killed in 1883 in the famous Thompson/Herrick murder at Pride. Also, the house still stands where the wounded sheepherder, Pete Swenson was taken after he was shot in 1907 by one of four local cowboys. This secret is still kept.

So, from the years Keith's grandfather, William H. Clark, first surveyed this country in 1910 and 1911, the people who have lived here and raised their families were very sedate, very stable, progressive and highly respected. They were very proud in their resourcefulness, their independence and willingness to help one another. They loved the school, the community activities and projects, national affairs and made every effort to make it a better place in which to live. Each person is an interesting individual, and many fascinating stories can be told about each one. Each has contributed to a very unusual and unique *community.*

It has been said that time waits for no man, and as a person proceeds like a projectile down the trajectory of years, this truth is ever more evident. Sooner or later, one finds a pattern revealed in which all events have a sequence; where each event is — at once — an effect of previous causes and the cause of new effects. It is in the nature of things, if one stops to think about it, for individuals to compete. It is also in the nature of things for Mother Earth to react to overt pressures with great resiliency. History has shown both factors to be essential aids in the advance of civilization. Both factors, however, appear to be subject to temporary modification.

In the early 1940s, for example, this nation was in the process of becoming the arsenal of democracy. The free world had its back put to the wall, and the last hope for survival was centered on the industrial capacity of the United States. Could the impossible be done? Would the doctrine of competition and the master idea of natural selection flex to accommodate this epic struggle for survival?

The free enterprise system wiped away a decade of cobwebs, and seemingly overnight, government, labor and management had joined forces to produce the cold steel of war. The response was spontaneous all over the nation. In Gary, hard-eyed Poles fired the furnaces of freedom with determined precision, and in Detroit, dry-eyed Armenians — one generation off the boat — eagerly reported for work at General Motors. For the very first time, the gigantic melting pot was brought to a boil; it was indeed a time to remember. The natural and immutable theory of existing U. S.

economic law which stressed enlightened self-interest and freedom of action was beautifully modified to fit the occasion of united all-all effort. When the dust had settled, it was generally acknowledged that the greatest war in history had definitely been won on the potent production lines of U.S. industry.

Now, production is an all-encompassing word which includes, "meat on the table", and Americans had been keenly aware of the fact from the beginning. U. S. expansion from the Erie Canal to the Twentieth Century Limited, may well have been a study in motion, but that motion was fueled by the farmers and ranchers of this nation, men and women whose roots were anchored, deeply, in the soil. Today, a goodly number of those roots are still in place; but, as they have throughout history, the pendulum of events keeps swinging, and the winds of change continue to blow.

Now, in the eighties, the national back is once again being put to the wall. The United States is face to face with an economic crisis which threatens to change a way of life. It is a crisis sustained by rumor and aggravated by indecision; a messy pot of porridge kept at the boiling point with internal bickering by a nation of experts. The entire nation is criss-crossed with formal organizations, and a veritable legion of individual specialists, all dedicated to providing first-aid for those groping in the dark for answers. The rhetorical broadsides cover a whole plum pudding of contrasting viewpoints. The fever reaches its peak in our nation's capital. The reasons are basic.

Washington is a magnet, the very air of the city crackles with excitement. It is unquestionably the economic as well as the political capital of the country, the focus of public attention. To it are drawn innumerable idealists, enthusiasts, national planners, super-savers of all degrees of hard- and soft-headedness, each with an infallible prescription for saving the nation. Financiers and their lawyers and briefcase-toting assistants disembark from their planes and hit the ground running. Specialists of all sorts attend receptions, conferences, dinners where they participate in long discussions between groups of experts, in endless and fatiguing succession. At first glance, one is aware of the force of self-interest at work, but hidden in the "depths" are special groups dedicated to saving "gluttonous Americans" from themselves; their concern has to do with the food we eat. It is, apparently of some importance.

The issue seems to center on the point that in the process of feeding ourselves, as in almost all other areas of activity, we (gluttonous Americans) thus have a disproportionate impact on the ecosphere. Once the point has been made, they zero in on the wasteful livestock industry. The attack comes from all directions and in many forms. For example, an article on "Tofu", made from soybeans, entitled, "It's a Food of the Future", states:

"It takes 21 lbs of feed to produce one pound of beef to feed one or two people."

Then it goes on to say that 21 lbs of that same feed would feed 34 people, if made into tofu. Tofu?

A book entitled, "Diet For a Small Planet", quotes several "certified" experts on the subject as follows:

"The Dean of Agriculture of Ohio State University has estimated that 40 percent of world LIVESTOCK PRODUCTION is derived from vegetable sources suitable for human food. If made available to man directly, he concludes, the world food supply could be increased by 35 percent."

And:

"According to Don Paarlberg, a former U. S. Assistant Secretary of Agriculture, just reducing our LIVESTOCK POPULATION by one-half would release about 100 million tons of grains for human consumption. This amount would meet the caloric deficit of the 'non-socialist' developing countries almost four times over."

This continual pounding on the evils of meat eating covers the full range of emotional impact on the activist calendar. It probably peaks in the following statement in a "letter to the editor", date-lined Washington, and written by a man named, Hershaft:

"Phaseout of animal food production will free land, water, and energy for more beneficial uses, reduce the stress on our environment, and bring an abundance of food, not only for ourselves, but for the starving millions in Asia and Africa, as well."

It might be noted as an afterthought that Alex Hershaft, PhD, is

President of the Vegetarian Information Service based in Bethesda, Maryland — a mere stones-throw from our nation's capital.

It is time, one supposes, to set the record straight, once and for all, about the West and such things as tall tales. True Westerners, and here we get right to the nitty-gritty, cherish a myth about life. In that myth, men are brave, women are fair, everyone eats beef and, whatever the reason, those tea-sipping, paper-pushing dudes from the east have no business butting in. And there's more.

Sensible Westerners know the value of tradition; they have a practical sense of history. Now in a period of stress, they can gain strength from a long look back. The view is clear and precise.

When the great war of the forties drew to a close, the American dream took to wheels as never before, and the road to glory was quickly paved over. But life in the fast lanes required nourishment, and out along the by-ways (and damned near every crossroad) American enterpreneurs began to build a network of new-style food dispensers. Slowly and surely, fast-food chains covered the country. Hamburger has become a national resource. Tofu not withstanding, it's still a fact of life.

Tofu?

Holy Nellie!

*   *   *

DISPATCH

January 20, 1981
Washington, D.C.

On this day, the Great Sagebrush Rebellion died aborning.

CHAPTER ELEVEN

THE END OF AN ERA

Mount Garfield in the distance glows
At Sunset like a crimson rose;
While far off Washington gleams bright
Touched by the roseate sunsets light.

So wrote W. E. Pabor of that special moment which occurs in the Grand Valley most every evening shortly before sunset. Just as the sun sinks on the western horizon, as though from some heavenly quirk, slanting sun rays cast a great transparent cloak of glowing color over the Bookcliffs. In the distance, everything comes to a stop as the ragged cliffs take on the appearance of a giant cameo which has been carved by nature's hand. The fading light seems to fall in place with measured precision as it touches the high red walls of the Monument and gradually covers the broken rims of Grand Mesa. Now is the time for silent thoughts as the twilight spins its magic.

The spell subsides slowly as if being filtered through a million shades of mauve stained glass. Finally, all that is left are flowing lines of purple mountains, rhythmically meeting, crossing, parting as your spirit is carried far into the still distance. And such is the magic of the moment that each person is sure it belongs to him or her alone.

Today, this special moment at last light is one of the few things left unchanged since the days of Mr. Pabor. True, the skyline looks the same, the desert still has long empty stretches, and there are wild places out in the "Books", but even in deserted areas, one is not sure what will be found over the next rise. Follow an old trail today, and it may lead to a picnic table or a natural gas pumping station. The slick rock country has been penetrated by jeep trails, and air-inflated rubber rafts glide down the fast-moving waters of the Colorado. Change has come, and who is to say whether for better or worse. The amazing thing, if one stops to think about it, is that much of it happened within the span of one lifetime.

It is, of course, absolutely true that we measure our speeds and directions in life by references to events of the past. Still, there are times when a person must fall back on the right of private judgement and make a stand on a living belief of the moment. For the straight truth of the matter is that dreams are, invariably, the better part of experience. Nowhere is this more clearly demonstrated than in the world of horses. For Stan and Margaret Hellman of Grand Junction, Colorado, involvement in that world came about primarily as a result of the dreams of their four lively daughters — Janet, Judy, Connie and Donna. To Janet, especially, the dreams centered on getting a horse of their very own. The dream became a reality when Janet, aged 12, found an old horse which could be bought for seventy-five dollars.

Janet recalls at the time:

He was an old horse — all of 17 years, but beautiful to us, and we just had to have him. Somehow, I had to raise that $75.00. Now there was this trumpet I was learning to play, and all of a sudden I developed an intense dislike for that instrument. At this same moment, my little sister decided she couldn't possibly live a day longer, unless she could learn to play the trumpet. The upshot of it was that sis got her musical instrument, and the family got their first horse. It was a fine tradeoff, so far as I was concerned.

So, the girls got their horse to ride — to love — to learn on, and the Hellmans were in the horse business, whether they were aware of it at the time or not. For the next move was to get a mare capable of producing foals — one for each horse-lover in the family. Sooner than anyone could imagine, this would include dad and mom.

The old horse was sold for $100.00, and the new mare cost $150.00. The first hurdle in the production cycle was passed, but it now became apparent that the foals had to have sires. And a half-Arab mare ought to have the best. The dilemma was solved when Stan traded some accumulated "building material" for the stud fee. But now the die was cast. For the magic in the words of "Arab" and "foal" can only lead to thoughts of a purebred operation. To understand fully, one must "sweat out" a birthing and actually observe the first movements of a new-born foal. The experience is visibly heightened when the foal is of Arab blood.

There is something special about the Arab horse. Renowned for its physical beauty, endurance, intelligence and almost touching devotion to its master, the Arabian purebred is the origin from which all Western ideas about the good breeding of horseflesh have been derived. Celebrated in literature as the desert horse of the Bedouin, the Arabian has left its mark on many breeds. In the Eighth Century, the purebred desert Arab was introduced into Europe through Spain, where it left permanent traces in its Barb and Andalusian descendants. Even the English Thoroughbred can trace its beginning to outstanding Arabian purebreds.

For the Hellmans, the purebred notion began to sprout when Janet went to the All-Arabian Horse Show in Scottsdale, Arizona, and returned with photos of a two-year-old filly owned by Charlie Steen, the Uranium King. The pictures and description struck a chord; this just might be the one. It was time for a family conference.

Says Stan:

I felt we needed a new car more than anything, but agreed to put it to vote. The final tally was, five for the horse, and one for the car, and I damn-well knew who voted for the car. At any rate, I agreed to go and take a look at the filly. Just looking wouldn't hurt a thing, and I could always decide I didn't like her. But first, I had to get out to the Steen Ranch in Reno, Nevada.

Now, we had a friend who was looking for an Arabian, and he had a friend who was a pilot and had access to an airplane. A deal was cooked up, and one Saturday about noon, we received a call to get ready for a trip to Reno. Margaret decided to come along, so we packed a bag and headed for the airport. The flight started okay, but over in Utah, the weather roughed up and along about Hanksville, the pilot decided we had better head for

Las Vegas. We got in without trouble, so it was decided to spend the evening doing the town.

The next day, we flew up to Reno and went out to the Steen Ranch. Charlie had built up quite a place. The horses were housed in a big Spanish-type barn that was built in a circle. It was pretty fancy, but someone had fouled up somewhere along the line, since they had to carry water to the horses in individual buckets. I suppose they eventually got it all straightened out. At any rate, I looked the filly over, and she was everything we had been hoping for. After looking her over and spending some time examining her papers and blood lines, I got around to asking-price. The man in charge said twenty-five hundred dollars without batting an eye, and I came near fainting. Finally, I said, "Lord, I can't cut that; but I've got $500 now, and I can go $50 a month." That old trainer just looked at me and said, "Can't be done."

Well, I figured Ol' Charlie ought to have a say in the matter, so I suggested he just take the offer up to the main office. It took twenty minutes to get Charlie's OK on the deal. While they were fixing up the papers, I decided to ride my luck, so I sided up to the trainer and said, "Of course, for that kind of money, you gotta deliver to Grand Junction."

The trainer agreed to deliver, and the Hellmans were in the horse business for real. Abu-Kiri was a purebred; she had the pure, clean blood-lines of a champion. Now it was time to go home. But the March winds were still kicking up and getting there was not going to be easy.

Marge Hellman continues:

It seemed like we were just not going to be able to get out of Reno. We took off in that little plane and just circled around over the mountains. The wings iced up, and we couldn't see a thing in the storm. I was scared stiff, and I guess it showed. The pilot finally decided to turn back, and when we landed back in Reno, I was much relieved.

Our friend had bought a Polish filly from Steen, so we went back to the ranch and asked the manager to deliver both horses right away. In the matter of an hour, we were on the road with both horses in a trailer and four of us in the front seat of the towing pickup. The roads were bad, and it was not exactly an easy trip, but for me it sure beat bouncing around the mountain tops in that light plane. All in all, it was a trip I'll never forget.

We should probably note at this time that the Hellmans did not have stable facilities on their home place. Nor could they devote full-time to the business of horses. Stan held a full-time job in maintenance for the Rio Grande Railroad. Marge worked for the school district. After years of moving from one railroad town to another, Stan had acquired the seniority status to enable them to stay put. And after years of living in rented houses of every description known to God or man, they had finally acquired a brand-new home of their own. But now they were in a business which required elbow room.

Stan Hellman continues:

We boarded the new filly out, but I knew it was just a matter of time before we would have to get acreage of our own, so I began to look around. We finally found a place out on 29 Road. The guy who owned it wanted to sell, but I offered to trade places — our new house for his old farm — and one-hundred dollars to boot. I figured we would need that $100 to move on, so I stuck to it, and the deal went through just that way.

The new place was pretty rundown. The house was eighty years old and not too modern. So we had to fix it up. That first summer, the girls bunked in the barn, and Margaret and I slept in a little housetrailer while we all worked at making that old place into a home. Everyone worked, and that's the way it has always been.

Thunder Mountain Ranch took shape on 29 Rd., and the Hellman family raised purebred Arabians. A breeding program was established, and the operation grew in size. Then, as so often happens, it became time for a larger place. The little ranch on 29 Rd. was sold, and the Hellman operation moved to a larger place on 31 Rd. Now they could raise their own feed. In view of rising prices, it was a good plan.

It is a double-barrelled fact of life, however, that as time passes, conditions are bound to change. The girls went off to college, and one by one became engaged and then married. And while love and concern for Thunder Mountain Ranch continued, new priorities took over.

In 1975, Stan and Marge Hellman sold the big place on 31 Rd., keeping five acres on which to build a new home. It's a beautiful house with plenty of room for visiting grandchildren, and the five acres is fenced and cross fenced to hold purebred Arabs. Slowly but surely, the Hellmans intend to cut back on the number of horses, although Stan has plans to keep at least two mares around just to keep his hand in. Thunder Mountain Ranch will continue to raise foals to show, to enjoy, and to keep ol' grandpappy active. The experience gained over the years will be put to good use.

Stan Hellman sums up:

When we first started out, I didn't know anything about Arabians. I didn't even know there was such a thing as an Arabian breed. So the only thing I could do was get some books and start studying.

When I first started out in breeding, I couldn't think of anything better than to set the girls up with a horse business. Horse shows for us have always been a family affair and kind of a hobby. We all sacrificed for it. When we started, Margaret asked how long it would be before I could made this pay. And I said, "About ten years." We've been at it for ten years, and I don't know if it's paid or not. It took a lot of hard labor and long hours, but how can one possibly measure such things when placed against the value of working together for a common purpose.

The value of two people working together! These are special words in the American scheme of things; words that echo throughout this collection of stories. They are words that tell of family. They tell of tradition. They tell of roots. Nothing is more vital to our survival. Nothing hangs stronger in the mind — not even childhood memories. It is a value tied closely to all human progress.

If we look back over the pattern of man's history, we can detect from earliest beginnings an instinctive concern for the family unit. From the start, this concern imposed conditions such as range of possibility and risk. Yet, invariably, the response has been innovation, experiment, and invention. Discovery, undoubtedly, reached its peak in the United States, because of a unique two-headed American capability which allowed individual initiative to mingle freely with family responsibility. Invention is an individual function. It takes only one to make a discovery. But, at the heart, incentive is the basic and most essential ingredient. It is the ingredient that makes our system work. Yet even here, balance must be sought for Americans have a tendency to swing in a wide arc.

Seventy percent of our population, it is claimed, live on one percent of the land. Way back in the mid-sixties, a Gallup Poll found that a majority of residents of large cities would rather live in a smaller town, or in a suburb, or in a rural area. Everyone, it seems, is distressed by threats of overcrowding, and we read and hear ever more about the need for open space and wilderness. This need appears to have focused on the mountains of our Western states.

It is a bit difficult to explain the spell of a mountain, but just place an urban-oriented greenhorn on a remote peak, and invariably he becomes possessed of a madness which defies all reason. This is the wilderness, and suddenly, it all belongs to him. Such a person can stand in the cold ashes of countless campfires, supremely confident that all around is virgin territory. He can gaze off into the blue distance, thinking he is first, even as a booted toe edges an empty beer can into the brush. The spell of upland enchantment can last but an hour or continue for a lifetime. There is a mystique here. The facts are self-evident.

The impractical dream of a wilderness paradise is supported by a staggering amount of environmental nonsense. It is an emotional theory based on the assumption that nature is a kind and provident healer. Nature is in reality a system operating upon the principal of the survival of the fittest. Mother Nature is cruel and demanding and perhaps the greatest polluter of all. The driving force behind the natural phenomenon known as, nature, is and always has been the generation of the new and vigorous at the expense of the old and weak. Still, a veritable legion of environmental activists insist that man can be saved only through a return to natural balance in the land.

It is in the disposition of the land itself that the environmentalist organizations outdo themselves. The charges are made continually that ruthless business interests are gobbling up all the land in our nation and depriving the people of adequate park and recreational areas. Now, what are the facts?

There are roughly two and one-quarter billion acres of land in the fifty states of this country. More than 750 million acres of this total is in Federal ownership. One in every three acres in our land, therefore, is set aside for the benefit of all. In addition, 150 million acres are owned by city, state and county governments. It is quite evident that the charges of ruthless gobbling are a gross misrepresentation. This obsession over land use appears to be the dominant theme of the entire environmentalist movement. Concern for the land, however, does not seem to include an understanding of the value of planned management.

Environmental organizations, and this includes much of the media, have shown little interest in a major bark beetle epidemic which has been roaring through Yellowstone Park for several years. They seem to be concerned only with man's interference in the matter. Meanwhile the beetles chomp away undisturbed as the epidemic picks up an ever-increasing momentum. The stricken trees, cut off from their life blood, fade and turn slowly to the red hue which signifies death in a conifer forest. At the very end much of Yellowstone will become a wilderness boneyard containing vast areas of grey broken snags extending to the horizon. The bugs will have been but an instrument in the cycle of regeneration. This is nature's way of reaching an ecological balance in the land. It is a sad and unnecessary process in an age of reason.

It is ironic that those who protest man's participation in the ecological balance of the land have the loudest voices in the constant demand for more outdoor recreational facilities. The inconsistency reaches its height when those who insist they are conservation experts refuse to accept the basic premise of professional forestry. This premise is as elemental as life.

Timber is a crop. It is life. A tree has a beginning. It lives, it grows, it matures, and it does have an ending. Nature's way is to provide that ending with fire or disease in order to prepare the way for the new. All things, including man, are subject to the same law of nature. The old must give way to the new. Modern forestry is a proven science designed to promote new and vigorous forest growth through controlled and selective cutting and utilization of mature, unfit or disease-prone trees.

The organized opposition — those superbugs of the environmental movement — reject this science out of hand. With practiced precision, they cry, "Rape," in unison. They cry, rape, and in the same breath demand complete control and total set-aside preservation of the nation's forested lands. This outcry continues, despite proof of the fallacy of such a policy. To those Westerners who live on the land, this overdeveloped emotional fixation with an untouched wilderness is most difficult to understand.

There is not an area in the Rocky Mountain West that remains untouched by man. The virgin wilderness is a myth. Urban-based wilderness eagles may stand where they wish and lay claims to the spot, but some of us have been there before. These western mountains have sustained life in local areas and made vital and absolutely essential contributions to the nation for more than one-hundred years. They are still here. They have survived. They did so under the concept of multiple use which provides for the greatest good for the greatest number.

Now, dedicated supersavers take one look and demand this great Western backyard be placed in a state of limbo for all eternity, lest it be contaminated by those who developed it. It is gospel fact that once branded with the wilderness iron, this "untouched" land is marked for an ultimate disfiguring death by fire, pestilence or saturation. In the end, the central theme of the activist thrust appears to be a general downgrading of individual effort. Its sharpest attacks are leveled at those who deal with the elements; at those people who live and work with nature. Two such people are Bill and Leone Hamilton of Gateway, Colorado.

Gateway is a small rural-oriented community located at the foot of the Uncompahgre Plateau in extreme western Colorado. Although the immediate area is devoted to cattle raising, this small town in the rock-rimmed valley of the Dolores River is quite literally the gateway to the uranium country of Colorado West. The Hamiltons do run cattle, and their ranch headquarters is situated along the Dolores River about a mile north of Gateway. It is a beautiful spot, overlooked by towering rock formations which often at dusk appear as night sentinels; silhouettes in dark red standing guard over a silent land.

The Hamilton spread is a working ranch. It is operated as a going business with records kept on every animal on the place. When a calf is born, it is tagged, and all information about that particular animal is recorded, including weight gain. These records are invaluable in picking replacement heifers and making decisions at market time. To Bill Hamilton, keeping full records in this manner is the only way the cow man can survive in today's precarious economy. A very important factor in this matter of survival for the Hamilton operation is the ranch permit to run cattle on National Forest and B.L.M. grazing lands. In the end, however, it is know-how, ability and dedication to purpose which keep things going. For to the Hamiltons, this ranching operation is a dream come true. The realization of that dream did not come easily.

Bill Hamilton grew up in the western Colorado town of Cedaredge under circumstances that were less than affluent.

Says Bill:

We were pretty poor. I guess even the poor families in town called us poor. We had a two and one-half acre place where we grew a garden and kept a milk cow, and I always had a dog. Even though things were hard, I remember it as a happy life — a country life where we learned to make do and to care for ourselves. We had a large family, and by the time I was twelve, I left home and made my own way. I would walk in the hay fields all summer and then work out on one of the farms or ranches for my board in the winter months. I managed to get through high school in this way.

•

Shortly after graduation, Bill married his high school sweetheart; he was nineteen; Leone was seventeen. Their first job was working on a ranch for thirty-dollars a month. Then, after several years as a ranch hand, Bill went to work in the Rangely oil fields driving a winch truck. The wages were much better in this line of work, but the die was cast, and the inner dreams of the man revolved around Delta, Colorado. By 1970, the sand and gravel business had expanded to include a redi-mix concrete operation of considerable magnitude.

Bill Hamilton comments:

In 1970, the Holly Sugar Company decided to put up the concrete silos which dominate their plant in Delta today. We agreed to supply the material, although I knew it would require special planning. The base alone took 1037½ yards of concrete, and we poured it in one day, working from 4:00 AM until 9:00 that evening. The silos were put up in one continuous pour which took a total of 5000 yards of concrete. It was one of the high points of my life, and one I shall never forget. Those silos have now become a landmark in Delta, and I believe they will remain so for a long, long time.

I always liked this business and enjoyed the challenge, but always in the back of my mind was the thought of being a full-time cow man on a ranch of our own. We had for several years been running a few head of cattle, but it was strictly a sideline operation. In 1972, I figured it was "now or never," and we put the redi-mix operation up for sale.

The ranch in Gateway was bought in 1973. The home place on the Dolores River consists of eight-hundred acres, two-hundred of which are in cultivation. This part of the operation, irrigation, haying, etc., is handled by Don Byers and his family who live on the ranch. The grazing permit, which is at the heart of this ranching operation, allows for 325 head on National Forest land from May to October. Each year, the cattle are trailed up Birch Creek to Calamity Basin, Massey Bench, and on to the open grass country on the Ridge

Allotment. Summer camp is at 9000 feet elevation, and it is here that Bill and Leone Hamilton spend the season. They ride every day, checking range conditions, keeping cattle spread out, and enjoying every moment of it. They live in a 28-foot camp trailer, but the life in general is much as it was in cow camps in days of old. Deer come in to camp, and elk are spotted every day. Camp is a mere fifty miles by road from the main ranch, but just being there is like going back fifty years in time. This is especially true when it comes time to gather and brand new calves:

Leone tells of this special time:

We gather and brand just like it was done years ago. The neighbors come to help, and we have some of the best cowboys left in the West riding this high country at branding time. Bill and Winifred Raber usually come over from Grand Junction to lend a hand. We're always glad when they can make it. There's no better cattleman in the country than Bill Raber, and Winifred handles a cutting horse like she was born to the saddle. It's hard, dusty work, but all in all, there's nothing quite like this special get-together at calf-branding time each year.

The hold of the old frontier ethic on the average American has confounded sophisticates and a generous assortment of professional critics for several decades now, and it is likely to do so for many more years to come. It is a "thing" difficult to put a finger on in some ways, and yet so clearly definable in others. To some of us who have bellied up for a closer look, it is tied tightly to that American phenomenon known as, diversity, and perhaps even more closely to that elusive something called, spirit. At any rate, it is clear that the Hamiltons have achieved more, much more, than financial success in the long struggle to make a dream come true. In the truest sense of the words, they personify the character and spirit which are at the very heart of the old ethic. They are each considerate of the other; they are concerned about those around them. Of all of Colorado's wealth, this spiritual background of refuge and freedom is the greatest of its treasures and goes to the very heart of the nation. Much of this feeling shows through in Leone's "homespun" poetry. In 1975, a number of her poems were assembled and published in a little book entitled, **Country Livin.** The book was dedicated to "Bill, my husband," and Leone noted: "because of his continual encouragement and gentle persuasion, this book was born."

Here she assigns the responsibility:

HE'S TO BLAME

He took me by my little hand
and led me to the table
He sat me down in a kitchen chair
and said, "I know you're able!"

He found a piece of paper
He found a pencil too:
He shook his finger at me
And said, "I mean it, too!"

He said that surely someone
Around this countryside
Would like my kind of poetry
Right then — — I nearly cried!

I told him poems don't grow on trees;
And rhymes don't come in gushes:
You got to think them out awhile
Won't do no good to rush us!

He said he'd go and milk the cow
And feed my chickens too,
And when the chores were finished
He'd 'spect a word or two!

So I've given him the message
And the words are plenty plain.
If he thinks this is poetry
That man ain't hardly sane!

In the mountain and valley lands around Gateway are remnant landmarks of a frontier past that have survived changing times and mounting taxes. They remain as a wistful read-guard fighting for the last genuine luxury left to man — simple privacy. In April of 1977, Bill and Leone Hamilton celebrated their fortieth wedding anniversary. In May, they made ready for a summer of riding herd high on the Uncompahgre Plateau.

Will this "last retreat" survive? Even as this is written, there are indications that it will not. For despite the obvious economic importance and the time-honored historical place of the livestock man in the development of the West, there are forces and groups constantly at work against him. These forces have been prowling the perimeter of his campfire for some time.

It is absolute fact, for example, that a consistently successful livestock producer is and must be a true conservationist in the most complete sense of the word. Yet, environmentalist organizations and much of the media constantly portray all stockmen as arrogant, deluded, plunderers of the American West. It is fact that the balanced operation of most western ranches depends upon the permanence of grazing rights on Federal lands which adjoin or are near privately-owned base property. Range grass, which is one of our greatest and most perishable crops can be utilized only as livestock feed, and genuine conservation dictates that it be used for the benefit of all. Yet, forest permits, which have traditionally supported the carrying capacity of home-base properties have been cut to the bone in the interests of the single-use concept.

How easy it has been for urban Americans to forget our history, or at least that part of it which relates to the pioneer accomplishment in the development of this great land. How easy it has been to bury our "men of the soil" in the rubble of modern statistics. Sooner or later, the American people must realize that if this system is to survive, the farmer and the rancher must also survive.

History in the Colorado-Utah border country has not yet been entombed in monuments, and the traditions of the old West always seem very near. Change has come, but it has had to fight every inch of the way. For tradition clings to this land and the people; it is upon them all the stamp of the frontier, the outdoor stamp. In perspective, even the aberrations can be understood. One needs only to go back a short time, as time is counted in history books and recollections of men. Remember again the frontier, and that this frontier was hard and raw, and that it began to recede only about sixty years ago. History and the old traditions are very near indeed. In 1961, a young oldtimer of fourteen years named, Jay VanLoan, wrote:

> I have heard my mother repeat many hair-raising tales told by my grandfather, Ross Huffman, and some very amusing ones. For instance, Walt Squires and Hank Carr (who was my grandfather's uncle) were chasing a calf through the brush in an attempt to rope it. Hank got ahead of Walt and swung his loop, but missed the calf and tangled his rope in a tree. As Walt caught up and passed Hank, still in hot pursuit, he asked him if he thought that was the tree he went up. It's a good thing he had the calf as an excuse to keep going!
>
> Grandpa Huffman also tells about a man he always felt sure was Butch Cassidy, driving herds of horses through this region. He would trade the horses for local horses and then leave with them. Occasionally, when someone had traded for one of the horses, some cowpoke from far away would come in and try to claim the animal.
>
> In the early days of this region, all stock were wintered out. In summer, they were pushed down on the benches toward the river. Sand Flats, in Utah, and the Sinbad country. There were very few fences then. And, of course, there were quite a few footloose cowboys who weren't too particular about what brand a cow wore, if they could catch the calf and put their own brand on it. I understand that was called, <u>mavericking.</u>
>
> In the old days, ranchers had to drive their stock to summer and winter camps and to market with only horses; wagons usually trailing along. Now, roads over most of the country

permit them easy access to their destinations by truck, car or jeep in a short time. Even in this modern day, though, the horse is very much a necessity. They haven't as yet invented anything to take a good cow pony's place, and I hope they never do.

One can almost feel the same sentiments echoed in the following excerpt taken from a letter dated December 6, 1982 and sent to me by Winifred Raber. In this final sequence, Win relates the hazards of a modern-day cattle drive on her brother's (Crafts Black) ranch operation near Whitewater:

I helped Crafts get his cattle out of Wagon Park and down the Dominguez and home from Bridgeport. One should figure out a "game" similar to Monopoly, with all the hazards that my brother has to contend with, before he gets his cattle back to winter range and home. He has hunters while at "Winter Camp," and then has to move them through Wagon Park and some oak brush pasture, through the fence where they can drift down through Big Dominguez Canyon, which is eighteen miles long. Before putting them in the canyon, he picks a poison called, Copper Weed, so they won't eat that and die. He gathers them out of the canyon one day, so they are in a holding pasture, ready to bring in the next day. (Of course, these days are from before sun-up to after sundown). To bring them in, we start by finding out if there is a train coming or not, so we know whether to put them in the corral, or let them drift after they cross the bridge.

Getting them across the bridge is time-consuming, since only six or seven are put on at one time, because it is a very old, narrow, swinging bridge. After getting them across and trains out of the way, we take them out of the canyon toward Highway 50 South (Delta Highway), trail them by the old Indeer Place, move stray cattle out of the way, and cross them across the highway with a flagman on either side. By the time we get them to the east side of the road, we have traffic stopped for quite a distance. After taking them four or five miles along the east side of the highway, we put them on the highway and take them about two miles toward Whitewater, past Kannah Creek, until we get to where Crafts' B.L.M. pasture is. Perhaps you don't think herding those cows through the traffic that there is today, with all the semis and etc. — impatient to be on their way — is an easy job! We do this by having a flagman in the lead and in the rear. About a couple of years ago, a fellow moved out to the right on the highway at Kannah Creek and established a zoo. It doesn't really bother the cows too much, but believe me, one's horse is all but out of control when one of those big cats or camels or whatever comes toward the fence at them. I've even had trouble leading my horse past the animals.

Didn't mean to get carried away telling you about the hazards of a trip in from Bridgeport, but it is quite an experience. Sister Nita and I laugh and tell our brother that when they put in the Dominguez Dam at Whitewater, and we have to ferry his cows across the lake a few at a time — we're through!

It is now time to wind down this story of people who settled and developed the rugged range country west of the Divide; time to review, to sum up. Out front, we have learned that the old-time cattleman was a natural storyteller. Perhaps it was due to the endless expanse of the land, or exposure to mountains that reached the clouds. Maybe it was due to the essential loneliness of life on the range. At any rate, cowboy humor grew out of daily exposure to natural elements. It expressed itself in pungent, vigorous language, in practical jokes and in tall tales which grew and grew around the campfires. How else could a man survive in a great grassland which took days to cross and was so flat in places that — "you could see the water in the bottom of a forty-foot well ten miles away."

Whatever the reasons for the popularity of such humor, armchair appetites demanded more, and supply has a tendency to follow demand in storytelling as well as in the livestock business. As the stories became better and taller, many legends grew to be outsized and lopsided, containing about nine parts fiction to one part fact. In such a manner, the tall story carried the impress of the frontier into the Twentieth Century.

On today's scene, the New West is a curious mixture of progress with both feet thrust firmly into high-heeled boots. There is a cumulative atmosphere clinging to our wide open spaces as if the past had been dragged along on the end of a long rope. For many people, the spirit of the frontier is still embodied in the rancher of the West; the man on horseback is closely tied to memories of old values and basic tradtitions. At its root is the frontier ethic, finely seasoned by a blended literary sauce made up of fact and fiction, legend and humor.

It has been our purpose here to probe the Western legend, to find and examine those key links in that invisible chain connecting past, present, and future. At first glance, the balance sheet would seem to indicate a great deal of wheelspinning, waste, and personal greed. But the past experienced and the past remembered are two very different things. Certain telltale scars may attest to the early boom or bust years, but time will soon eliminate even these silent witnesses. That which remains in retrospect, and in the imagination, may well be legend and symbol. That which remains in practice and tradition is surely knowledge.

END

EPILOG

It has been said that it takes at least thirty years for a newcomer to be accepted in most parts of the Intermountain West. This is an arbitrary and inexact rule of thumb. The actual length of time depends on the newcomer's background, personality, manners, and way of life. Some people have actually made it in twenty-five. Cattlemen — like a certain species of plants that grow on a particular kind of rock — have always flourished in this desert and mountain country. They are the elite, and "you" had damn-well better remember the fact.

The impact of this tradition on successive decades of American life and progress has amply proved the frontier's existence in the hearts and minds of Americans. In a classic sense, the frontier ethic has been the only mythological tissue available to this nation over the years. The man on horseback, the conquest of nature and the law of the gun have appealed from the first. Certainly, the Old West was settled by hard-nosed individualists possessing every degree of cussedness known to God or man. Rugged and direct, they lived in a time when the risks and dangers of daily life had to be met boldly. Those who made it became specialists in the art of survival. Then, slowly out of the mists and shadows that gather over all persons and events with the passing of time, they also become part of an ever-growing legend.

Cowboy! Cowboy! a cowboy to the end. One of a rare breed who invariably created more than they inherited. The spirit of such men can best be summed up in the following poem written sixty-odd years ago by an unknown author:

> Now, come all you cowboys that live near Gateway,
> And I'll tell of some fun that happened one day.
> 'Twas their annual roundup down in the flats,
> Where they wear spike-heel boots and big Stetson hats.
>
> Pack automatics and lariats, too,
> And ride Bradbury saddles, as most cowboys do.
> Each man owns cattle and horses galore;
> So, in this bunch of cowboys there's no one so poor.
>
> The wrangler brought horses at half past five,
> The cook yelled, "Chuck," and the boys came alive.
> They washed their faces and combed their hair.
> Then they were ready for another square.
>
> Hot biscuits and beef steak and gravy they had,
> With Karo corn syrup and butter to add.
> Canned peaches, too, and condensed milk, I think,
> And coffee so strong it looked black as ink.
>
> Some cottontail rabbits fried nice and brown,
> And some kind of preserves manufactured in town.
> Stewed raisins they had as a kind of dessert,
> So they could decently fill out the slack in their shirts.
>
> They sat on the ground with their plates in their laps,
> Some had on spurs and some had on chaps.
> Although they were sunburned and dressed rather rough,
> They didn't act smart or try to be tough.

*As the fun went 'round with laughter and jest,
They treated each other as honored guests.
At last, breakfast was over, each rose to his feet,
And rolled him a smoke so dainty and neat.*

*When up spoke the cook — good-hearted old Dan,
Said he, "Boys, throw your plates in this pan.
For soon I must hook up and be on the road,
For those long sand gulches I've a heavy load."*

*Bert Graham started to the cavvy, a rope in his hand,
Said he, "I'll ride old Stockin's from no-man's-land."
So he made a good throw with a big round loop,
And he choked old Socks 'til he wheezed like the croup.*

*He at last got a hack on the pony's bald face,
And said, "My, my, Stockin's, but yore a disgrace.
To this outfit you're not a bit of good,
We can't rope off you, and you won't drag wood.*

*"But some hot day I may use you perhaps,
To pack my old bed, my slippers and chaps."
So he eased his saddle on old Stockin's back,
And he cinched and cinched 'til there wasn't no slack.*

*Then he said to Pete Hanson, the wrangler boy,
"Go tell John Gallagher or Willard Foy
To come twist the brute's ears so he can't spin round;
For I don't like the looks of this rocky ground."*

*So Johnnie came a-running to the aid of his pal,
Said he, "Say Bert, what'll I tell your gal?"
Then Bert replied, "See here, friend Johnnie, quit your kiddin'.
This old hoss had to do my bidding."*

*Bert mounted the saddle with quirt in hand,
And I'll tell you that pony did dig up the sand.
I stood and gazed and felt sorry for Bert,
For he didn't have time to use his quirt.*

*But his spurs were busy clawin' out hair,
'Til he lost his temper and began to swear.
Then the pony quit pitchin' and started to run;
So that was the end of most of the fun.*

*Up spoke Ed Gordon, "I'm captain today,
So, if you boys are ready, we'll drift away.
We'll ride the river and the chaparral,
Comb the mesas and rims, as well.*

*So they rode away with hearts care free,
Each one expecting some maverick to see.
Then, what a race and O, my! what fun,
'Til the maverick was caught and the brand was run.*

*There was Bill and Bert Graham and Willard Foy,
Old Dad Gallagher, Johnnie and Roy,
Bert Hubbard was there, the long lank galoot,
With an old floppy hat and run-over boots.*

*With his teeth out in front, he looked like an ape,
But for a genuine cowboy, he had the right shape.
A good broncho twister, the best in the land,
He could keep the right tally and read any brand.*

*There were Ed and George Gordon, and the two Steele boys,
And quite a number of the younger Foys.
There were the two Yarbroughs, Billy and Lute,
Ray Loveridge was there in his corduroy suit.*

*Bill and Ray Doke, from the Sinbad side,
And old Sid Pace, who would always ride
With the boys on the river and pick up a few;
Now I think this finished out most of the crew.*

*Excepting Dan Boyd, our cook, you know,
He was a wizard with the sourdough.
Without any joking, he was a dandy cook,
But I don't think he learned it from any book.*

If the wood was shy, or the water was low,
He'd never ask one of the boys to go.
Some thought he was grouchy, but it was just his way,
And then he would say, "I'm just earning my pay."

With a gun or a butcher knife Dan wasn't bad,
A friendly feeling he always had
For some hungry cowpuncher, who'd come into camp,
Or some weary prospector, or even a tramp.

They were always welcome to a meal and a smoke,
Then Dan would crack some comical joke,
Which would make them laugh 'til they shed big tears,
And lengthened their lives for several years.

The roundup went on through days and days,
With the branding of calves and the herding of strays,
Though the work was hard and the days were long,
Each day was finished with laughter and song.

At last we pulled in at old Monty's place,
The one that belonged to old Sid Pace,
Just across the river from Oscar Foy's,
Here we said goodbye to most of the boys.

When the last calf was tallied and we'd turned loose the bunch,
We decided to go to the wagon for lunch.
Then we turned loose our horse and the cavvy was gone,
We finished our supper with a smoke and a yawn.

As the moon shone brightly on the rims in the west,
They rolled out their blankets and lay down to rest.
I rode with these cowboys, in this rugged land,
But I've long since departed, so guess who I am.

*   *   *

A LIST OF WESTERN COLORADO BRANDS

All brands beginning with a letter are arranged alphabetically; those beginning with a number are arranged numerically, while those beginning with a character are arranged, as follows:

—, ⌒, ⌢,), (, +, ♡, ◇, □, ▽, ᨆ

miscellaneous brands beginning with "one", "circle" or with a "horseshoe" will be found under the letters I, O, and U, respectively.

* * * * *

My source of information was a 1914 and a 1938 brand book. The date following each brand is when it was recorded. A brand without a date is the result of local inquiries and knowledge of 'old-timers'. Most names were familiar, but those that were not, I made an effort to trace, and have added that bit of information. Those with 'no record' following a name were those I was not able to locate anyplace.

* * * * *

Compiled by 'Nita Clark
Kannah Creek
Whitewater, Colorado

WESTERN COLORADO BRANDS

J. E. Wiley, Whitewater, 1914. Father Tom came to Kannah Creek in the early 1980's. They lived at Pride.

August Johnson, Whitewater, 1914. He came in 1898 and bought a small ranch on Whitewater Creek from Will Meserve (who was a storekeeper in Whitewater). This ranch is known today as "Swede Hill", or "Johnson Hill". Mrs. Effie Silzell was a daughter. **Martin Johnson** was a son to whom the brand was transferred in 1938.

Alex Mettras, Whitewater, 1914. They lived on Kannah Creek. The house is now abandoned at the foot of "Sullivan Hill". The brand was transferred to a **Antone Hoagland**, Grand Jct., 1938.

Leon E. Booth, Whitewater, 1914. No record.

Ica M. Cox Click, Whitewater, 1938. Ranched on Purdy Mesa.

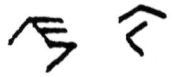

Art Lewis, Delta, 1938.

Warren Wright, Whitewater. North Fork of Kannah Creek.

Frank Benton, Eagle, 1914; to Foster Evans, 1938: to Dick Sommerville. The Evans, Sommerville ranch is on upper Whitewater Creek, range on Grand Mesa.

Dick Sommerville, Whitewater.

William E. Schoolfield, Delta, 1914 and 1938. Schoolfield came before the 1900's, worked as a cowpuncher, helping to ship cattle to eastern markets, later an agent for a Denver Livestock Ass'n. He ran cattle from Kannah Creek to Delta and built the chimney's on Indian Creek in the late '90's. "Schooley Draw" was named for him. He camped at the present Keith Clark ranch, and the wire for his horse corral is still visible in the old oak trees.

Will C. Watts, Montrose, 1914. Transferred to **Lawrence Mash**. Mr. Watts is the father of Esther Mash.

S. W. Ashley, Whitewater, 1914, to **Charlie Ashley**. Ranched on Purdy Mesa.

Mrs. Albertine Wolfe, Whitewater, 1938. Daughter of J. A. Laurent.

Tom C. Casto, Whitewater, 1938.

H. B. Evans, Whitewater, 1914. He owned a section of Earl Lucas's ranch on Kannah Creek. Howard Brouse now owns the ranch.

B. H. Wood, Whitewater, 1914. No record.

Taylor Cattle Co., Whitewater, 1938.

(B   Chas. W. Woodring, Whitewater, 1914.

(†   A. J. Taylor, Whitewater, 1914.

aa   Warren Watkins, Whitewater, 1914. To Watkins Cattle Co., Meeker, 1938.

D-D   Theodore L. Sullivan, Whitewater, 1938.

D-4   Cashious C. Sampson, Delta, 1914. Shot and killed Ben Lowe in a gun-fight in Escalante Canyon, June, 1917.

DEM   R. F. Burford, Whitewater, 1914.

EAC   Ethan Casto, Whitewater, 1914, Unaweep Canyon.

EG   Earl H. Grant, Whitewater, 1914. Ranch in Unaweep Canyon between Taylor and Heskett Ranches.

EIF   Chas. Rinderle, Whitewater, 1914 and 1938.

EJ   Earl Lucas, Kannah Creek, 1914 and 1938. Son of Benjamin Franklin Lucas who came into the valley as a pioneer.

ЧJ   E. N. Lavender, Uravan, 1914. Owner of the famous Club Ranch, and father of David Lavender who wrote "One Man's West". Brand now owned by **Jerome Craig Ranches**.

Brand	Description
∃<	**G. W. Ponsford**, Whitewater, 1914. Came into the area in 1884 and lived at Pride and owned one of the 1st water rights on Kannah Creek.
FLC	**Lottie M. Rambo**, Bridgeport, Whitewater, 1914 and 1938. Still living on Dominguez Creek.
FL\	**Jack Casto**, Whitewater, 1914 and 1938. Unaweep Canyon.
f-	**Wilbur (Bill) Raber**, Kannah Creek Rancher, 1938. Owned the Elk Glen Ranch.
∏▽	**Forrest (Bus) Click**, Collbran, Whitewater, 1938.
FИ	**Mrs. R. T. Smith**, Whitewater, 1914.
F<u>N</u>	**W. E. Schoolfield**, Delta, Whitewater, 1914, transferred to **Earl A. Johnson**, Austin, 1938.
⊥ F	**Francis (Punch) Holland**, Whitewater, Pride, 1938. Son of M. D. Holland and was killed on the Granite Quarry Hill in an automobile wreck. Brand transferred to **Alta Wadlow**, Whitewater.
H<u>I</u>	**George Barnard Hughes**, Whitewater, 1938.
⊥ b	**Hugh Jones**, Whitewater, 1914. Jack Wadlow purchased this ranch. (Hugh Jones daughter, Sarah, married Carl Farmer and they ran the old North Fork Store.)

Brand	Description
⌐⌐	F. E. Anderson and W. L. Anderson, North Fork of Kannah Creek, 1938.
HJ\	W. H. Laramore, Whitewater, 1938. (Related to present owners of local feed-lot, and at one time owned "Casey Glen" on the North End of Grand Mesa.
HUH	Jack Casto, Whitewater, 1938. Edward Casto, Grand Junction, 1973 by notice in CATTLE GUARD'
H-B	H. H. Burch, (Henry Houghton), Niwot, (Mom's foster parents) 1914-1938.
H-I	W. E. Schoolfield, Delta, Whitewater, 1914.
H→	Charles Fields, Whitewater, 1938. No record.
I⊆	John L. LaFair, Gateway, 1938.
IIЯ	Eva Wines, Gateway, 1938.
IIX—	Fred Click, Whitewater, Purdy Mesa rancher, 1938. To Howard Brouse to Buck Catt.
II⊥	E. D. Stewart, Mesa, 1914-1938.
II⊥	E. H. Stewart, Mesa, 1914-1938.

11⊥< A. H. Stewart, Mesa, 1914-1938.

IKC Robt. Sanders, Mack, 1938. (Wanda's father-in-law).

IRΛ Ira Vincent, Whitewater, 1914-1938. Ranch on Whitewater Creek, Crafts Black present owner of the ranch.

TT (Spur double T) Morrison, (Earl Lucas's lower place, on Kannah Creek), to **J. W. Sullivan**, 1914 to **Taylor Cattle Co.**, 1938. The Sullivan range was the Uncomphagre at one time. This brand is called the "Spur double T." This Morrison married a Sullivan girl and the log cabin where they lived still stands.

TW Geo. Pickens, Whitewater.

⊥X Geo. W. Ponsford, Whitewater, Pride, 1914 to **Irma J. (Clyde) Hooker**, 1938.

JEF J. D. Dillard, Delta, 1914, Nephew of Cash and married Ben Lowe's daughter, Maxine.

ĊĊ John L. Luvey, Whitewater, 1914. No record.

⌐⌐ John L. Williams, Whitewater. No record unless he was a brother of Bill and Huey Williams of Kannah Creek.

Jb Frank Lucas, Whitewater, 1938. Purdy Mesa

rancher, owned the Elk Glen ranch. Brand transferred to **Crafts Black.**

◡**Y**   Jerome Craig, Unaweep, 1938.

⊂)−   Wes and Eban Massey, Unaweep Canyon, 1938. (Craft's horse, "Minister" wears this brand.)

◡◡   Jay Olson, Kannah Creek.

K L K   C. D. Clark and son's. Whitewater, 1938. No record.

K N   Mrs. Silman Renick (Dode), 1938. **Dode Lockhart.**

K I N   Kenneth J. Moblitt, Whitewater, 1938. No record.

⋀ E   Kitt Casto, Unaweep, 1914.

∇   Raymond Woodring, Unaweep Canyon, 1938.

J̲F̲   W. M. Cox, Grand Jct., 1914 to **Bob Bowen,** Whitewater, 1938.

L − X   C. V. Hallenbeck, Whitewater, Purdy Mesa.

L M J   John W. Musser, Escalante, 1914-1938.

L V L   Bill La Fair, Gateway - **J. W. Sullivan,** 1914 to

Taylor Cattle Co., 1938, to **Dr. E. H. Munro**, Grand Junction, Purdy Mesa. Bill La Fair killed Wes Massey's father at the Bowman Hill on the Uncomphagre.

JY   **Vic Laurent**, Whitewater, 1914 to **Oscar Laurent**, 1938. Sons of J. A. Laurent. They were French-Canadians.

L7)   Mrs. E. R. Sullivan, Whitewater, 1914.

J-⅄   D. B. Burford, Whitewater, 1914.

L-Я   Al Rhodes, Pride, 1914.

L(U   Floyd Blair, "Whiskey Flats", Whitewater, 1914.

L/D   Eugene C. Davis, Whitewater, 1938. No record.

J(-   Ernest Oldland, Meeker, 1938.

MH   Michael Holland, Pride, came from Ireland in 1889.

M/H   J. W. Musser Jr., Escalante, 1938.

ИK   W. H. Treesh, Whitewater, 1938. Married a Riddle girl (Jack Treesh was a range boss on the Uncomphagre for several years, also a brand inspector.)

NK   Charles F. Bowman, Whitewater, 1914.

NK (overlined)   Mrs. W. E. Flanagan, Craig, 1938 to **Pat Dalton**, Whitewater.

O 4 O   Matt Casto, Unaweep Canyon, 1914-1938.

oTs   Samuel Dodgins, Whitewater, 1914. His father A. J. Dodgins came to Colorado in 1869 and to Whitewater in 1880. Another child, a daughter was Ruby Burford.

O→   Ernest Oldland, Meeker, 1938.

R̞   James Davis, Whitewater, 1938.

R-∧   Rollie and Amy Miller, Whitewater, 1938. No record.

↑S↓   John Brown, Mesa, 1914-1938.

⊣A   C. M. Raber, Kannah Creek, 1914-1938. She and her husband, J. J. Raber came to this country as pioneers from the Black Hills of South Dakota. Sons, Bill and John, owners of the Elk Glen, became prominent stockmen in the area.

S-4   J. A. Laurent, Whitewater, Purdy Mesa, came to this country, 1892.

VH   Sawtelle Bros., Escalante, 1938.

S/4   **J. A. Laurent**, 1914 to **G. J. Wolfe**, 1938. He married Albertine Laurent.

St   Sieber Cattle Co., Pueblo, Mesa County range, 1914. Sieber was killed by Joe Harris in 1902. Joe Pace killed Joe Harris in 1908.

⊥B   **Fred Simineo**, Kannah Creek, 1914-1938.

TF   **G. L. Moore**, Whitewater, 1914, to **G. Lamore Moore**, Clovis, New Mexico, 1938.

TIV   **Alden Leonard**, at the mouth of Wells Gulch along the Gunnison River, range on the Uncomphagre, 1914. The water sheels he used for irrigation are still visible, which he built. Believed he owned the present Crafts Black camp on the Uncomphagre, as Crafts saddle-shed is reported to be the oldest cabin on the Uncomphagre.

LT)   **Geo. and Robt. Lockhart**, Delta, 1938.

⊣M   **Thomas McDonald**, 1914, **Roy Renick** (son of W. E. Renick who came to Renick Flats in 1882. **Henry and Francis Holland**, 1938, to **Claude M. Hathaway** to **Whiting** family. Thomas McDonald built the McDonald Pond south of Kannah Creek up on the mesa, and also many years ago left a pile of poles on the trail to the Point, on Grand Mesa, which is still referred to as the "McDonald Poles". These are still barely visible.

O T S   **Daniel Dodgins**, Whitewater, 1914. Son of A. J. Dodgins who came in 1880.

T X —   **W. E. Schoolfield**, Delta, Whitewater, 1914. To **R. C. Butler**, Delta, 1938.

T ⌒   **A. J. Taylor**, Whitewater, 1914, to **Warren Fifield**, Whitewater.

T + L   **John Holland**, Whitewater, Unaweep Canyon, 1914-1938.

T △   **Frank B. Grant**, Whitewater, Unaweep Canyon, 1914-1938.

U P   **James Page**, Whitewater, 1914. To **Ernest Hildebrand**, Kremmling, 1938. James Page came to Whitewater in 1886 and was the Whitewater depot-agent and postmaster for 25 years. John Page, 90, of Steamboat Springs, died there Aug. 16. He was a member of the pioneer Whitewater family of the James Pages. The family operated the Whitewater depot and mail service before there was rural mail delivery. He is survived by his wife and two daughters. Although he had moved to Steamboat many years ago, he attended the annual Whitewater picnic until this year. August 20, 1975.

⊃ S   **Samuel L. Dodgins**, Whitewater, 1914.

U K   **Marie Scott**, Ridgeway, 1938.

U R A   Wes Massey, Unaweep Canyon, 1938.

U   J. D. Dillard, Delta, 1914.

Ute Osborn, Grand Jct., 1914. Ute was a cattle buyer for many years.

UX   R. T. Anderson, Reeder Mesa, Whitewater, 1914-1938. Father of W. L. & R. E. Anderson.

U2   W. S. LaFair, 1914 to John L. LaFair, 1938.

U+U   Paul Craig, Gateway, 1914-1938.

VJ   E. E. Chambers, Whitewater, Purdy Mesa, 1914. (Roxie's brother, Ernest.)

V⌒   Lyle Vincent, Palidade, 1938.

VL   Geo. Colleps, Whitewater Creek, 1938.

VJ   Hazel Lucas, Kannah Creek, Whitewater, 1938.

>   J. V. Geiger, Whitewater, 1914, 1938. Married Minnie Virden, also surveyed many of the early Kannah Creek Ditches and roads.

<<   Ute Osborn, Grand Junction, 1938.

Brand	Description
✓Z	**Patrick Lynch**, Lily, Moffot Co., early hermit of Brown's Park and Pat's Hole, 1914.
⊻⁄‖	**C. C. King**, 1938.
>S	**W. J. Wolf**, Snipes, Mesa Co., 1914. Dad's Uncle? who at one time owned and operated the big feedlot by the old sugar mill on the Indian School Road.
⊴	**James A. Cavanaugh**, Whitewater, 1914, to **W. A. Rigdon**, Hughes, Colorado, 1938. James was a son of Martin Cavanaugh, here between 1892-1898 and lived among the Utes and spoke their language fluently.
W∧T	**Warren Watkins**, Whitewater, 1914.
W̲E̲	**Orville J. Pettingill**, Whitewater, 1914.
W/J	**Geo. Wolfe**, Whitewater, 1938.
W//	**J. T. Wadlow**, Whitewater, 1938.
W)	**W. W. Wolf**, Boulder, Colo. 1914. (Dad's Uncle Will).
W W W	**Manuel J. Woodring**, Whitewater, 1914.
W + P	**John Holland**, Whitewater, 1914 to **Geo. Ponsford**.

W̱   **J. B. Claybough**, Whitewater, (Actually, Claybough purchased the cattle, but not the brand from **Florence Fuller and Joe Pace** at Westwater, Utah. In the 1914 brand book it read: ₩ and in the 1938 book it was recorded as: W % Leola Scarlett, daughter of Mrs. Fuller.)

X H /   Raymond Woodring, Unaweep Canyon, 1938.

X I H   **Picket Ranch** on Whitewater Creek, **Frank Bradbury** 1914-1938 to **Walter (Bud) Bradbury**. Frank Bradbury was a son of Daniel Bradbury who came before 1900, he was also the brother of Lon Bradbury, saddle-maker.

X / /   **James Nelson**, Whitewater, 1914. **Foster Evans**, 1938.

X / Z   **Ruby Burford**, Whitewater, 1914-1938.

X L)   **Don W. Mart**, Whitewater, 1914. No record.

X L X   **Walter Farmer**, Pride, 1914 to **John Cox**, Whitewater in 1938.

X̱ -   **James Nelson**, Whitewater, 1914 to **Foster Evans**, Whitewater, 1938.

—313—

Brand	Description
X ⟩ /	W. J. Devenney, 1938. Whitewater.
5 X	Phil Massey, Whitewater, 1938.
X ⊲	Oscar Laurent, 1914 to **Grace Learned**, 1938 to Davidson?
X ⌒ /	Don Musser, Escalante, 1938.
‿X‿	Lawrence (Dutch) **Learned**, Whitewater.
Y / U	R. D. Lucas, Whitewater, 1914-1938 to **W. L. Anderson** R. D. (Ray Lucas married Lon Bradbury's daughter, Hazel.
Y̶ / S	Samuel L. Dodgins, Whitewater, 1914 to **Harry Spayd and son**, Garo, Colo. 1938.
≤ / W	Lola A. Lucas, (Mrs. B. F.), Whitewater, 1914.
—⟨+	Dave S. Hall, Whitewater, 1914. To **Albert Peters**, Stratton, Colo., 1938. Son of Augustus Hall who came in 1893 and ran a blacksmith shop in Whitewater.
Z — K	A. H. Bassett, Ladore, 1914 to 1938. Old-timers in Brown's Park during the hay-days of Butch Cassiday. (Queen Ann's brand)

SΛ'   Silman Renick, Whitewater, 1938. **Warren Fifield.**

ZUZ   W. P. Honsinger, 1914 to **Henry and Francis Holland** 1938. Bill Honsinger came to Kannah Creek from the Klondike in 1897.

Z   Williams, Bill and Huey's father on Kannah Creek.

ZV   Alden Leonard, 1914 to **Z. R. Moon**, Fort Lupton, 1938.

ZX†   W. E. and W. J. Silzell, 1914 to **Chas. Silzell**, 1938, Unaweep Canyon.

Z/   Chas. Silzell, Unaweep Canyon, 1938.

Z/7   Ellery Burford, Whitewater, 1914.

Z+L   C. V. Hallenbeck, Whitewater, Purdy Mesa.

ZC   Ernest Coffman, 1914 to **Biggs and Kurtz Co.**, Grand Junction, 1938.

29   G. F. Bowman, 1914 to **Dr. E. H. Munro**, 1938. Bowman purchased the ranch from Dave Peugh. Rustlers ran several of Bowman's cattle into ravines and branded them with a D reverse B. Bowman offered a reward but results unknown. Old times believe Bowman ran both brands for several years.

Brand	Description
2 E	James Armstrong, Whitewater, 1938. No record.
2V⌢	Dean Vincent, Whitewater, 1938.
2X6	Mrs. Alice Sullivan, Whitewater, 1938.
2⌣	Charles Rump, Bridgeport, 1938.
2̄	Lawrence Mash, Whitewater.
3U	Gertrude Timbrel Krohn, Whitewater, 1938.
3X3	J. M. Byler, Debeque, 1938, to **Crafts Black**, Whitewater Creek.
EX/	Glen Armour, Collbran, Whitewater, 1938.
4-U	O. M. James, Jr., Whitewater, 1914, married Roxie Chambers sister — built the house on the Elk Glen.
4/X	Will Van Pelt, Kannah Creek, 1914.
5◇	Ed Craig, Whitewater, 1914, 1938.
5T	Francis Holland, 1938.
67⌣	W. H. and Lorna Laramore, Whitewater, 1914.

F. H. Lucas, 1914 to 1938 later transferred to **Raber Bros.** then to **Ken Johnson**. This brand came into the country about 1872 with **Henry Bolen** who previously owned the Anderson Ranch.

M. D. Holland, Whitewater, 1914.

Fred Bowen, Verva Bowen, Rifle, 1938.

Pete Middlemist, Whitewater, 1938.

Roy Grant, Whitewater, Unaweep Canyon, 1914.

W. H. Clark, Meeker, 1914 — to **Chas. Auckland**, Olney Springs, Crawley Co., 1938. W. H. Clark was Keith's Grandfather, pioneer of Rio Blanco Co., who was shot during the Meeker Bank Robbery.

D. F. Blair, Whitewater, Whiskey Flats, 1914. Mr. Blair came to Whitewater in 1882.

J. D. Bean, Indian Hunting Grounds, Pride, 1914-1938.

Wm. Van Pelt, Kannah Creek, 1914.

Will Silzell, Mesa, 1938.

Gail C. Murray and **Vaughn C. Kersetter**, Whitewater, 1938. (Isom Dart, colored cowboy of Brown' Park's brand was **ID**

⊙𝚄   **J. H. Herron**, Grand Junction, 1914.

E̅6   **Geo. Bryan**, Whitewater, 1914, Grand Junction, 1938. No record.

I̅T   **Byrl Casto**, Whitewater, Unaweep Canyon, 1938.

K̅₁   **Orval Herron**, Whitewater, 1938.

M̅)   **Vern Woods**, Grand Junction, 1938.

W̅   **B. F. Lucas**, Kannah Creek, Whitewater, 1914.

X̅N   **Ben Lowe**, Escalante, 1914, to **J. W. Musser, Jr.**, Es. 1938. Ben Lowe killed Cash Sampson in a gun fight in Escalante Canyon June, 1917. Craft's horse "Gomer" wears this brand, minus the bar.

−2̲   **A. A. Silzell**, Whitewater, 1914.

∼−   **Floyd A. Blair**, 1938. Son of D. F. Blair.

−𝓌   **Claude Timbrel**, Kannah Creek, 1938.

Q̅   **Roy Renick**, Renick Flats, Whitewater, 1914. (Where the radio-towers are now).

Bulkeley Wells, Telluride, 1914. He was the famous bank swindler.

Carl V. Farmer, 1938. Sargents. Married Sarah Jones of Whitewater and operated the North Fork Store.

J. A. Recher, Eads, Colo., 1914 to **Walter Raber**, Whitewater.

D. Mitchell and **Frank Grant**, Whitewater, 1914.

Dennis Sullivan, Mesa Co. 1914. (Bob Coburn's place). Mr. Sullivan came before the 1900's.

John H. Sievers, Burn, Eagle Co., 1938, to **Howard Brouse**, Whitewater.

Walter V. Simenio, Kannah Creek, Whitewater,

C. C. King, 1938.

Howard Scott, Debeaque, 1938.

Joe Pace, Westwater, Utah, 1914. Called the "bell" brand.

O. E. Chambers, Whitewater, 1914. (Roxie)

Claude Timbrel, Whitewater.

⊙ Foster Evans, Whitewater Creek.

⌒a Matt Casto, Whitewater, Unaweep Canyon, 1938.

⌒w W. W. Burch, 1938. Mom's kinfolk, (Foster parents), Boulder, Colorado.

+> Henry Holland, Kannah Creek, Whitewater—1938.

↑ Harold E. Bryant, Appleton-1914. He was the famous artist who did the excellent western, cowboy paintings.

⋏ Lottie Rambo, Bridgeport, 1914.

⌒3⌒ S. L. Farmer, Grand Jct., 1914.

L7 Bob Bowen, Whitewater, 1938.

OL Ruby Lowe, (Mrs. Ben), Escalante, 1914, to J. W. Musser Jr., 1938.

⌣K Joseph King, Whitewater (End Deer)—1938.

⌣P J. J. Wines, Gateway, 1938.

⌣⌣ J. J. Wines, Gateway, 1938.

B. D. (Barny) Marlowe, Montrose, 1938.

Foster Evans, Whitewater Creek, 1938.

Silas and Fina Bayington, Whitewater, 1914. No record.

James Davis, Whitewater, Reeder Mesa, 1914-1938.

James Davis, Whitewater, Reeder Mesa, 1914-1938.

Glen Coffman, Whitewater, 1938.

Marie Scott, Ridgeway, 1938.

Taylor Cattle Co., 1938. Whitewater.

Huber Dale Holland, Whitewater, 1938. Son of Henry Holland.

M. D. Holland, 1914 to Mrs. Margaret Holland, 1938 to Clyde Hallenbeck.

Belle B. Ennor, 1914 to J. J. Wines, 1938 to Stadelman Hereford Ranch. (Dr. E. H. Munro also owned this brand) (x Eugene W. Spencer, Whitewater, 1938 to Lawrence Mash.

+/- J. M. Cunningham, La Salle, 1914 to **Charlie Redd**, La Sal, 1938.

+◇ Sieber Cattle Co., Glade Park, 1914.

+H+ Bert Hubbard, Gateway, 1938.

+// Chas. F. Bowman, 1914 to **Dr. E. H. Munro**, 1938.

+2̲ Aaron and Chas. Silzell, Unaweep Canyon, 1914 to **Mary and Massey Wright**, Gateway, 1938.

+ - + Wm. Ternahan, Kannah Creek, 1914 to **J. B. Clay**-bought in 1938 to **Claude M. Hathaway** to Whiting Family all of Kannah Creek. Wm. Ternahan was a son of John Ternahan, who homesteaded the Elk Glen in 1889. This is supposed to be one of the oldest brands in Colorado.

+/- Tom Ternahan, Whitewater to **C. V. Hallenbeck**, Whitewater.

-ɔ W. L. Farmer, Kannah Creek, 1914.

->-\\ Mont Wright, Whitewater, 1914, No Record.

-2̲ A. A. Silzell, Whitewater, 1914.

 Wes and Eban Massey, Unaweep Canyon, 1914-1938.

 Starr Nelson, Delta on Alkali Creek, 1938.

 "Cap" Gillespie, Kannah Creek, Whitewater. This place is now the girl Scout camp.

 Goldsborough Bros. Gateway, 1914-1938.

 Geo. Gordon, Gateway, 1914 to **J. J. Wines**, Gateway, 1938.

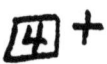 Gilbert Laurent, Kannah Creek, 1914 to **Anderson Bros.**

⊔K   John P. Raber, Kannah Creek, Whitewater, to **Ken Johnson** to **Bill Shelnett**.

⊐<   Charles Ashley, Whitewater, 1914-1938.

⊔⅄   E. J. Heskett, Whitewater, 1938.

∇H   Jerome Craig, Unaweep Canyon, Whitewater, 1938.

△∣⌐   Donald Dowd, Kannah Creek, Whitewater.

 Otis and Casement, Unaweep Canyon, 1914-1938. Dan Casement married Major Thornburgs daughter, born 1874. Major Thornburg was killed in 1879, at the time of the Meeker Massacre on Milk Creek, north of Meeker, while coming to give aid. Dan Casement raised the famous Steel-dust horses at the Unaweep ranch. Casement was also a work foreman on the UP Railroad when it was built through Wyoming.

 Manuel J. Woodring, Unaweep Canyon, 1914 to **Martha Belle and Raymond Woodring**, 1939. Believe this Martha Belle married John Holland.

 Walter C. Black, Kannah Creek, Whitewater, 1938, to **G. Keith Clark**, Kannah Creek.

 Frank Calhoun, Delta, 1938.

 Pete Middlemist, Whitewater, 1938.

 Milo Vincent, Palisade, 1938.

 Alden Leonard, Grand Junction, 1914 to **Watkins Cattle Co.**, Meeker, 1938.

The naming of Whitewater is attributed to John Ross Penniston. He arrived in Whitewater as a 'Shack' cook for the D. & R. G. Railroad track layers. He used the muddy Gunnison River water for cooking. He chose the name because after a rain the water became white from the alkali soil washing into it.

By the early 80's Whitewater was said to be the largest cattle shipping point in the West.

Bridgeport Tunnel was built in 1884, took 350 men, 6 months to build, and at a cost of $200,000. It is 2300 feet long, 16 feet high and 21 feet wide.

In 1907 Edward Martin began a stage line to Gateway via team. He made two trips each way a week and changed teams three times. The 'Martin' place belongs to Crafts Black now.

Thomas Virden came to Kannah Creek in the early 90's and homesteaded on 'Whiskey Flats'. He was one of the very first pioneers in this area. His wife is one of the first buried in the Whitewater cemetary.

Jo. Gill was one the first settlers in the Unaweep Canyon, arriving there in 1881 and moving to Kannah Creek in 1885.

A man by the name of Sawyer built the Elk Glen Barn between 1910 and 1913.

John Terhahan came to this county in 1889, built an 8 strand fence on Purdy Mesa, placed some elk there and called it the Elk Glen. The tall cedar posts necessary for such a fence are still there.

* * * * *

INDEX
(Reference Names and Titles Listed by Chapters)

—A—
Across the Wide Missouri — 1
ANDERSON, Elizabeth — 10
ANDERSON, Pearl — 10
ANDERSON, Walt — 3, 10
ASHLEY, Lee — 2, 4
ASHLEY, William — 1
Axial Basin — 2

—B—
BAXTER, Anne — 6
BECKER, Peter — 4
BENNIT, Lee — 3
BLACK, Crafts — 3, 10, 11
BLACK, Walter C. — 10
BLAIN, Nan — 4
Blue Mountain — 3
Bloom Cattle Co. — 3
BOGART, Humphrey — 6
BOND, Ward — 6
Bookcliff Mountains — 1
BOWMAN, Charles — 4
BRADBURY, Frank — 10
BRENNAN, Walter — 6
BREWSTER, Bob — 3
BRIDGER, Jim — 1
BROUSE, Howard — 6, 10
BROWN, Harry — 19
BROWN, Maude — 4
BROWN, R. C. — 2, 3, 20
BROWN, R. O. — 2
Buffalo Bill — 3
BULL, Dr. — 2
BURG, Charles — 4
BURKITT, Mose — 1, 4
BYERS, Don — 11

—C—
CANUTT, Yakima — 6
Carlisle's Place — 9
CAREY, Harry — 6
CARPENTER, Ferry — 5
CARR, Hank — 2, 11
CARSON, Kit — 1
CASSIDY, Butch — 3
Castle Valley — 4
CASTO, Matt — 4
CHAMBERS, Roxie — 10
CHAPLIN, Charles — 1
CHIPETA — 5
CLARK, Anita — 10
CLARK, Keith — 10
CLARK, William H. — 10
CLAYBAUGH, Bruce — 4
Cleveland, Colorado — 3
CLICK, Bus — 3
CLICK, Lincoln — 4
COBB, Bill — 1
COFFMAN, William — 4
COLLIER, John — 4
COLTHORPE, Ed — 3
COOPER, Gary — 6
COTTON, Joseph — 6
CRAWFORD, George A. — 1
Cuddy & Land — 3
CUDDY, Tom — 2
CUNNINGHAM, Wallace — 2
CURRIER, Chastine — 5
CURRIER, Tom — 2, 5

—D—
DAVIS, Cap — 1
DEE, Frances — 6
DELANEY, Frank — 5

—C— (cont.)
DENNIS, Vint — 2
Denver & Rio Grande RR — 3
DILLARD, Jefferson D. — 3
DINE, Dan — 4
DIX, Richard — 6
DOAK, Bill — 4
DODDS, J. S. — 4
Dolores River — 1
Douglas Pass — 2, 3
DOUGLASS, Sam — 4
DOWLING, John — 2
DUCKETT, Thad — 9
DUFFY, Barney — 10

—E—
ERNEY, Chris — 4
Escalante Canyon — 3
EVERITT, Wiley — 3

—F—
FAIRBANKS, Douglas — 1
FISH, Mart — 4
FISHER, Burns — 2
FISHER, Cheesy — 2
Flying W — 3
FONDA, Henry — 6
FORD, John — 6
Forest Service, U. S. — 10
FOX, William — 1
FRANCE, Jennie — 4
FROMM, Mike — 8
Fruita, Colorado — 1, 3
FULLER, Bob — 1

—G—
GABLE, Clark — 1
GAVIN, Doc — 2, 5
GAVIN, Nina Turner — 5
GEIGEL, Ray — 3

—G— (cont.)
GERRY, Minta — 5
GILPIN, Col. William — 1
Glade Park — 3
GLASS, Charlie — 2, 6
GORDON, Ed — 1
GORDON, George — 4
GORDON, John — 4
Goslin Sheep Co. — 1
GOSS, Bob — 3
GOSS, Jake — 2, 8
GOSS, Morgan — 3
GOSS, Rose Pritchard — 5
GOSS, Ruth — 7
GOUCHER, Louis — 2
Grand Junction, Colorado — 3
Grand Mesa, The — 1, 10
Grand Valley, — 1
GRANT, U. S. — 1
Great Train Robbery, The — 1, 2
GREELEY, Horace — 1
GREY, Zane — 2, 6
GROSS, Arthur — 3
GROSS, Cecil — 1
GROSS, Shorty — 2, 3, 6, 7
Gunnison River — 1

—H—
HAMILTON, Bill — 11
HAMILTON, Leone — 11
HAMMER, Anne — 4
HAMMER, Ted — 4
HARRIS, Joe — 1
HASKELL, Charles W. — 1
HART, William S. — 1
HARTMAN, Bose — 2
HAYDEN, Lyman — 9
HELLMAN, Connie — 11
HELLMAN, Donna — 11
HELLMAN, Janet — 11

—H— (cont.)
HELLMAN, Judy — 11
HELLMAN, Margaret — 11
HELLMAN, Stan — 11
HENIKER, Henry — 4
HERSHAFT, Alex —10
HIGHT, Ike — 3
HITCHBORN, Gladys — 8
HOBBS, Mart — 9
HODIAK, John — 1
HOLT, Berdee — 6
HOLT, Jack — 1
HOLT, Tim — 6
HOWELL, Bart — 1, 3
HOWELL, Dode
HUBBARD, Bert — 1
HUDSON, John — 2
HUFFINGTON, Oscar — 3
HUFFMAN, Ross — 11

—J—
Jacobs Ladder — 4
JESUI, Felix — 6
JOHNSON, Ben — 5
JOHNSON, C. C. Windy — 2
JOHNSON, George — 4
JOHNSON, R. W. — 3
JONES, Buck — 6

—K—
KELSO, R. S. — 3
KIEFER, Mabel C. — 5
KILBY, Ellen White — 5
King Bros. Wild West Show — 3
KIRBY, Albert — 5
KIRBY, Ruby Rector — 4, 5
KIRK, Doc — 2
KIRK, Lee — 4
KNIGHT, Harry — 2
KNIGHT, Nettie — 2, 8

—K— (cont.)
KNOWLES, Emery — 3

—L—
Land's End — 10
LANE, Matt — 2
LASSITER — 2
Last of the Duanes, The — 2
LAWRENCE, M. H. — 4
Lazy Y S — 3
Lone Star Ranger, The — 2
LUSTER, Jim — 1
Mack, Colorado — 3
MAHANNY, Bert — 1, 2
MANTEY, Fred — 5
MARTIN, Ed — 4
MASH, Lawrence — 3
MASSEY, Jim — 4
MATURE, Victor — 5
McCARTHY, Jerry — 4
McCREA, Joel — 5
McKENZIE, Jennie — 4
McTAGGART, Ethel — 4
MEEKER, Nathan — 1
MENJOU, Adolph — 1
Mesa County Democrat — 1
MIDDLEMIST, Andy — 3
MILLER, Johnny — 1
MITCHELL, Mattie — 7
MIX, Tom — 1, 2, 5
Moab, Utah — 4
MOCK, Enola — 2, 3, 5, 8
MOCK, John — 3
MOGENSEN, Gertrude — 5
MOGENSEN, J. M. — 5
MONTALBAN, Ricardo — 1
MOORE, Catherine — 1, 3, 4
MOORE, Frank — 2
MOORE, Sam — 1
MOORHEAD, Agnes — 6

—M— (cont.)
Mt. Whitney — 2
MUHR, Franz — 2, 3, 5, 8
MUSSER, John — 3

—N—
NEARING, Jay — 2
NEARING, Sy — 2, 3
O'CONNOR, Walter — 2
Oh You Tony — 2
OLSON, Jay — 10
OSBORNE, Laura — 7
OWENS, Bart — 2,3,5

—P—
PABOR, W. E. — 11
PACE, Joe — 6
PACE, John — 4
PACE, Lucile Hanson — 4, 5
PACE, Sid — 4, 5
PENNISTEN, John Ross — 4
Pinon Mesa — 2
Pittsburg Cattle Co. — 4
PORTER, Edwin S. — 1
PURDY, Will — 10
PYSERT, Ollie — 2

—R—
RABER, Bill — 3, 10
RABER, Winifred — 8, 10, 11
Ranch Life in the Great Southwest — 1
Rangely, Colorado — 3
RAY, Charley — 2
RECTOR, James — 4
REESE, Claude — 5
RICE, David - 5
Riders of Death Valley — 2
ROBB, Nathan — 10
ROGERS, Roy — 6

—S—
S Cross — 2, 3
Sagebrush Rebellion, The — 10
SANDERS, Wanda — 10
SAYLES, Al — 2, 3, 4
Santa Fe R.R. — 3
San Miguel Cattle Co. — 3
SAXBURY, Ida — 4
SCHOOLCRAFT, Iva — 4
SEIBER, Charles — 1, 4
Seiber Cattle Co. — 1, 3
Selig Co. — 1
SHEETS, Percy — 4
SHROPSHIRE, Clyde — 4
SILZELL, Charles Stewart — 4, 8
SILZELL, Effie — 4, 8
SLEEPER, Frank — 4
SLEEPER, John Frank — 9
SMITH, Byron — 6
SNYDER, Henry — 4
Softboiled — 2
SQUIRES, Walt — 11
STANIFRED, Ethel — 5
STARR, Lester — 2
STEEN, Charlie — 11
STEVENS, Harold — 4
SULLIVAN, Katherine — 5

—T—
T Cattle Co. — 1
TAYLOR, Andrew — 4
TAYLOR, Barbara — 2
TAYLOR, Claude — 2
TAYLOR, Ed — 5
TAYLOR, Joan — 2
TAYLOR, Lester — 4
Teller House — 2
TERRY, Bill — 4
Thatcher Bros. — 3
THORNOCK, Clarence — 10

—T— (cont.)
TOMLINSON, Leslie — 2
TONY (Tom Mix's Horse) — 1, 2
TRAGY, H. S. — 2
TURNER, Albert — 2
TURNER, Charles —
TURNER, Jim — 2, 5
TURNER, Oscar — 2

—U—
Uncompahgre Plateau — 1
Union Colony — 1
Universal Pictures — 2
Ute Trail — 3

—V—
VAN LOAN, Jay — 11
VIRDEN, Bert — 4

—W—
WADLOW, Jack — 3
WALSH, Ed - 1
WATSON, Tom — 5
WATTS, Lyle F. — 10
WAYNE, John — 5
WEBB, Gibb — 1
WEIMER, Don — 2
WELLMAN, William — 1
WELLES, Orson — 5
WETZEL, C. E. — 3
WHITE, John — 5
White River — 3
WHITING, Perry — 1, 4
WILCOXSON, John — 3
WILLEY, Lute — 4
WILLIAMS, Bill — 1
WILSON, Lois — 2
WRIGHT, O. S. — 4
WULSTEN, Carl — 1

—Y—
YOUNG, Ed — 2, 3, 4
YOUNG, Lafe — 5
YOUNG, Lew — 2, 4, 5
YOUNG, Lottie — 5
YOUNG, Kenneth — 5
YOUNG, Marie — 4, 5
YOUNG, Nina — 4
YOUNG, Will — 4

—Z—
ZINKE, August — 3

SPECIAL ANNOUNCEMENT

A new book by, Jim Curtis

THE LAST TALLY
a novel

A colorful evocation of the life and times of Charlie Glass, the legendary black cowboy, as based on fact, but told in fiction. The ranching and rodeo days, the gunfight, the trial, the private and public hi-jinks are all covered in a tale as authentic as it is engrossing.

Coming soon from
Rocky Mountain Books

....

SPECIAL EDITION
Advance Order Card

To: Rocky Mountain Books
   Box N
   Windsor, CO 80550

Yes, I would like a copy of **THE LAST TALLY**. Please enter my name on your Special Edition Mailing List.

Advise when ready for delivery .... ☐

Send C.O.D. .... ☐

Name: ─────────────────────────────

P.O. Box: ───────────────────────────

Address: ────────────────────────────

City ──────────── State ──────────── Zip ───────